The Scottish Lochs

Also by Tom Weir

Highland days
The ultimate mountains
Camps and climbs in arctic Norway
East of Katmandu
Focus on mountains
The Western Highlands
Scottish islands
Batsford colour book of the Highlands

The Scottish Lochs

Tom Weir

Constable London

The Scottish Lochs first published in
two volumes in 1970 and 1972

This one-volume edition of *The Scottish Lochs*
revised 1980

Published by Constable and Company Ltd
10 Orange Street London WC2H 7EG

ISBN 0 09 463270 7

Photographs by the author

The author wishes to acknowledge the help
given by the North of Scotland Hydro-Electric
Board, and officers of the Nature Conservancy
Council in Scotland

Contents

The lochs of this book are the equivalent of lakes—which by definition are 'masses of still water situated in depressions in the ground'. The arrangement of the chapters is by drainage basins, beginning in southern Scotland, travelling north to the Pentland Firth, then west to the Hebrides and finishing with Orkney and Shetland.

Within these boundaries between Atlantic and North Sea is found a variety of loch-scenery unequalled elsewhere in the world. They vary from shallow kettle-holes like wooded Loch an Eilein trapped in glacial undulations of the Spey Valley, and the corrie lochans of the Cairngorms which are the highest in Britain, to the gouged-out rock basins of Loch Ness and Loch Morar in whose dark waters unidentified monsters are believed to lurk.

The human history of the lochs begins with the remains of the Iron Age lake dwellings known as 'crannogs', and primitive canoes dug from the mud. The people who left these relics built stockades on artificial islands at a time when most of Scotland was a jungle of pine forests and swampland vegetation inhabited by beavers, bears, wolves, northern lynx, caribou, great elk and red deer superior in stature and antler to any we know today.

In the Christian era, islands on many lochs became places of holy retreat and pilgrimage. And sometimes they became prisons and places of refuge. Mary Queen of Scots had sad knowledge of both, on the Lake of Menteith and Loch Leven. With written history, the role of the Scottish lochs becomes important. This book is aimed at the intelligent traveller who wants to know more about the cause, and the effect, of the most striking feature of the Scottish landscape.

Science has come a long way in the last hundred years towards an understanding of how the Scottish lochs were formed. The evidence has been painstakingly gathered from the leavings of the glaciers and the ice, which shovelled out rock basins now occupied by all our grandest lochs. Some lochs have vanished, leaving only shorelines like the 'parallel roads of Glen Roy' near Spean Bridge. Charles Darwin pondered on these 'roads' and came to the conclusion that they were ancient seashores. It shook his confidence when he was proved wrong from the evidence in Glen Spean, Glen Roy and Glen Gloy which supported a glacier dam, impounding behind it great lakes, whose levels fell as the Nevis ice melted. Each 'road' is the shoreline of former lochs.

Man has taken a leaf from nature's books hereabout by building a dam of concrete to make a reservoir at Moy covering part of the site of the former loch. Adjacent to Loch Laggan is an example of the ugliness which results from hydro-electrification when natural shorelines are lost and replaced by straight edges of grey 'tide-mark' caused by rapid rise-and-fall.

Hydro-electricity in the main, however, has been carried out with sensitive regard for landscape values, with an emphasis on good architecture. This book gives a fair outline of what has been achieved since 1943 when the North of Scotland Hydro-Electric Board was formed. The lochs today serve 400,000 customers with power, a quarter of them living in the remoter parts of the Highlands and Islands. Half the total water of the Highlands is in use to date, with a generating capacity of 1,064 megawatts and an average output of 2,911 million units. The preoccupation today with nuclear and other methods of generation should save further plunder of our scenic reserves.

The reprieve is also important to science, for new information on the lochs is coming to light all the time, even in accessible waters like Loch Lomond, which has a community of plants unlike any other in Britain. They hold the shifting sand of the south-eastern corner and have played a vital part in shifting the River Endrick a full mile in the last 200 years.

One of these plants is a tiny waterwort with a pinkish red flower and reddish green leaves which was undiscovered here until 1968. It is an annual, like its companion *Pelplis portula*. These two, with the perennial *Eleocharis acicularis* are able to withstand the fluctuations of Loch Lomond. They flower and seed when the sand is exposed, but even when floods come and seeds are washed away, enough adhere to continue the process of flowering and seeding when they get the chance. They hold the sand *in situ* long enough for the grasses and sedges to take over, accelerating the process of land-making. Secrets have still to be learned about every loch in this book, so we must be thankful that many of them have not been touched by man, as yet.

Much of this north and south country of Scotland is still remote. In the Uists for example, where the trout, sea-trout and salmon fishing has the quality of legend, there are half a dozen lochs unfished for every one fished. Fair Isle and Shetland are a crossroads for arctic bird migrants, but strange things have been happening here of recent years. The snowy owl has become a nester, redwings have established colonies in the woods of Ross, Sutherland and Inverness-shire, the wood sandpiper has become established in wet floes, the bluethroat has nested and a brood of great northern divers has been reared.

The wanderer in the lonely north country will find himself surrounded by echoes of the past. On an island on a loch he may see a stone fortification, an ancient 'dun' with an underwater causeway leading to it. On the shore there may be a stone circle or a megalithic burial tomb. This is the country of the 'brochs', mysterious round towers which occur only here in the world. Archaeologists still puzzle over who built them. Their latest findings are described in this book.

In country where there are distinctive valleys, as in most of the mainland dealt with, it has been easy to arrange the lochs by their drainage basins, but in peat blanket covering Lewisian gneiss where the lochs are mere hollows and connections hard to trace, this system breaks down, especially when many of the lochs have no name. So in the lochscape of Sutherland and the Outer Islands I have chosen representative samples to give a picture of the whole.

It is the author's hope that readers will be attracted by the new motorways to explore the south-west and the Borders. High Galloway is in fact a miniature of the Cairngorms. The rock is granite, and though the scale is only half that of the Grampian massif, the atmosphere is the same when you get up among the lonelier lochs where the rounded boulders look like curling stones on the ice-scored slabs round the shore of Loch Enoch under Craignaw. The best of it can only be reached on foot, which is all to the good.

Although the Scottish Lochs purport to deal only with freshwaters, this definition has been stretched a little in the Outer Hebrides and North Isles where some lochs are marginally salt because of the tide spilling in from time to time. No loch has been described which does not support a freshwater fauna, which I think is a fair criterion.

Gartocharn
August 1979

Map of the main loch regions

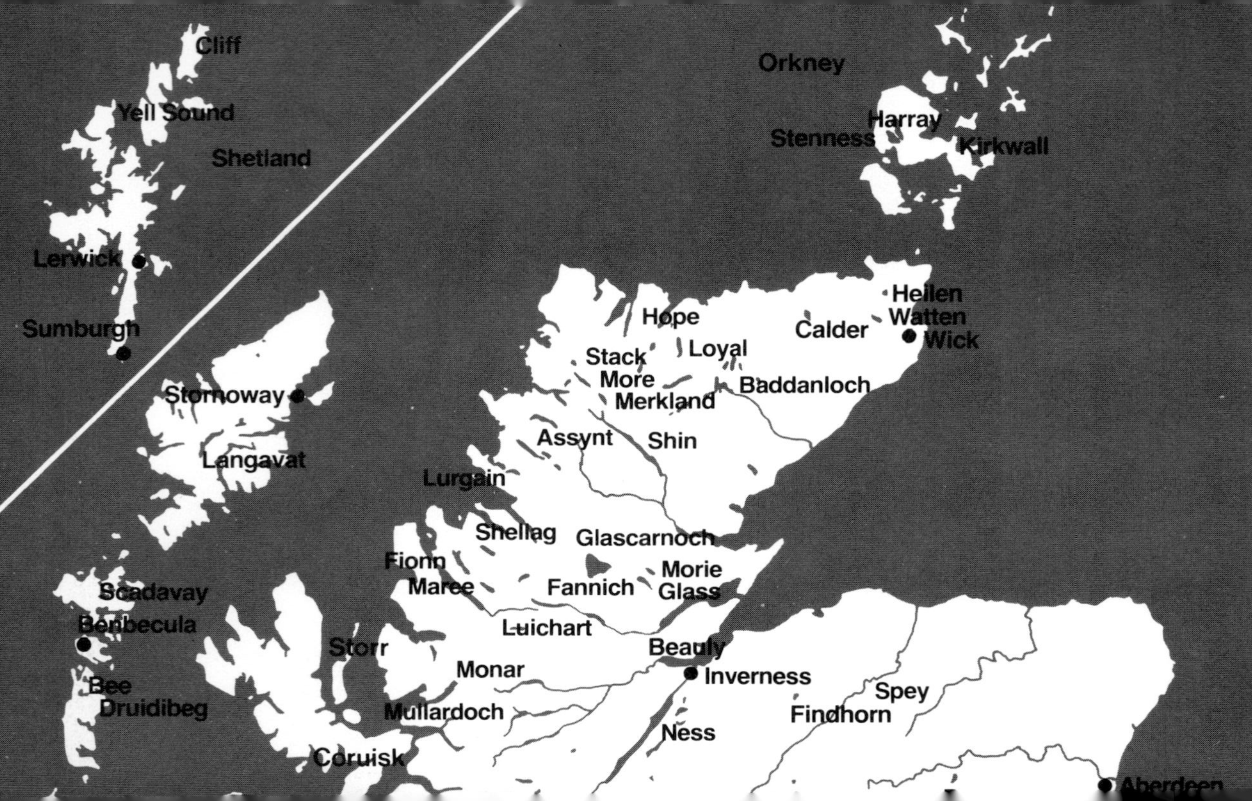

Cliff
Yell Sound
Shetland
Lerwick
Sumburgh
Orkney
Harray
Stenness
Kirkwall
Stornoway
Langavat
Heilen
Watten
Wick
Hope
Calder
Loyal
Stack
More
Baddanloch
Merkland
Assynt
Shin
Lurgain
Shellag
Glascarnoch
Fionn
Morie
Maree
Fannich
Glass
Scadavay
Benbecula
Luichart
Storr
Beauly
Monar
Inverness
Bee
Spey
Druidibeg
Mullardoch
Findhorn
Ness
Coruisk
Aberdeen

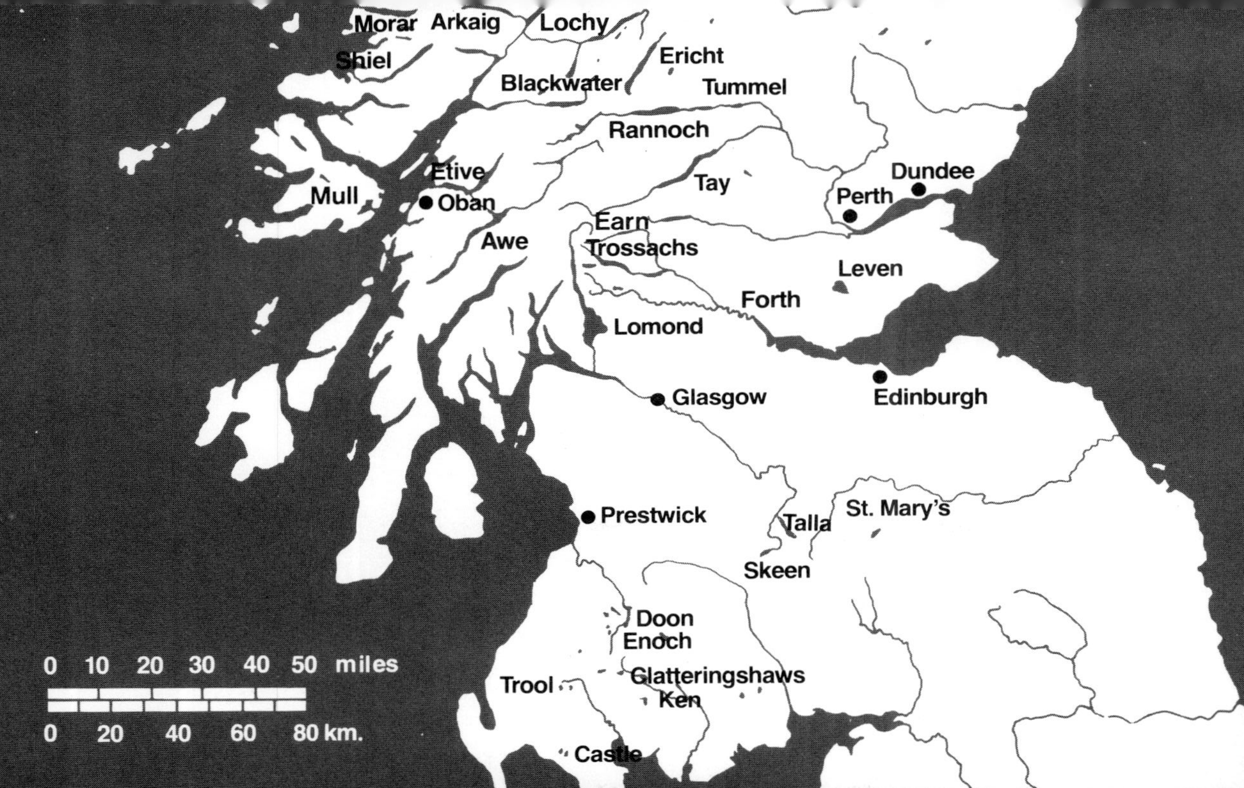
Morar
Arkaig
Lochy
Shiel
Ericht
Blackwater
Tummel
Rannoch
Etive
Mull
Oban
Tay
Dundee
Perth
Earn
Awe
Trossachs
Leven
Forth
Lomond
Glasgow
Edinburgh
Prestwick
Talla
St. Mary's
Skeen
Doon
Enoch
Trool
Glatteringshaws
Ken
Castle
0 10 20 30 40 50 miles
0 20 40 60 80 km.

Metric Conversion Tables

The bold figures in the central columns can be read as either the metric or the British measure. Thus 1 inch = 25·4 millimetres; or 1 millimetre = 0·039 inches.

Inches		*Millimetres*
0.039	**1**	25.4
0.079	**2**	50.8
0.118	**3**	76.2
0.157	**4**	101.6
0.197	**5**	127.0
0.236	**6**	152.4
0.276	**7**	177.8
0.315	**8**	203.2
0.354	**9**	228.6

Miles		*Kilometres*
0.621	**1**	1.609
1.243	**2**	3.219
1.864	**3**	4.828
2.486	**4**	6.437
3.107	**5**	8.047
3.728	**6**	9.656
4.350	**7**	11.265
4.971	**8**	12.875
5.592	**9**	14.484

Feet		*Metres*
3.281	**1**	0.305
6.562	**2**	0.610
9.843	**3**	0.914
13.123	**4**	1.219
16.404	**5**	1.524
19.685	**6**	1.829
22.966	**7**	2.134
26.247	**8**	2.438
29.528	**9**	2.743

Sq feet		*Sq metres*
10.764	**1**	0.093
21.528	**2**	0.186
32.292	**3**	0.279
43.056	**4**	0.372
53.820	**5**	0.465
64.583	**6**	0.557
75.347	**7**	0.650
86.111	**8**	0.743
96.875	**9**	0.836

Yards		*Metres*
1.094	**1**	0.914
2.187	**2**	1.829
3.281	**3**	2.743
4.374	**4**	3.658
5.468	**5**	4.572

Sq yards		*Sq metres*
1.196	**1**	0.836
2.392	**3**	1.672
3.588	**3**	2.508
4.784	**4**	3.345
5.980	**5**	4.181

Cu feet		*Cu metres*
35.315	**1**	0.028
70.629	**2**	0.057
105.944	**3**	0.085
141.259	**4**	0.113
176.573	**5**	0.142
211.888	**6**	0.170
247.203	**7**	0.198
282.517	**8**	0.227
317.832	**9**	0.255

Gallons		*Litres*
0.220	**1**	4.546
0.440	**2**	0.092
0.660	**3**	13.638
0.880	**4**	18.184
1.100	**5**	22.731
1.320	**6**	27.277
1.540	**7**	31.823
1.760	**8**	36.369
1.980	**9**	40.915

Lochs of the Annan Basin

Loch Skeen, Mill Loch, Kirk Loch, Castle Loch and Hightae Loch

Loch Skeen is a rarity for the Southern Uplands, a corrie loch 1,750 ft high between 2,600-ft hills. Moreover, in the Grey Mare's Tail dropping 200 ft into space it has the finest waterfall outside the Highlands. Add to that rare flowers, wild goats, a glacial tangle of moraines and you have a place of exceptional interest, especially with St. Mary's Loch lying only a short distance to the north-east.

Ponded by moraines, elongated Loch Skeen is $\frac{3}{4}$ of a mile long by only $\frac{1}{5}$ of a mile broad, with a centrally placed maximum depth of 36 ft and a mean of 18 ft. The best way to it is by the path known as Fraser's Brae which traverses the hill about 2 miles west of the Grey Mare's Tail. It is also practicable to take the National Trust path up to the east side of the Tail Burn, enjoy the sight of the foaming waterfall, and carry on beyond, picking your way as best you can. Warning notices telling you to beware of the steep ground below the path should be carefully regarded, as deaths have occurred here from slipping into the ravine. There is a shorter way of seeing the waterfall by taking the west side of the Tail Burn, and it is all the more impressive for the viewpoint being low down since you get the full roar and spouting vigour of the fall.

The remaining lochs are grouped round Lochmaben near Lockerbie, a trim Royal Burgh with a proud statue of Robert Bruce who built his castle here, and the local tradition is that the hero was born in Lochmaben. The Castle Loch has the ruins of the Bruce stronghold on a wooded promontory, all that is left of a much besieged place. The loch itself is the largest in the basin and is a fine example of a eutrophic (mineral rich) lowland loch said to contain pike, perch, roach, bream, chub and trout, though its vendace is now extinct, killed off by pollution apparently. It is a local nature reserve now, with Hightae Loch. The accent is on conserving the plants and wildlife, especially the large numbers of wildfowl which winter here. Castle Loch statistics are: length just over $\frac{3}{4}$ of a mile, maximum breadth $\frac{2}{3}$ of a mile, maximum depth 18 ft in the central part. The mean depth is $8\frac{1}{2}$ ft.

The Mill Loch still has vendace in it, the only loch in Scotland where *Coregonus vandesius* occurs, a 6- to 8-in. fish which spawns in November and December. Brown-backed, sides tinged with yellow, it has a heart-shaped mark between the eyes. There is a tradition that they were introduced here by Queen Mary, no doubt as a tasty dish, for they were once netted in fair numbers, and there was even a club devoted to catching enough for an annual banquet. Situated immediately north of Lochmaben, the length is ½ a mile by ⅕ of a mile with a maximum depth of 55 ft at the southern end. It is a kettle-hole in fluvio-glacial gravels.

Kirk Loch is edged by a modern housing development now, in good taste to match the quality of the view from their windows. The length is just under ½ a mile by ⅕ of a mile, the maximum depth being 25 ft though over half is covered by less than 10 ft of water.

Hightae Loch is shaped like a narrow upside-down pear, only ⅓ of a mile at its broadest where the water is deepest at 13 ft, with an overall mean of 7 ft. Hightae Loch takes its name from the Royal Town to the south called Hightae, just a hamlet like Greenhill, Smallholm and Heck which are the other three 'Royal Towns' of Lochmaben. Much of the troubled history of the Scottish border was made here at this western frontier with England. Even in 1628 fines imposed upon cattle drovers were allocated to the upkeep of the King's castle at Lochmaben. A lot of money would be taken this way, for the cattle trade to England was considerable. In 1663 something like 18½ thousand beasts passed through the Carlisle toll gate. How many slipped across the border without paying will never be known.

Lochs of the Galloway Highlands

Lochs Trool, Valley, Neldricken, Arron, Long Loch and Round Loch of Glenhead, Enoch, Twachtan, Macaterick, Fanny, Finlas, Derclach, Riecawr, Goosie, Ballochling, Gower, Muck, Doon, Kendoon, Carsfad, Earlston, Round and Long Loch of Dungeon, Clatteringshaws, Ken, Girvan's Eye, Cornish, Skelloch, Lure, Bradan and Brecbowie

Here in south-western Scotland is an outcrop of the Highlands, a combination of Trossachs and Cairngorms in a sudden outcropping of granite between the Clyde and the Solway, where the turfy farmlands swell behind Girvan to a rocky hinterland of lochs and glens before dropping in another green apron to Wigtown Bay. The best of it belongs to Glen Trool Forest Park which is the largest of its kind in Scotland, and it has never been easier to explore, thanks to a network of forest tracks which penetrate from all directions, notably around the head of Loch Trool.

Loch Trool is one of the great scenic transformations of Galloway. Following the River Cree north from Newton Stewart among yellow reed beds and green foothills of cattle and sheep, you swing east in 8 miles to face a sudden rise of Trossachs-style country. It is unmistakably the Highlands, yet Loch Trool is only 250 ft above high-tide level, so the steep hills have a scale of grandeur out of all proportion to their true height.

Yet it is perhaps the change of colour which makes the greatest impact, the sudden feast of bronze, reds, and yellows, reminiscent of Loch Katrine in autumn. But the spring comes earlier here, with a rush of flowers as the oaks break bud, and happy the person who has a tent or caravan at Loch Trool then in the delightful clearings of the natural forest which make this one of the finest camp sites in Scotland. And there is lots of room and privacy, thanks to the imaginative way the sites have been laid out.

Deciduous woods fringe the narrow road all the way up the loch, screening the thick mats of sitka spruce and larch. The road ends at Bruce's Stone and now you are on the fringe of the Cairngorm country, except that there are more lochs hidden in that granite cauldron than in the Cairngorms, some draining to the Clyde and some to the Solway. The spattered lochans occupy what was once a great reservoir of ice like Rannoch Moor, and Loch Trool—at your feet—is a rock basin dug by one of the masses of ice which drained the cauldron.

The floor of the loch has been carved into three basins, the deepest at the eastern end where the steep hillsides flatten out in a depth of 55 ft below water, then shallowing to 24 ft, deepening again in the mid-basin to 48 ft, shoaling again to another barrier covered by only 12 ft of water, then sinking in the third basin to 36 ft.

The total length of the slightly curved loch is roughly $1\frac{1}{2}$ miles, with the broadest part at $\frac{1}{4}$ of a mile east of the Maiden Isle opposite Bruce's Stone. It was on the far side of the loch Bruce

Loch Trool, one of the great scenic transformations of Galloway

ambushed an English force by rolling stones down on them from above—a victory that was to lead to the success of Bannockburn and the return of Galloway to Scotland. Just 200 years before Bruce, the Viking rule which had lasted for 300 years was coming to its end. The place names today are derived from Norse and Gaelic, as in the Rig of Jarkness, where 'Rig' is Norse for 'ridge' and 'Jarkness' comes from the Gaelic 'Uachness', meaning 'lonely desolate waste'.

No fishing is permitted in Loch Trool, but anglers who enjoy a walk will find a wealth of free fishing in the upper lochs by following up the hanging valley of the Gairland torrent to the staircase of lochs which feed Loch Trool. The lowest in this series is Loch Valley at 1,050 ft, and the highest Loch Arron at 1,450 ft with Loch Neldricken in between at 1,146 ft.

Loch Valley is a trout loch a mile long and much indented by bays on its north shore, fed to the east by the slightly higher Loch Narroch. Loch Neldricken discharges into it in half a mile of short turbulent stream. Both lochs are about the same size and nearly equal in sinuosity, except that Neldricken is nearly cut in two by a peninsula projecting from the north, while just west of it is the strange cut-off known as the 'Murder Hole' of S. R. Crockett's fiction story *The Raiders*. The Galloway novelist has given a sinister atmosphere to the place.

In fact it is a cheery place by reason of the rocky character of Craignaw whose granite rises above the east shore and breaks down into silver sand edging the lagoons. True the hollow is marshy and the stream from the 'Murder Hole' leads up to Loch Arron, which, tiny as it is, has its bay of granite sand beneath the Nick of the Dungeon, 'Nick' meaning 'neck', an exciting pass into the Dee Valley.

On the return journey you could link the other two Trool lochs by crossing the bouldery Rig of Jarkness to the Long Loch and the Round Loch of Glenhead which are 960 ft and 980 ft respectively above sea-level. These lochs are only 200 yards apart but occupy separate rock basins, the marshy Long Loch under Jarkness and the Round Loch under Craiglee.

The Cairngorm feeling of this country is mainly due to the strewn blocks and the granite escarpments of the central spine stretching from Craiglee over Craignaw to Mullwharchar and the

Tauchers forming the highest cliffs above strings of lochs. The pale biotitic granite has resisted erosion, but the lochs occupy depressions where it has been under chemical attack.

To appreciate it fully you must take a look at the lochs of the Doon Basin, which should include Loch Enoch, the remotest and the finest of all the hill lochs yet not much further to walk than a mile beyond Loch Arron. Here is a very special place indeed, a strange ragged loch with islands at 1,617 ft ringed by naked rock slabs and strewn with boulders as if the ice had melted yesterday. And above it on the west, the Merrick, 2,770 ft, highest peak in Galloway, able to withstand denudation because, when the molten granite was intruded in the adjacent cauldron, its sedimentary rocks were metamorphosed by the heat into harder material, as happened too on Corserine, its near rival in height.

So Loch Enoch, like the Dungeon lochs over the hills below Corserine, is on a boundary of rock types, though it is by far the

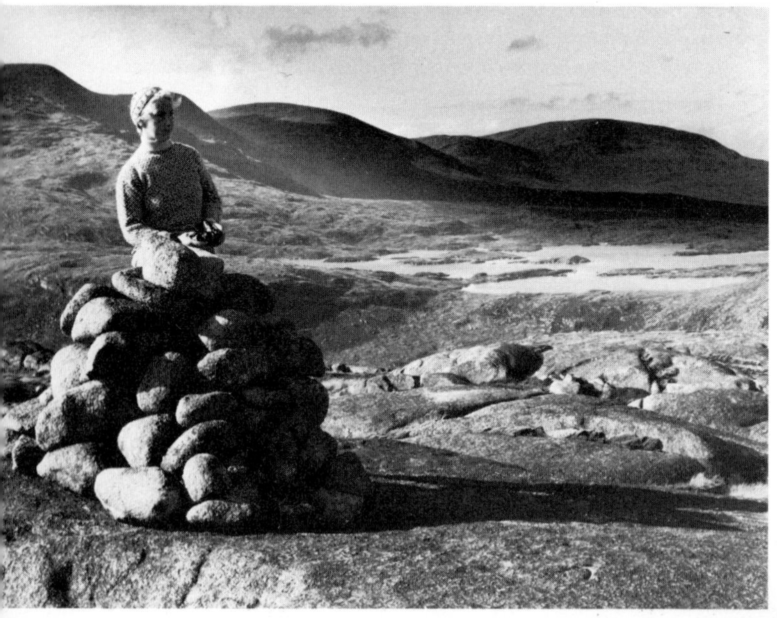

Loch Enoch, the most remote of the Galloway rock basins

most uneven loch in Galloway, like a ragged butterfly pinned on a mount of granite, flecked with black spots which are islands. The biggest island has its own loch on it. Mr. J. McBain in his informative book, *The Merrick and the Neighbouring Hills* tells the crafty story of how he chiselled through the ice in March 1918 to measure Loch Enoch for depth, since the absence of a boat had prevented any surveyors from doing so.

He proved it to be the deepest loch in South Scotland at the time, 20–30 ft deeper than Loch Doon before the hydro-electric alterations deepened the latter loch. McBain was able to cross the deep water on the ice to the big island, and in that lower wing of the butterfly was able to get soundings of 63, 85, 96, 127, 105 and 57 ft, while in the opposite wing to the south-east he got 50, 56 and 64 ft on a loch not quite covered over with ice, so he was a brave man working all alone up there. That night he stayed with the shepherd at Backhill of Bush in the Dee Valley, tramping the 17 miles to Dalmellington next day.

Loch Doon

Great changes have come on this land since he wrote his book published in 1929. The shepherd has long since gone from Backhill of Bush and vast plantations of commercial trees have spread up the loneliest lanes, 'lane' meaning a stream in Galloway, though the term is meant to denote one connecting two lochs. The outlet from Loch Enoch to Loch Doon is by the Eglin Lane in which was caught a 4 lb Loch Enoch trout a long time ago.

These trout described by McBain, though not from personal knowledge, are said to have had no lower half to the tail, nor complete ventral fins, and he speculates that the adaptation may be due to the rock and sharp sandy bottom of this rock basin. It certainly seems strange that they should now be extinct if they managed to live long enough in this high loch to adapt.

Anyone visiting Loch Enoch should walk over the naked rock slabs and look at the strewn rocks of the icefall left by the shrinking Merrick glacier. Better still go on and climb nearby Mullwharchar, the highest of the pure granite peaks situated in the centre of the aureole of metamorphism. From here you have Merrick to the west and Corserine to the east and the cauldron lochs at your feet, with the crags of The Tauchers falling into Gala Lane. Here indeed is a Cairngorm feeling, intensified if you walk the ridge to Craignaw and drop to Cornarroch Strand, itself a miniature Lairig Ghru.

Under the Fang of the Merrick lies tiny Loch Twachtan, one of a dozen lochs draining into Loch Doon. This circular little loch swarms with tiny fish which are said to have large heads in proportion to their size—perhaps another effect of extreme isolation. The smallest loch and the largest, Loch Macaterick, drain into Eglin Lane, the latter covering half a square mile with the large Blaeberry Island. Macaterick receives the outflow from Loch Fanny at its north end, and both contain trout.

From here we enter the field of domestic water supply and hydro-electricity developments, with Loch Doon sending its water by tunnel to power 4 generating stations *en route* to the Solway, while some of its catchment goes the other way to Ayr from Lochs Finlas, Derclach, Riecawr, Goosie, Ballochling and Gower. The only loch feeding Loch Doon from the east side is Loch Muck on the Dalmellington–Carsphairn road where the

Water of Deugh is harnessed to feed Loch Doon.

The raising of Loch Doon by the building of dams at the north and north-eastern ends gives it a possible variation in level of 40 ft. In pre-reservoir days its measurements were as follows: length 6 miles, maximum breadth 1½ miles, mean breadth ⅓ of a mile, maximum depth 100 ft, mean depth 27 ft. The main visual difference today is that the loch has a greater superficial area giving it more width and dignity. The salmon and brown trout fishing from the banks is free and boats can be hired.

Geologically the loch is of special interest, since the aureole of metamorphism passes through it, so that one basin is granite—the deep one nearest to the high hills—while the north basin is in softer Silurian strata. The famous fourteenth-century castle, removed from its island and rebuilt on the shore, overlooks the granite area. Its stones were relaid in the original manner and show the unusual shape with 11 unequal sides 26 ft high and over 7 ft thick. The entrance is by a fine pointed doorway. The island on which it stood may always have been a place of refuge for early man judging by a find of nine tree-trunk canoes on the loch bottom close to it.

The water of Loch Doon released eastward by an outlet valve is used 4 times through a chain of 4 power stations before discharging into the Solway at Kirkcudbright. Built between 1931 and 1936 it has long since repaid the £3m. spent on it and was the only big development in those days of depression. It took maximum advantage of catchment in this southern hill country, establishing a completely new loch at Clatteringshaws as a second reservoir, with a third in Loch Ken, giving ⅓ storage against ⅔ river to produce 226 million units annually.

Once the water has been released from Loch Doon through the valve in Carsphairn Lane it goes through the headponds of Kendoon Loch, Carsfad Loch, Earlston Loch and Loch Ken to Tongland. Clatteringshaws is broadly triangular and lies to the west of the Ken Valley, the water being led by 3½ miles of tunnel to Glenlee power station before joining the Ken. Good places to stay are the villages of St. John's Town of Dalry and New Galloway, two of the most architecturally delightful in Galloway, superbly situated in gentle farming country and looking out on river and hills. Fishing permits for lochs and rivers can be had at

Milton Park Hotel, Dalry, and Cross Keys Hotel, New Galloway, or from the Dalry Angling Association for Carsfad and Clatteringshaws. The salmon and sea trout fishing in Loch Ken is free to hotel guests.

Loch Ken belongs to the Dee drainage system, which by hydro-electric engineering begins nowadays at Loch Doon as has been explained. To trace the original drainage we must go back into the heart of the hills and look at two Loch Dungeons. The remotest is the Round Loch of the Dungeon under Dungeon Hill. It lies close to the watershed of the Great Valley separating the granite of the Mullwharchar and the baked rocks of the Rhinns of Kells and contains trout and pike. Just below it is the Long Loch of the Dungeon, said to be infested with pike, and with maybe a salmon among the trout. The height difference between the lochs is only 30 ft, and the Long Loch trails into the sinister Silver Flow, the most dangerous raised bog in Galloway and one that has claimed at least one life.

It takes its name from the glitter of pools in the centre of the bog which is actively growing west of Cooran Lane though one part lies in the loop where the Cornarroch Strand joins the Lane. The Nature Conservancy has leased Silver Flow in order to study it, and one of the methods used has been to take low level aerial photographs of the pools with an automatic camera suspended from a balloon. Sheep avoid the place and the largest dragonflies in Galloway buzz around the bladderwort in summer.

Loch Dee is a pleasant walk from the head of Loch Trool or from Clatteringshaws and contains trout, salmon, pike and eels. It is a true rock basin, broadest at the south-west end where it is deepest. Length just over a mile with a maximum breadth of $\frac{3}{4}$ of a mile, more than half the loch is covered by less than 10 ft, the maximum being 36 ft west of the big peninsula which nearly divides the loch into two. Fishing can be arranged with the Cross Keys Hotel, New Galloway.

Another Loch Dungeon is in the Rhinns of Kells, approached from above Earlston Loch from Polharrow Bridge by one of the most delightful glens in Galloway. The road ends at Forrest Lodge beyond which it is a walk of 3 miles or so into the hills, through forestry plantations at first. Nestling under the steep screes of Milldown and Millyea it has great character, 1,000 ft up and nearly a mile long by $\frac{1}{3}$ of a mile maximum breadth, a big peninsula almost dividing its irregular shape. As might be expected the rock basin is deepest under the peaks, reaching 94 ft, shallowing to 34 ft in the centre and deepening again to 45 ft. Two smaller of the Dee lochs lying northward are Loch Minnoch and Loch Harrow, the latter a rock basin with a maximum depth of 29 ft. The fishing appears to be private.

Loch Grannoch takes us back to the granite again under Cairnsmore of Fleet in the Cairn Edward Forest, a narrow rock basin 2 miles long by over $\frac{1}{3}$ of a mile broad with a maximum depth of 68 ft. Brown trout fishing can be arranged with Cally Estate Office, Gatehouse-of-fleet, also from Cally Hotel in the same country town.

Winter at Clatteringshaws reservoir

Loch Skerrow lies further east and the brown trout fishing is from Cally Estate Office as above. This loch is $\frac{3}{4}$ of a mile long by $\frac{1}{2}$ a mile in maximum breadth with a greatest depth of 33 ft, although 40 per cent is less than 10 ft deep. All this is noted wild goose country, attracting ornithologists from autumn to spring when pink feet, greylags, barnacle, Greenland whitefronts and even the rare lesser whitefronts may be encountered.

Woodhall Loch lies below New Galloway on the Laurieston road and is $1\frac{3}{4}$ miles long by nearly $\frac{1}{3}$ of a mile broad, partly a rock basin with a maximum depth of 49 ft. And now we come to Loch Ken, greatly elongated to make a reservoir for the Galloway Power Scheme but still the finest wildlife loch in the neighbourhood thanks to the diversity of its shores and rich feeding for birds. Loch Ken contains enough water to run the Tongland Power Station for 24 hours at full load, controlled by barrage gates at its southern end. Yet it does not look like a reservoir.

In pre-hydro-electric days Loch Ken was just over $4\frac{1}{2}$ miles long with a maximum width of $\frac{1}{2}$ a mile and a maximum depth of 62 ft near the top end in the deepest of 6 rock basins. And beneath where the loch ended there were expansions of the Dee, one of them nearly $\frac{1}{2}$ a mile in width, with depths of 44 ft and 42 ft, in parts separated by a mile of winding. The barrage and added inflow from the north has made a 10-mile loch of all this, narrowest near Parton where the disused railway crosses by bridge. There is no monotony in any stretch of this loch, with its farmlands and forests and grassy hillocks often thronged with cropping grey geese and sleeping wigeon duck. Glass the loch and you will find pintail, teal, shoveller, mallard, golden eye and many another in the bays or out on the narrow loch. Over the hills you may see buzzards or spot a peregrine falcon. Man has superimposed himself graciously here, even on architecturally satisfying villages like Parton and Crossmichael. Just a few miles on is shallow Carlingwark Loch at Castle Douglas, 17 ft at its deepest and popular for fishing and boating. The extensive National Trust for Scotland gardens at Threave nearby should be visited for its views and parklands as much as for its wealth of exotic flowers. Part of the estate is a wildfowl reserve.

Before leaving Galloway a mention must be made of the

connected lochs of the Girvan basin which begin just north of the Merrick on the hill called Shalloch on Minnoch with Loch Girvan's Eye nearly 1,500 ft up, a tiny sheet of water full of trout and relatively accessible from the high-climbing Straiton road in a walk of less than 3 miles. In the connected staircase of lochs below, the next is Loch Cornish $1\frac{1}{2}$ miles distant and three times as big, though the length is only $\frac{1}{4}$ of a mile by $\frac{1}{7}$ of a mile broad, with a maximum depth of 7 ft. Below it in another $1\frac{1}{2}$ miles is Loch Skelloch about the same size and holding good trout.

Another $1\frac{1}{2}$ miles down is Loch Lure and Loch Bradan, now joined together to make a reservoir to supply domestic water to Troon. Bradan fed by Loch Brecbowie was originally a few feet lower in elevation than Lure. Joining them together has not submerged completely the ruins of a building on the island purported to be a castle. The original depth of Lure and Bradan was 7 ft maximum and 8 ft maximum respectively. Raised by 10 ft they make one loch of just under 2 miles connected by road to Tairlaw. Fishing and boats may be had from the Forestry Commission, Craigard, Straiton, Maybole.

Galloway is in the process of change and there are two extreme views about the huge-scale forestry operations which are crowding up valley after valley in a dark green tide of spruces. The forester says you cannot have too many trees, and points out the 205 sq. miles of Glen Trool Forest Park, which was a region in decline when the Commission took over. Until then the vast areas of hill land had been divided into sheep farms. There are five productive forests now, yet the country of Kirkcudbright as a whole still carries the same population of sheep. Grazings have been much improved, says the Forestry Commission, due to the use of lime and fertilisers to reseed the fire-breaks which are let out to local sheep men. The network of forestry roads have also been of use to the farmers by reducing their isolation.

In human terms there is a new village of 47 houses with shop and school in Glen Trool. Eighteen smallholdings have been let to forest workers. The population has gone up here but has decreased elsewhere in Kirkcudbright. On the recreation side there has been a steadily increasing use by caravanners and campers using the Glen Trool site, so that the whole area is being enjoyed as never before in its history.

Against this, however, is the view of the shepherd and the naturalist. The first would say that the plantings are going too far and that there will soon be no room left for his sheep. They plead that the time has come when positive conservation is required to save the farms and preserve the habitats before they disappear under trees, diminishing the wide views of moors and sky which are such an inspiring feature of Galloway. It is said now that there is two acres of productive forest for each of the 58,000 inhabitants in the two counties of Wigtown and Kirkcudbright. Forestry is expected to provide for 4,000 people in Galloway eventually, including workers and their families.

The establishment of the Cairnsmore of Fleet National Nature Reserve, comprising 2,850 hectares unafforested and pastureland extending to the granite of the high tops, means that a Grade 1 site noted for its wild life remains as a fragment of old Galloway. Its birds include golden eagle, peregrine, merlin, raven and a variety of waders which are disappearing from tree-planted areas. It gives a yardstick by which to measure the effects of afforestation on wildlife, as well as being varied and beautiful.

St. Mary's Loch, Loch of the Lowes and Talla Reservoir

Anyone with an eye for country travelling north-eastwards along Moffatdale will notice the deep 'U' shape of the valley, its straightness the result of glaciation along the shatter belt, the same influence that gives us the Grey Mare's Tail, most conspicuous of several hanging tributaries above the road leading to St. Mary's and Loch of the Lowes—two separate lochs which used to be one. The barrier between the lochs at Tibbie Shiels Inn which carries the road is no more than debris pushed out by the Ox Cleuch Burn to the west and the Thirlstane Burn to the east meeting together to form a natural dam.

Even St. Mary's Loch as it is today is divided into two basins by a big fan of alluvium built up by the Megget Water where it enters half way down the loch. Similarly the loch level has been raised by the deltas which pond its outlet. The dam in this case has been built up by the Kirkstead and Dryhope Burns to the north, and the Thorny Cleuch to the south. The glacier which dug the trench containing St. Mary's Loch spilled over from Moffatdale and Megget to make a rock basin continuing its digging action into Yarrow to leave a mass of morainic litter.

In this country of fine glens and rounded hills with its few lochs, two great native writers, Sir Walter Scott and James Hogg, drew inspiration here for their novels. They would often meet together to carouse at Tibbie Shiels, and delight in each other's opposites, Scott the man of infinite culture, Hogg the self-taught Ettrick shepherd and poet who wrote the amazing *Confessions of a Justified Sinner* now regarded as a classic. It is a psychological horror story, haunting in its conviction of evil turned on its perpetrator to madness and suicide. Nothing like it had been written before, or since.

Hogg's seated statue in bronze, with his '. . . auld, towzy, trusty dog' Hector, looks over the Loch of the Lowes outside Tibbie Shiels Inn, as if reflecting on all the big trout he caught. Permits are available by applying to the Gordon Arms Hotel, the Rondono Hotel, the Glen Café or The Old Schoolhouse, Cappercleuch.

Loch of the Lowes is a mile long by ¼ of a mile broad with a maximum depth of 58 ft at the southern end. St. Mary's is just under 3 miles with a maximum breadth of over ½ a mile and a maximum depth of 153 ft in its widest part where the Megget glacier joined the Moffat glacier. This shallows to 88 ft where the ridge of gravel brought down by the Megget has built up a ridge, beyond which is the southern basin which drops to 112 ft and continues deeply for ½ a mile.

St. Mary's Loch with its ruins of the old chapel and Dryhope Tower is a popular motor run today, but it does not yield its full charms by this flighty mode of travel. To catch the spirit of the place you should leave the car at Tibbie Shiels and take a walk along the foot-path following along by the March Wood to the farm of Bowerhope. South of the Gordon Arms Hotel above the Yarrow is a farmhouse called Eldinhope. James Hogg who died in 1835 lived there. A memorial service to persecuted Covenanters who died for their faith is held every year in the ruins of St. Mary's Chapel.

A narrow road running from Cappercleuch climbs through the hills to Talla Reservoir and drops by waterfalls into the deep glacial gouge now occupied by a long narrow loch impounded behind 1,300 ft of embankment to supply Edinburgh with water. The natural drainage is into the Tweed. Begun in 1895 the work was finished in 1905, and the brown trout fishing is in the hands of the Corporation Water Department, 6 Cockburn Street, Edinburgh, 30p per boat and 20p per rod.

Talla Reservoir is 959 ft above sea-level and 14 miles south of Peebles in Tweedale. Length 2½ miles by ¼ of a mile broad, the maximum depth of 73 ft is near the embankment. It is an easy matter to climb the highest hill in the Southern Uplands from Talla, Broad Law, 2,754 ft, by striking north from the Megget Stane on the highest point of the road above the Talla Linns.

The lines to the Galloway novelist S. R. Crockett written by Robert Louis Stevenson sum up the feeling of this rolling country of secret glens:

Grey recumbent tombs of the dead in desert places,
Standing-stones on the vacant wine-red moor,
Hills of sheep, and the howes of the silent vanished races,
And winds, austere and pure . . .

Stand with me on the summit of Ben Lomond on a May day of crisp visibility. On this most southern of the Highland Munros you command the Highlands and Lowlands. Out there on the Firth of Clyde, beyond the high ridge of the Arran hills and the dark hump of Ailsa Craig, is the Antrim coast from whence came the Celts who gave Scotland its name. Below us are the dark corrie crags of the Ben, with a wee burn tumbling down it—the beginning of the River Forth. In the distance its course to the sea is signposted for us by the rocks of Stirling Castle, the Wallace Monument and the chemical complex of the Grangemouth Refinery. Westward are the Hebrides, the Paps of Jura and the Bens of Mull.

From up here we can see clearly how man had such easy access to the Highlands from the Firth of Clyde, with salt-water Loch Long threading inland for 16 miles to end below the rock prongs of the Cobbler—an invitation to the Vikings to sail in, haul their longships 2 miles overland from Arrochar to Tarbet, relaunch in Loch Lomond, sail south and sack the shore and island settlements. Nor did they have to retrace to Loch Long after their raids, since they could navigate down the outflow of Loch Lomond by the River Leven, regain the Clyde below Dumbarton Rock, and join the main Viking fleet for the Battle of Largs, where powerful retribution was meted out to them.

It would be illuminating to know what the human population of Loch Lomond was in these thirteenth-century times. It would be even more so if we could look back another 5,000 years to the sight that met the eyes of the first Stone-Age men to paddle their dug-out canoes on the loch, primitive bows and arrows at the ready, against human enemies or dangerous animals.

Perhaps these bold colonists from the Baltic numbered only a few dozen when they settled at Balmaha, at Luss and at Inchlonaig. We know about them from the stone tools they left behind. Probing forward would be a cautious affair, with 27·45 square miles of water and 33 islands to explore, in a heavily wooded country with brown bears roaming and wolves preying on elk and reindeer. The tree-line would be much higher than we know now, and the red deer would be larger and more heavily antlered than those today.

Why is Loch Lomond so narrow and ravine-like in the north and so very spacious in its broad southern base? The answer is in the sudden change of rock strata from hard Highland schist to soft sandstone. The glaciers of ice-age times which dug out the depression that was to be Loch Lomond dug deep where the rocks were hard, down to over 600 ft below the present sea-level between Tarbet and Inversnaid. But when they came to the softer material they had room to spread. The islands which are one of the glories of Loch Lomond are the gritty masses which withstood the passage of the broadening glaciers.

One fish reflects the ice-age past, the powan or fresh-water herring. The theory is that this plankton-eating white-fish was forced to adapt to a fresh-water existence when the land level rose with the removal of the great weight of ice as it melted. Thus when the salt-water hollow of Loch Lomond became fresh water, the powan was cut off from the sea. By spawning in mid-winter when the loch is coldest it reflects its ice-age past.

Powan are the commonest fish in the loch and are good to eat when freshly caught, but to get them you have to use a net since, being plankton eaters, they rarely accept a fishing fly. Pike on the other hand are notably good, the British record being held by a Loch Lomond fish at 47 lb 11 oz. The roach reaches its northern limit here, but for the game fisherman the real challenge are the salmon and pink-fleshed sea trout. No other Scottish loch can list so many species of fish as Loch Lomond, with sea lamprey, brook lamprey, lampern, brook trout, minnow, perch, loach, eel, three-spined and ten-spined stickleback, roach and flounder.

Loch Lomond was probably a relatively small loch when powan were impounded in what may have been gravelly water and decaying ice-lobes. The separated basins would become one when the ice melted. Glen Luss and the River Endrick, originally one east-flowing stream draining from a high plateau, were severed when the valley which was to become Loch Lomond was gouged by the last ice-age which ended 10,000 years ago.

The story of that final phase, when pieced together, shows that a long period of melting which began 20,000 years ago came to an end in a return to glacial conditions known to science as the

Loch Lomond Readvance, when fast moving rivers of ice 2,000 ft thick moulded the mountain shapes and valleys we know today.

Perhaps the best place to view the transition between Highland and Lowland rocks is to climb the small hill called Duncryne on the southern shore, above the village of Gartocharn. From its 462-ft top you have the Lowlands at your feet and the Highlands rising northward in a bristly wall above the dotted islands. The line of the Highland Boundary Fault is clearly seen, running along the crest of the islands of Inchmurrin, Creeinch, Torrinch and Inchcailloh and eastward over the ridge of Conic Hill. No other change from green fields to sudden mountains is more striking.

It has been computed that if you could stop up all the streams draining into Loch Lomond it would take the river Leven two years to drain it from Balloch—the only natural outlet. Speculate on what you might see if this were to happen. Immediately below Duncryne where the fields meet the shore you would make such a

The rise of Ben Lomond and the adjacent Highland peaks from the Lowland shore at Gartocharn

shallow descent to the loch floor that all the way north to Luss the islands would never be as high as Duncryne over your head.

But north of Inverbeg you would be plunging downhill in a narrow trough so deep that Tarbet would be 500 ft above you, and for the next 3 miles you would be more than 600 ft below sea-level, stumbling over the rock and rubble left by the glacier which excavated the bed. Although Loch Lomond dates back only 10,000 years, the glacial period which led to its formation began approximately 3 million years ago, as valleys were carved from the plateau. The rock types are obvious in the slate quarries at Luss, in the grey schist rock faces outcropping everywhere northward, quite unlike the gentler country of the sedimentary Old Red Sandstone stretching from Helensburgh through the

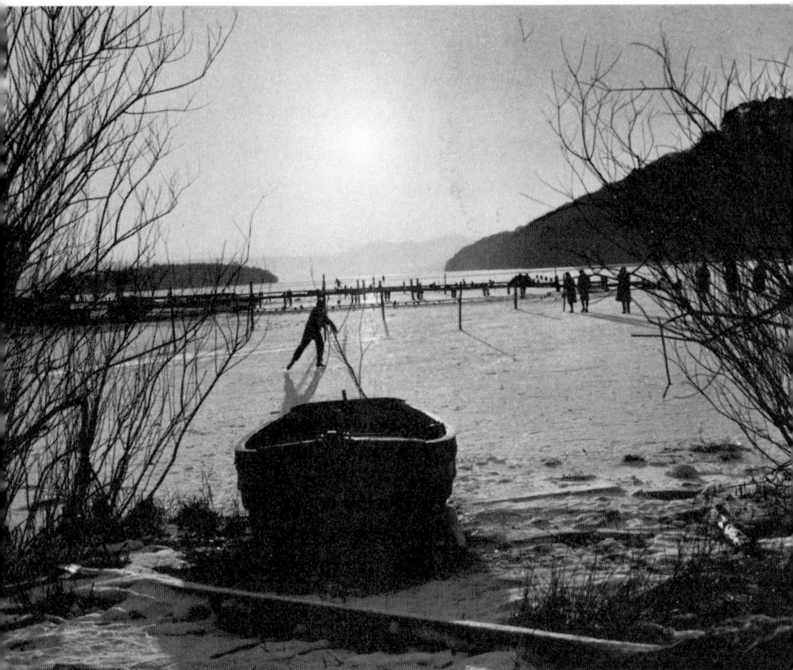

The hard winter of 1963 from the foot of Balmaha

southern chain of islands to Balmaha, whose crests are the serpentine of the Highland Boundary Fault.

Balmaha Bay is the picturesque natural anchorage for boats on the eastern side of the loch. Separated from the holy island of Inchcailloch by no more than a short strait of water, it is edged on the south by the sandbars and marshes of the Endrick mouth where the river sweeps broadly into the loch, and is one of Britain's finest plant- and bird-rich National Nature Reserves.

No other Scottish loch has such a mixture of little sandy bays, lagoons of semi-aquatic vegetation and shallow pools pink with persicaria and yellow with water lilies in summer. This 'Mainland' part of the reserve is a natural holding-point for birds of passage and wintering wildfowl, situated as it is at the junction of four flyways.

February is a time of peak activity, when the marshes are loud with the baying of geese, perhaps a thousand or two of greylags, and the softer calls of Greenland whitefronts, with a few pink feet and Canada. Add to that the duck—wigeon, shoveller, teal, tufted, golden eye, mallard and the odd vagrant like smew, gadwall, long-tailed duck or pintail. Nesting time brings goosander and merganser and an inland colony of shelduck sail with their flotillas of striped young, as common terns and occasional Arctic tern incubate eggs nearby. Late May and early June are the most delightful times, when the dunlin are reeling and the marshes are loud with the cries of curlews, redshank, peewits, oyster-catchers and drumming snipe. Anything can turn up here, red-necked phalarope, avocet, curlew, sandpiper, godwits, knots, goshawk, peregrine, merlin, little gull or gyrfalcon. Ospreys fish for pike and powan most summers off Balmaha.

Get the man who hires boats at Balmaha, to run you over to the near island of Inchcailloch, and explore it with the help of the Nature Trail booklet available there. Inchcailloch is from the Gaelic: Innis means island, and the cailloch refers to old women, probably followers of St. Kentigerna, mother of St. Fillan and daughter of the King of Leinster who retired to the Loch Lomond island at the end of her life and died here in AD 763.

In the ancient graveyard with names of MacFarlanes and McGregors on its weathered stones, is the foundation of the church built in 1225 to honour St. Kentigerna, 300 years after her death. It remained the parish church for the next 500 years. During these early days of written history we know that the monks of Paisley Abbey shared with the local churches the right to exploit the Loch Lomond woods. In the fifteenth century timber from Loch Lomond was brought to the Dumbarton shipyards. A century later we hear of Inchcailloch being farmed, and the trees may by then have been completely cleared.

But what we see now on Inchcailloch is a semi-natural oakwood grown originally for its bark, used in tanning; the trees being coppiced at twenty-four years. Nature brought it back to forest with the abandonment of the bark industry in the nineteenth century. Its feature is the exceptionally high density of woodland birds. Note the tiny speck at the nose of the adjacent island of Clairinch, which is shaped like a flounder. That speck is a crannog, where a fragment of Roman pottery was found recently. Crannogs are ancient lake dwellings. Another can be seen at Strathcashel Point in heaps of stones 85 ft by 65 ft. They were usually built on sunken rocks, to make artificial islands, or wooden stakes might be driven down to support an Iron-Age house and stockade.

Inchmurrin is the biggest of the Loch Lomond islands, and water buses operate to it from Balloch railhead, or it can be reached from Duck Bay. Run as a farm with holiday homes to let and licensed hotel, it is popular with water-skiers and has a nudist colony in a remote corner. The ivy-clad ruin of a castle on its extremity reminds us of Duncan, Earl of Lennox, who was executed by James I; his male heirs were exiled or imprisoned, but his widow was allowed to live on in the castle.

Luss village is one of the gems of Loch Lomond in the Colquhoun lands whose family home, Rossdhu, and beautiful parkland are open to the public in summer. This family has a proud record of wise land-management which has always taken account of public interest and conservation. To them we owe much of the charm we are apt to take for granted in this part of the loch. Notice the wooded island of Inchtavannach where the Irish monk St. Kessog settled in the sixth century, perhaps the first of the Celtic missionaries to work in these parts.

North of Luss the Loch Lomond road becomes difficult and

dangerous, because of increased summer traffic and the congestion caused when two long vehicles meet each other on the numerous bends that are tight even for cars. Realignment is to take place in the 1980s, and it can only be a painful process for trunk road users, with long delays on the A82.

There could be traffic congestion on the eastern side too, if the North of Scotland Hydro-Electric Board fulfil their plan to build Europe's biggest pumped-storage scheme on Ben Lomond. If this comes to pass, it could mean widening the road from Balmaha to Rowardennan, plus driving a new road upwards round the shoulder of the hill to 1,600 ft, where a great hollow in the hill would be dammed to make a reservoir.

On Loch Lomondside itself, dug into the mountain a great underground powerhouse would be built, to pump water from Loch Lomond up through the mountain into the high reservoir, then to bring the water down again to turn the generators and produce electricity at peak demand. Output in the first phase of this scheme would be 1,600 megawatts, and construction would take eight years, or more.

Opposers of this scheme make a good case for all development on Loch Lomond being kept to the western side, leaving the Ben Lomond side of the loch a free wilderness of natural beauty. They would prefer a conversion of Loch Sloy to pumped storage, as was proposed by the North of Scotland Hydro-Electric Board in the 1960s. Sloy is a conventional scheme at the time of writing, producing a mere 130 megawatts of electricity from its powerhouse on the Inveruglas shore. But by conversion to pumped storage, its output would be around 1,600 megawatts, equal in capacity to the Ben Lomond proposal.

Arguments have centred around comparative costs, but there has been no break-down of figures. If the Ben Lomond scheme is accepted, it means that we shall have two power schemes facing each other across our finest loch; yet Ben Lomond in European conservation terms is a number one site, and has been protected since the 1940s by a National Parks Direction Order because of its distinction. A big argument for Loch Sloy is that it is already served by road and railway.

For a drive from Loch Lomond to Loch Sloy, call in at the Inveruglas power-station and obtain a free permit to use their high climbing road going up nearly 1,000 feet into the heart of a wild rocky corrie. Above you the peaks of the Arroch Alps rise to 3,000 ft, and behind you is one of the finest views of Ben Lomond and the unsurpassed eastern shore. A full-scale pumped storage scheme utilizing an enlarged Loch Sloy could be a great magnet for tourists, and take some of the pressure off the busy main road. *Loch Sloy* was the warcry of the clan MacFarlane whose stronghold was on Inveruglas Isle far below, now a ruin after being sacked by Cromwell.

Loch Lomond, considering all the pressures put upon it, remains a scenic miracle as well as a waterway vital to our future economy. 100,000,000 gallons of it per day are used in the central belt of Scotland for drinking and industrial purposes. Glasgow gets electricity from it, and every year an increasing avalanche of tourists descends upon it. We envisage a world of increasing leisure in the future, when Loch Lomond will become more and more valuable for recreation, and its wilderness area on the eastern shore will be more important to urban dwellers looking for escape to the natural world.

Our planners are not unaware of the problem, but they are in the hands of the economists, without whom they would have no job—and neither would we.

Loch Lomond:
Loch Lomond is the third longest and third deepest loch in Scotland.

Length: 22.64 miles
Area: 27.45 sq. miles.
Height above sea-level: 27 ft.
Longest lochs respectively are Lochs Awe and Ness.
Lochs Morar and Ness come first in order of depth.

Ferry service: Inverbeg to Rowardennan.
Steamer:
Day tours on *Maid of the Loch* from Balloch Pier, in summer.
Calls at Luss, Tarbet, Rowardennan, Inversnaid.

Motoring:
A82 trunk road offers a scenic and direct route to the Western Highlands but is inadequate for summer traffic, and delays are common. Demands careful driving on numerous bends north of Luss. Long vehicles a problem. Realignment of road taking place during the 1980s.
Motoring on the eastern shore ends at Rowardennan. From there to Inversnaid there is a footpath.
Inversnaid may be reached by car by detouring to Aberfoyle and driving by Loch Ard.

Nature Reserve:
Warden, Telephone Drymen 428.
Inchcailloch accessible from Balmaha boatyard, Nature Trail booklet available on the island.

The Maid of the Loch at Rowardennan

Boating: Boats for hire at Balloch and Balmaha.
Local tours by water bus from Balloch and Tarbet.
Trips from Balmaha to the islands on the post boat.

Youth Hostels:
Auchendennan near Balloch.
Inverbeg, on west shore.
Rowardennan, opposite Inverbeg and accessible by ferry.

Hotels:
South shore: Balloch, Gartocharn, Drymen.
East shore: Rowardennan, Inversnaid.
West Shore: Duck Bay, Lomond Castle, Luss, Inverbeg, Tarbet, Ardlui, Inverarnan. Also private house bed-and-breakfast available on west shore.

Caravan sites:
A good range on western and eastern shores, including those of Caravan Club and Forestry Commission. Often congested at height of tourist season.

Trains:
Every half-hour, electric service from Queen St., Glasgow, and Balloch.

Cameron House Bear Park:
A safari park with restaurant and gardens near Balloch.
Exhibition of historic relics in Cameron House.
Open 10 am–7pm in summer.

Bus service:
Glasgow to Balloch (frequent)
Balloch to Luss (infrequent)
Balloch to Balmaha (infrequent)
Glasgow to Drymen (fair service)
Glasgow to Fort William via Loch Lomond and Glen Coe (one daily)
Glasgow to Oban via Loch Lomond (twice daily)

Angling:
Permits for the whole loch from
Loch Lomond Angling Improvement Association,
R. A. Clement & Coy,
224 Ingram St.,
Glasgow.

also from
Head Water Bailiff,
20 Luss Road,
Alexandria.

Peter Ewing, Ironmonger,
168 Main St.,
Alexandria.

Lochs of the Forth Basin (1)

The Trossachs, Lochs Arklet, Katrine, Achray, Venachar, Drunkie, Voil, Doine, Lubnaig, Chon, Dubh, Ard

Roads, reservoirs, a steamer service on Loch Katrine, car parks and laybys, tinkers in kilts playing bagpipes, ice-cream vans, strings of tourist buses and picnic parties have not destroyed the charm of this miniature 'Lake District', for the excellent reason that much of the country remains as remote as in the days of Sir Walter Scott and William Wordsworth who gave it to the world in prose and poetry.

True that in their day the best way to see the Trossachs was to sail up to Loch Lomond, disembark at Inversnaid, and be driven by horse and coach up the steep hill by a rushing waterfall to reedy Loch Arklet beyond which lay Loch Katrine. Sturdy boatmen took over, pulling down half a dozen miles on the oars into a defile of great rocks and mountain peaks drawing ever closer, to inspire Sir Walter with:

High on the south huge Ben Venue
Down on the lake in masses threw,
Crags, knolls, and mounds, confusedly hurled,
The fragments of an earlier world. . . .

All this was before Loch Arklet and Loch Katrine were commandeered by the Glasgow Corporation, and the Forth robbed of 90,000,000 gallons per day by diversion of its waters west through pipes and conduits to the city. To break down the story a bit we shall begin with Loch Arklet which used to flow west into Loch Lomond until a dam was constructed at its outlet so that the waters of an enlarged loch would be tipped into Loch Katrine.

Loch Arklet was originally a shallow loch, only 67 ft deep before it was enlarged to three times its original size by the dam. It lies almost mid-way between Loch Lomond and Loch Katrine and occupies a glacial breach. Stand at Inversnaid and look west to Inveruglas, and reflect that the stream beside which you are standing was once linked to the one exactly opposite, in an east-flowing valley. The water engineers have made history repeat itself by building a dam and making Loch Arklet flow east again—through a conduit into Loch Katrine.

From Loch Arklet to Loch Katrine is less than a mile, but the change of scene is striking. Loch Arklet is sombre and walled westward by the high mass of the Arrochar Hills, though these 'Alps' are actually beyond Loch Lomond, at the head of Loch Long. Loch Katrine at Stronachlachar, just down the road, is wooded with an intimate friendliness, even though the hills are rugged. This is the turning point for the steamer, *Sir Walter Scott*, which plies on the loch each morning and afternoon in summer offering a $1\frac{3}{4}$-hour sail at the lowest prices in Britain, owing perhaps to the fact that the little ship has been operating since the beginning of the century. Fishing Loch Katrine is likewise cheap, bookable at Stronachlachar where the rowing boats are kept. There is no driving allowed round Loch Katrine, though cyclists can use the good private road from Trossachs Pier to Royal cottage.

Loch Katrine near Trossach Pier

All this is Rob Roy's country. He was born in the house at the head of the loch, and nature favoured him with exceptionally long arms which he put to good use to lift other people's property. They say he could tie his garters without stooping or thrust a claymore further than most. Combining the trade of cattle dealer with riever, he was well-placed in this spot to whip across the hills into the Lowlands and spirit the cattle across the passes into secret hideouts between Loch Lomond and Loch Katrine.

Royal Cottage about two miles east of Stronachlachar commemorates the opening of the 'waterworks' on 14 October 1859 when Queen Victoria sailed with her retinue on the *Rob Roy* to land here and perform the ceremony. And as the water flowed, the consumption of soap was cut by half in Glasgow, thanks to its softness. However dirty Glasgow was, analysis showed that they had the cleanest water supply in Britain.

The route the water takes is west by tunnel to the pipe-track above Loch Chon and Loch Ard, where giant pylons march in the same direction. These pylons of the Cruachan Power Station have marred the unblemished skyline of Loch Katrine. At 250 ft high they are too dominating in this small-scale country. The electric cables should have gone underground. Sailing up the loch they are the only jarring note, coming in as they do from the north as part of the Cruachan Hydro-Electric Pumped Storage Scheme.

The name 'Trossachs' really applies to the narrow pass where the Achray Water emerges from the loch through rock bluffs. In olden days the pathway was so precipitous that it was known as 'the ladders'. The word 'Trossachs' is supposed to derive from 'Bristly', which is absolutely right for it. Alas, it was all too easily tamed, even though the blasting operations are said to have cost the Glasgow Corporation £2,000 a mile. I like to reflect however that as late as 1843 the native boatmen were still untamed enough to sink a small iron steamer introduced to Loch Katrine as a tourist attraction, just twelve years before the Act of Parliament authorising the raising of Loch Katrine to supply Glasgow with water.

Loch Katrine is 8 miles long with an average width of 1 mile, with its maximum depth somewhere around 500 ft. It is the only loch of this group whose floor is below sea-level—indeed half of its total length is over 400 ft deep in the narrow central depression which shows the loch to be a simple basin. The height above sea-level is 364 ft.

A short walk I can recommend is through the woods behind Achray Hotel, forking right over a stream, and right again at the first path junction. By this route you are following the south side of the outlet stream, and soon it becomes a grassy track beneath the crags of Ben Venue, getting wilder as you approach the Bealach nam Bo, a cleft in the mountain meaning the Pass of the Cattle, a bouldery notch in the rocks which was made good use of by Rob Roy, as you might expect.

Turning east down the same water you come to Loch Achray and the Trossachs Hotel, built in the grand baronial style, now a centre of dinghy sailing, water ski-ing and pony trekking. Loch Achray is 97 ft at its deepest, with a bit near the centre, marked

Loch Achray in the Queen Elizabeth Forest Park

by a buoy, which is only 2 ft. Length 1¼ miles by ⅓ broad, much of its charm is due to the trees on the steep slopes of each side, birch and oak to the north, spruce and larch to the south on the Queen Elizabeth Forest Park side, though the Commission are now planting on the north as well.

The outlet from Loch Achray by the Black Water leads to Loch Venachar by an interesting marsh, where whooper swans gather in winter. The distance is only a mile, and between the lochs lies the clachan of Brig o'Turk—no touch of the Orient but referring to Tuirc—the wild boar. There is a Youth Hostel here and a path climbing to Loch Drunkie and descending along the south shore of Loch Venachar.

Drunkie is 416 ft above sea-level, and shaped like a running goose. Rather remotely situated you would expect it to be entirely natural, but in fact it was raised 25 ft by the Glasgow Corporation to supply compensation water for the River Teith on which Deanston cotton mill near Doune depended. Smallest of the five Loch Katrine lochs, its maximum depth is 80 ft, 3 ft more than Loch Achray, in the westernmost of the three arms, or on the outstretched neck if like me you care to think of the loch as being shaped like a running goose.

Loch Venachar on the main road is much less picturesque, nor do the sluices which govern the compensation water at the eastern end help. It is 4 miles long and ¾ of a mile wide, the greatest depth here is 111 ft, at the eastern end while the west is reedy. It contains salmon and brown trout and is much favoured by fishermen. Drunkie also contains brown trout.

The Highland Boundary Fault cuts Loch Venachar near its eastern end. We are back in the Highlands in the Pass of Leny where Ben Ledi grits have resisted the passage of ice as in the Trossachs. Narrow Loch Lubnaig stretches north for 4 miles—shaped like a boomerang and compressed between rock bluffs on the west and steep conifer woods to the east.

For many people entering the north, this is the first Highland loch they meet on the drive from Edinburgh, and as the main road is well provided with laybys and inviting picnic spots it is apt to be busy. Walkers will prefer to use the abandoned rail track along the west shore, by crossing at the Pass of Leny. Better still they might climb Ben Ledi from the Stank Glen, through a little Switzerland of spruces, past a high waterfall into a corrie of pinnacles.

Loch Lubnaig is a loch almost separated into two basins by alluvial detritus brought down by the river descending northwards at Ardchullarie More. The maximum depth of 146 ft occurs in the northern basin. The southern basin reaches 108 ft. Silting up by the Stank and Anie burns at the south end of the loch has shortened Loch Lubnaig by $\frac{3}{4}$ of a mile, while the River Leny has allowed more of the loch to tip out by digging itself deeper and allowing more water to escape. By entirely natural means the Leny has lowered the level of Loch Lubnaig 20 ft. It contains salmon and trout.

Lochs Doine and Voil are almost one, lying at right-angles to Loch Lubnaig and separated by only five miles of low ground. The height difference between the three lochs is only 9 ft and there is plenty of evidence that they were once linked in one dog-leg. They are the most northerly lochs of the Forth drainage, and form the sides and base of a triangle whose other side is the chain of lochs we have discussed earlier in this chapter.

Loch Voil near Balquhidder where Rob Roy, most infamous of the Macgregors, is buried

To reach Loch Doine you take the Balquhidder road and follow it past the great forestry plantations of the Kirkton Glen, heading west towards a host of high peaks reaching 3,845 ft in Ben More. The end of Loch Voil is the beginning of Loch Doine.

The separation of the two lochs—if you can call it that—is due to a build-up of alluvium from the Monachyle burn, north, and another burn called the Monachyle Turach to the south, working towards each other.

Loch Doine is 1 mile long, by ¼ mile wide and has a maximum depth of 65 ft. The deep water of Loch Voil lies just over the alluvium cones built up between the lochs and continues for 2 miles of its total length of 3½ miles. The maximum depth is 98 ft. Both lochs contain salmon and trout. History sometimes asserts itself in heavy rains by flooding over all the alluvium and linking Doine, Voil and Lubnaig, and the waterfall in the Pass of Leny becomes a roaring cataract added to as every hillside spouts water.

To deal with the other Trossachs lochs we have to retrace our way and cross the Duke's Pass to Aberfoyle through the Queen Elizabeth Forest Park, an exciting road of zigs and zags in the Highlands yet commanding the Lowlands. A good stopping point is the David Marshall Lodge overlooking the village which was built with Carnegie Trust money and providing free picnic facilities, indoor or outdoor. Pillared verandas and large picture windows combat the weather and there is a fine exhibit of birds and animals of the Park.

The view-indicator on the 'Highland' side of the pass was also built with Carnegie Trust money, and offers tantalising glimpses of the Trossachs lochs between rocky or woodland bluffs. In former times the bark of the oaks was gathered for oak tanning. Forestry on the present scale did not begin until 1929, and Aberfoyle today is mainly a forestry village in an estate of some 45,000 acres. The slate quarries scarring the hills are now defunct.

The road to Inversnaid, west out of Aberfoyle twisting through a pass and wriggling along Loch Ard was well summed up by Queen Victoria. 'Certainly one of the most lovely drives I can remember, along Loch Ard, a fine long loch with trees of all kinds overhanging the road, heather making all pink, bracken, rocks, high hills of such fine shape and trees growing up them as in Switzerland.'

She would see considerably more forest today if she were to return, for the slopes stretching west and south along and behind the 'pipe-track' are growing spruce trees spanned by a maze of tracks which the public are encouraged to use. Walks of 8 miles and 3 miles have been marked, and a guide to them published by the Forestry Commission. Both begin at Cobleland Camping and Caravan Site near Aberfoyle.

For us it is logical to continue along the road to Loch Chon which inherits some darkness from Ben Dubh—the Black Mountain—rising in a steep face behind. The Loch Katrine aqueduct passes along under it, but is so self-effacing you would hardly know. The loch is $1\frac{2}{3}$ miles long, $\frac{1}{3}$ of a mile wide and is a simple depression with a maximum depth of 75 ft. The little dot at its southern end is the Lochan Dubh, 35 ft deep whose tadpole tail is the river.

Campers who like a little place of their own will enjoy this loch, with many delectable little green spots hardly bigger than the size of a smallish tent. The naturalist will find plenty to challenge his skill, for all this wild country has become a vast sanctuary for birds of prey, notably hen harriers, short-eared owls, sparrow-hawks, merlins, buzzards and even golden eagles and peregrine falcons.

The charm of Loch Chon is in its contrasts of scenery: woods, rocks, little bits of cultivation, and a mighty impression of the north face of Ben Lomond as you go south past 'The Teapot' to Loch Ard. The little white cottage called 'The Teapot' gets its name from the illicit distilling days, when it was an inn and recognised customers wanting whisky, asked for tea, knowing they would get something very different out of the pot, if it was available and the coast was clear. That was one kind of gold. Real gold was also mined here, but none too successfully, though some was obtained.

Kinlochard is a forestry village on the branch-road round the west end of Loch Ard, but there is no through route for cars by Culigarten where Glen Dubh winds down from Ben Lomond. This river is the true source of the Forth which begins high on the mountain, though it is not called the Forth until it joins up with the Avon Dubh flowing out of Loch Ard.

Loch Ard is rather a mysterious loch, with a back-end like the haunch of a cow complete with leg. It has a body to match, with a short foreleg, and there is even a head and a stubby tail. From hind leg to snout the length is 3 miles with a greatest depth of 107 ft, but the body proper is more correctly stated at $2\frac{1}{3}$ miles, with a mean breadth of $\frac{2}{5}$ of a mile.

Although of complicated shape it is a simple basin, the greatest depth coinciding with a belt of slate between bands of harder grit. Hotels, a Youth Hostel, and well-kept gardens along the rocky roadside contrast with the dark forest growing over hummocky moraines on the far shore, with the sheerest side of Ben Lomond rising behind, its northern corrie usually filled with snow until late spring.

The north side should be explored, and a good way is from the Covenanter's Inn where a rough track, passable for cars, runs past the Lochan Spling to the waterman's cottage where there are locked gates, but a foot wanderer is free to roam the maze of tracks.

Follow the Duchray into Gleann Dubh. Visit the Forth where it rushes over the rocks as a waterfall, and follow it the few miles to Aberfoyle where it loses its vigorous youth and flows sluggishly through the flattest land in Scotland, which is a more remarkable transformation than can be found in any other Scottish river. And just north of the flatlands where it winds lies the Lake of Menteith.

Angling:
In following lochs, Ard, Chon, Venachar and River Blackwater.
From: James Bayne, Fishing Tackle, Callander.
Aberfoyle Angling Protection Association.

Lochs
Achray and Drunkie:
Forestry Office, Aberfoyle and David Marshall Lodge. Also Post Office, Brig o'Turk.
Katrine, Arklet, Glen Finlas Reservoir:
From Lower Clyde Water Board, 419 Balmore Rd., Glasgow, N.2.

Lochans:
Spling, Gheannain, also rivers Forth, Duchray.
From Newsagents, Aberfoyle.

The Lake of Menteith and Loch Leven

An alien 'lake' in a country of lochs leads you to expect something 'different' from the Lake of Menteith, and this is how it turns out to be, for although there are hills round this large oval of water, they are gentle except for the steep escarpment in the north dividing you from the Trossachs.

The Lake of Menteith is only 55 ft above sea-level and occupies an irregular hollow where the ice from the Highland hills was lapped by the sea or shore. This is clear from the marine shells found in the glacial moraines which make such a tangle of hummocks at Aberfoyle. These moraines are most strikingly seen from the little golf course between Aberfoyle and the lake shore.

The hollow occupied by the lake is made up of stratified beds of sandstone with deposits of boulder-clay. It is not a rock basin, but a depression made by a great lobe of ice gradually decaying. Eastward you can see the black hulk of Stirling Castle, flanked by the distant Ochils and the nearer Campsie Fells—another misnomer in a land where mountains are hills, but never dales or fells.

For most people the interest of the Lake of Menteith is in the historical associations of its islands, especially Inchmahome which has a ferry service to it from the Port of Menteith. At 10p it is a bargain trip, thanks to the Department of the Environment, who maintain the old cloister of pinkish stones edged with wonderfully gnarled Spanish chestnuts. The sail is short, from the Port of Menteith, but the change of atmosphere is out of all proportion to the distance covered.

The Augustinian ruins, dating back 700 years are said to be the most beautiful memorials of medieval monastic life in Scotland. Their more famous connection of course is with Mary Queen of Scots who was brought here as a child from Stirling Castle following the Battle of Pinkie, in September 1547.

It was no holiday, for she was promptly put to school by the Prior for the three weeks she was here. The Monastery seems to have gone into rapid decline after this famous event, for by the end of the same century we hear no more of the black-habited monks who tilled the soil, cultivated the orchards, brewed beer, baked bread and netted pike and eels. But a boxwood tree planted by Mary is still growing, and her 'bower' by a little grove of trees looking to Inchtalla is still pointed out.

The name Lake of Menteith dates only from 1724 in written form. Before that the loch was always referred to as the Loch of Inchmahome. 'Menteith' of course derives from the noble earls who had their castle on Inchtalla, now in ruins. The 'Dogs Island' nearby was where they kept their hounds.

Inchmahome is their burial place. The founder of the Augustinian house was Walter Comyn, Earl of Mentieth, in 1238. What remains today is a tribute to the fine work of that century, including the magnificently sculptured tombstones of that time, commemorating Walter Stewart, first Earl of Mentieth and his Countess, dressed as in life, the Earl in armour, the Countess in robes. Another Menteith stone is thought to be that of the betrayer of Wallace.

Pike have always been a nuisance in the Lake of Menteith, but a big campaign of netting them, together with a restocking with rainbow trout opened a new era of fishing in 1968, with fifteen boats for hire at the Port of Menteith. Of 1,100 good fish caught in the first month the fishing was opened, 90 per cent were rainbows of around 1½ lb., the remainder being brown trout of over 2 lb.

This is how one angler described his catch: 'At last I was into a Menteith rainbow and the battle exceeded my highest expectations. One moment the fish was high in the air, the next tearing line from the reel in rushes of incredible speed. I breathed a sigh of relief when we finally netted the most beautiful broad rainbow, his silver sides flushed with the startling band of pink. This indeed was a fish worth waiting for.'

To stock the loch the rainbow trout are electrically stunned at the spawning season and artificially stripped of eggs and milt, then put back in the loch, while the eggs are taken to the hatchery at Malling at the western end of the lake, for subsequent rearing and restocking. Permits and boats are available at the Port of Menteith Hotel from 1 April to 30 September.

Most of the lake is shallow, but the maximum depth goes down to 77 ft which puts its bottom 22 ft below sea-level—fairly close to the northern shore at Coilledon, where the 50 ft depression extends for $\frac{1}{3}$ of a mile. The general impression is of a reedy lake, attractively fringed with woods and fields. Yet this is misleading for there is much bog on the north side where the wet woods have been deep drained and Cardross Moss planted with conifers.

No similar loch in Scotland, with a total length of only $1\frac{1}{2}$ miles and a breadth of 1 mile, has a comparable variety of habitat on and around its shores, comprising as they do agricultural fields, rough grazings, bogs, hills, islands, reed beds and a wealth of coniferous and deciduous trees. Quick to freeze in hard winters, it is a favourite among curlers.

A motor car run from the Lake of Menteith to Loch Leven follows the ancient sea shoreline of the Forth above Flanders Moss which begins just after the Goodie Water leaves the lake to wind sluggishly over the flattest land in Scotland. The route is by the A873, and in quick time you are looking down on the soggy peatland from which the jawbones of whales have been dug, and trees with the marks of Roman axes upon them.

Why the trees were felled no one knows—perhaps to prevent ambush by the Britons in the hills who could sweep down swiftly on the Romans, moving unseen amongst the great oaks which still lay where they had been felled. Another suggestion is that Severus may have tried to build a wall before Antonine's famous structure across the narrows of Scotland from the Clyde to the Forth.

A growth of peat covered this flat land all the way to Stirling, until about 1767 when a remarkable piece of reclamation was undertaken by destitute Highlandmen who were offered spades and the challenge of winning a living from the moss if they could dig down to the good clay beneath the peat. The landowner gave them ten acres each and the timbers for houses. Their reward was to be the land they reclaimed on which they were promised rent-free living until their nineteenth year of occupation, when a rent would be charged.

Lord Kames who instigated the reclamation had devised a most original way of disposing of the peat, by floating it into the Forth along canals in the moss. It was initially successful, but the river carried it into the estuary where the trouble began, because the peat became a filthy pulp, destroying the oyster beds and salmon fishing of the Forth.

But for the peat-floating being declared a public nuisance one hundred years ago, it is likely that there would be no Flanders Moss as we know it today. The 'mossers' had done so well that in fifty years over a thousand people were living on 1,440 reclaimed acres, and other landlords were copying Lord Kames. The Carse of Stirling which stretches as a fertile flat of fields all the way from the brown edge of Flanders Moss to the Castle Rock is the great result, and the farms today grow the finest Timothy grass in Scotland.

Now the Forestry Commission are trying to tame some of the 5,000 acres of wet land which is all that remains of Flanders Moss. Fortunately there are no big plans for reclaiming the whole area which is still a great reservoir of wildlife, alive with the shrilling of wading birds in summer and full of the noise of geese in winter. The nature conservationists must fight hard to retain some of the moss.

Past Stirling and along the foot of the Ochil Hills we come to Loch Leven.

Loch Leven

Apart from its less intimate size, this Kinross loch bears a remarkable resemblance to the Lake of Menteith, in the gentle character of the basin it occupies, with hills offsetting its shores which are agricultural and reedy, wooded and marshy. And its islands have historical parallels with those on Menteith. Mary Queen of Scots was held prisoner on one of them. The Culdee monks had a foundation on another, dating back to AD 760 or thereabouts. Castle Island has a ferry service operated by the County Council, similar to that on the Lake of Menteith.

There is one basic difference however. Loch Leven is not entirely natural. It was reduced in size between 1826 and 1836 to win land for agriculture and provide the paper mills with better water supplies. And in this process three more islands emerged, making seven where there used to be only four. Like the Lake of Menteith the floor of the loch is of the old red sandstone, and the maximum depth is only 6 ft more, 83 ft, though the loch is twice as long and twice as broad.

It is offering scientists a challenge to research all aspects of its hydro-biology as one of Britain's main contributions to the International Biological programme. Their task is to trace the links in creation which we call the food-chain, on a loch dense with plankton and fish and vast numbers of waterfowl.

In fact Loch Leven is too productive. Modern fertilisers are causing too much nitrogen and phosphorus to seep into the loch from the surrounding fields which causes a growth of algae which clouds the water and results in poor fish and poor fishing until it clears. Trout and Loch Leven are almost synonymous terms. Here is an excerpt from the Old Statistical Account of Scotland of 1793: 'The high flavour and bright red colour of the trout seem evidently to arise from the food which Nature has provided for them in the loch. What appears to contribute most to the redness and rich taste of the Loch Leven trout is the vast

Loch Leven from Vane Hill, an outstanding region for wildfowl

quantity of small shellfish, red in its colour, which abound all over the bottom of the loch, especially among the aquatic weeds. The trout when caught have often their stomachs full of them.'

In these distant times the fleshy trout was sold at 4*d.* per pound, twice the cost of pike, though perch were sold not by weight but by the dozen. Pike have fallen out of favour in our well-fed society, but something like 85,000 trout are still caught annually on Loch Leven, though the quality early in the season is not so good as it was.

Loch Leven was declared a National Nature Reserve in 1964, and in 1967 the Royal Society for the Protection of Birds purchased Vane Farm to set up Britain's first Conservation Centre, for this is the most important freshwater loch in Scotland, England or Ireland for migratory and breeding wildfowl. The Observation Post at Vane Farm overlooks an immense front of feeding birds, especially grey geese which assemble here from the Arctic in thousands. It is curious that of the seven islands of Loch Leven only St. Serf's carries a big breeding population of ducks, with something like 700 nests among the rough grass and marram. Most of these are tufted duck and mallard nests, but some 40 are of wigeon, with about the same amount of gadwall, plus 5,000 nests of black-headed gulls.

St. Serf's has an interest outside birds of course, since it was here in 1420 the Prior Andrew Wyntoun wrote *The Oryginale Cronykil* of Scotland, while on the east shore at Scotlandwell there is a bubbling spring of therapeutic quality where Robert Bruce bathed. This is the *Fons Scotiae* mentioned by Tacitus in the seventh Roman campaign.

The sluices at the south-eastern end replace the natural outlet of the River Leven and were designed to regulate the supply of water to flax mills and bleachfields below the dam at Auchmar Bridge in the days when the attractive villages of Balgedie, Scotlandwell and Kinesswood were engaged in wool and weaving. High quality parchment and vellum were manufactured in the latter village until 1930, by a secret process given by the monks over 400 years ago it is said.

St. Serf's, sometimes called 'The Inch', was given to Culdees, the Servants of God, by a Pictish king in the eighth century. Their foundation lasted for nearly 400 years—until Bishop

Robert of St. Andrews supplanted them with monks of the St. Augustine order, who no doubt used Latin instead of Gaelic for divine offices. By 1309 the Culdees had lost their land, privileges and books, but the ruins of the Priory remains on St. Serf's to mark their passing.

Loch Leven comes from Leamhan—the elm tree—the Loch of the Elms, and its parkland atmosphere is one of its charms. It is a rural landscape unspoiled, and the gliding club at the southern end does not detract in the least. Kinross at the north end is the county town, more or less linked to Milnathort, centred on wool spinning and linen manufacture.

The ferry service to Castle Island leaves from Kirkgate Park pier—summer only, and there is a resident guide to tell the tale of Mary Queen of Scots and her various wiles during the year she was in prison before her clever escape. She entered this castle in 1567 and was beheaded twenty years later, having spent only a fortnight of the intervening time in freedom.

A pageant of the escape was performed in 1967 to celebrate the 400th anniversary of the escape. The story even hit the headlines. Willie and Mary did an audacious piece of work. Willie, the pageboy, had the heavy end of the stick. A page at the table, his job was to lift the keys from the keeper of the castle as he supped his food. Willie had seen that he usually laid the keys beside his plate, so in the act of serving he dropped a napkin over them, whisked them away and joined Mary and her maid who were at the ready. Willie then locked in all the castle inmates and threw the keys in the loch from where they were recovered about a hundred years ago.

Friends and horses were waiting on the shore. Her freedom might have lasted more than a fortnight if she had not ridden south and crossed the Solway into England after the disastrous Battle of Langside. Her last night of freedom was spent in Dundrennan Abbey near Kirkcudbright. On 7 February 1587 the axe fell twice on her neck. Her words, 'Today you see the end of Mary Stewart's miseries', were all too true.

Loch Leven Castle consists of a courtyard and tower of the late fourteenth or early fifteenth century on the site of a still older castle. A mile east of Milnathort lies Burleigh Castle of about the 1500 period, now a roofless tower-house—once the family seat of

Balfour of Burleigh. The keeper of the key lives at the farm opposite, and free admission can be had at all reasonable times.

The vital statistics of Loch Leven are as follows. Greatest length $3\frac{2}{3}$ miles from south-east to north-west; greatest width $2\frac{2}{3}$ miles, pear-shaped area $5\frac{1}{3}$ sq. miles. There are two deep areas, the maximum 83 ft west and south of St. Serf's; and 79 ft in the north-western part of the loch. The main feature of Loch Leven however is its shallowness, 85 per cent of the bottom being covered by no more than 15 ft of water. The height above sea-level is 350 ft.

Historical note on the effect of the drainage scheme on the loch taken from the *Bathymetrical Survey*—Murray and Pullar.

'Extensive operations for the draining of the loch were completed about the year 1845 at a cost of £40,000, by which the loch was lowered $4\frac{1}{2}$ ft, and the area reduced by about 1,400 acres; some people maintain that the quality of the trout has been injuriously affected by the draining. Prior to 1856 rod fishing was disappointing, but about that time, from some cause that does not appear to have been satisfactorily explained, the fish rose more freely to the bait, angling became more encouraging, and Loch Leven became a resort for anglers from all parts of the country. Some years ago the fishing was taken over by the Loch Leven Angling Association, who pay a rental of £1,000 per annum. The statistics regarding the trout caught by rod in the loch, and their weight, show great fluctuations from season to season. In 1872 over 17,000 were taken, the average weight being nearly 1 lb.; in 1873 the take fell to 13,400, in 1874 to 6,400, in 1875 to 5,000, in 1876 even less. In 1877 the take rose again to 6,000, in 1878 to 13,000, and in 1879 to 21,000, but the average weight seems to have been less. The best year recorded during the last quarter of a century was in 1888, when 23,516 trout were taken weighing 21,074 lbs. In 1893, 1898, 1899, and 1900 the takes again exceeded 20,000, but the weight never equalled the 21,000 lbs. of 1888, the nearest approach being in 1893 when 23,100 trout, weighing 19,500 lbs. were caught. Last year (1900) the trout taken by the rod numbered 23,811, weighing 15,584 lbs., an average of 0.654 lbs.'

Kilconquhar Loch

The pronunciation of Kilconquhar is Kinneuchar, and the village with its red pantiled roofs and ancient church on the north shore gives great character to the reedy loch in a wholly agricultural setting.

It has great fields of barley and oats to the east and west, with the neat village on the north and fine woods to the south. The loch is like a garden in summer when the crowfoot is white and the pink spikes of the *Amphibious persicaria* are to be seen. Unfortunately, the marshes and reeds make the loch difficult to approach but the church lawns are a fine viewpoint, and the ornithologist will be thrilled at the amount of wildlife, especially at migration time.

Only the centre of this circular loch, which is ½ a mile in diameter, attains a depth of 7 ft. Mostly it is from 3–5 ft, and the plants which distinguish it grow on a muddy bottom—less so in the south and east which is firmer and sandier. The water may lack Highland sparkle but it is clear and attractive in this lowland environment.

Over it may be seen an astonishing collection of unusual birds, black terns and little gulls, dipping and swooping after flies; while on the water I have seen all the British grebes at one time and a host of duck including gadwall.

In a visit to Fife Kilconquhar village and loch should not be missed. A fine view of the Bass Rock and the Lothian shore may be had from the high ground just above the loch.

Lake of Menteith

Height above sea level: 55 ft.
Length: 1.6 miles.
Breadth: 1 mile.
Maximum depth: 77 ft.
Volume: 562 million cu. ft.
Area: 1.02 sq. miles.

Fishing

Port of Menteith Hotel.
Telephone Port of Menteith 214.

Boats for hire. 10 a.m.–5 p.m. and 6 p.m.–10 p.m.
No boats let to single fishermen.

Brown trout and rainbow trout.

Hotels
Port of Menteith.
Aberfoyle (several).

Other activities: Golf.

Loch Leven
Height above sea-level: 350 ft.
Length: 3.65 miles.
Breadth: 2.6 miles.
Maximum depth: 83 ft.
Volume: 2,195 million cu. ft.
Area: 5.30 sq. miles.

Loch Kilconquhar, noted for its birds

Fishing
Kinross Estate Office, Telephone Kinross 2256.
The Pier, Kinross, Telephone Kinross 3407.
Green Hotel, Telephone Kinross 3467.

Charges on application.

Brown trout.

Hotels
Kinross—three hotels.
Green.
Bridgend.
Kirklands.
Kinesswood.

Other activities: Golf, gliding.

Lochs of the Tay Basin

Lochs Ericht, Lochan na h-Achlaise, Ba, Laidon, Eigheach, Rannoch, Dunalastair, Errochty, Tummel, Faskally, Daimh, Stronuich, Lyon, Lochan na Lairige, Tay, Breaclaich, Earn, Dochart, Iubhair, Essan, Broom, Ordie, Derculich, Loch nan Eun, Lochan nan Cat, Craiglush, Lowes, Butterstone, Clunie, Drumellie, Rae, Fingask, White, Black, Long, Thrieply, Benachally, Lintrathen, Forfar

The last traces of corrie glaciers vanished from Scotland only a few hundred years ago—perhaps as recently as the mid-eighteenth century. The nearest approach to them left to us are the summer snowfields of Ben Nevis and the Cairngorms in the deepest recesses of the high corries. Relics of glaciation are everywhere in the high mountains. But the most obvious evidence in the lower glens are the innumerable rock basins, now filled with water, which we call 'lochs'.

There have been other lochs which disappeared, but not without trace. One in Glen Roy was probably deeper than Loch Morar at its maximum, measured from its highest shoreline, which is the highest of the 'parallel roads'. There were others in Glen Gloy and Glen Spean, where you can see similar 'parallel roads'—each denoting a different lake level as the glaciers from the Nevis range which formed a gigantic natural dam slowly melted and the water drained away.

Man copies nature when he blocks the outlets of valleys to make reservoirs, and in this way most of the 2,508 sq. miles of Tay drainage is controlled, for this is the watershed of Scotland, with seventy lochs draining into four superb rivers, the Garry, the Tummel, the Earn and the Tay, each harnessed at some stage for hydro-electricity, with dams and aqueducts between lochs where rivers surge through rock gorges, in waterfalls and dark pools beloved of salmon fishermen.

This is central Scotland, with big heather moors, high plateaux, fine forests, open glens, peaks containing corries of rare alpine plants and lochs of many shapes and sizes, many untouched by hydro-electricity. Here too is Rannoch Moor—once covered in Caledonian pines, but now they are mostly grey skeletons in a raised bog which is the wildest in Britain. Rannoch was a great centre of ice dispersal in the glacier age, sending streamers into the Spey Valley and breaching high mountains to create beds for future lakes.

Loch Ericht is exactly such a lake, a glacial breach against the natural drainage line. It points in a north-easterly direction in 15 miles of narrow water, and like Loch Katrine in the Trossachs and Loch Ness in Inverness-shire is said never to freeze, though it is situated in one of the coldest regions of Scotland. Height 1,179 ft above sea-level, it is one of the most elevated and remotest of the larger Scottish lochs, yet is said to be as good as Loch Leven for trout. Its *Salma ferox* are also renowned.

Access is not easy however, since the only motor roads are private, from the north at Dalwhinnie, where you may walk the road that leads along the shore for about five miles to Loch Ericht Lodge: or from Loch Rannoch in the south where there is a road to the hydro-electric dam from the Bridge of Ericht. Walkers may use either road freely, but permission has to be obtained for cars.

However you cannot know a loch by merely touching its north or south end, and Loch Ericht being roadless on both shores for most of its fourteen miles of length, has to be explored on foot. And for the man who is prepared to carry food and sleeping bag there is the perfect lodging at Ben Alder Cottage, an empty house in the south-easterly corner beneath Cluny's Cage.

If you go to the cottage do not expect anything more than a fireplace, a good roof, and pine roots in the bogs for firewood. The best way to it is on the track which becomes a narrow footpath from the west end of Loch Rannoch. The approach to Loch Ericht over a wide moor of lonely lochans with mountains on every side is softened by straggling pines when Loch Ericht comes into view. But the walking gets harder as the loch is reached, because the path vanishes, and there is roughly two miles of peat-hopping to reach the welcome haven of the cottage.

This region of extreme remoteness was the secret hideout of Bonny Prince Charlie in his last days in Scotland before escaping to France. Hard walking from the Great Glen and over the mountains by Loch Laggan brought him here to a bower woven in the rocks somewhere above the site of the present cottage. I believe the Ordnance Survey mapped the site correctly and a scramble a few hundred feet from the house takes you to it.

The description certainly tallies with the details of the view briefly given in a manuscript in the Cluny Charter Chest, believed to be written about 1756 while Cluny MacPherson was in France. The relevant portion reads thus:

'It was in this forest where the Prince found Cluny with Locheill in his wounds and other friends under his care. He was afraid that his constitution might not suit with lying on the ground or in caves, so was solicitous to contrive a more

Alder Bay, Loch Ericht. The figure stands on the site of Cluny's Cage

comfortable habitation for him upon the south front of one of these mountains, overlooking a beautiful lake of 12 miles long.

'He observed a thicket of hollywood, he went, viewed and found it fit for his purpose; he caused immediately waive the thicket round with boughs, made first and second floor in it, and covered it with moss to defend the rain. The upper room serv'd for salle à manger and bed chamber while the lower serv'd for a cave to contain liquors and other necessaries, at the back part was a proper hearth for cook and baiker, and the face of the mountain had so much the colour and resemblance of smock, no person cou'd ever discover that there was either fire or habitation in the place.'

The site fulfils all the specifications in the Charter Chest MSS except one, the holly trees, but as there are no thickets of holly on the slopes of Ben Alder nowadays it must be presumed that these trees have died out in the passage of 200 years. The other specifications are covered:

(a) The cave was sited on a southern spar of Ben Alder.
(b) Was on the face of a rocky hill.
(c) It overlooked the loch.
(d) Was openly situated and sentries could easily give warning.

Examine the boulders carefully and it is not difficult to conceive how effective the lower caves would be for cookery, with a natural hearth and fireplace in stone to obviate the risk of fire, while there are enough openings to let the smoke disperse in dribs and drabs. Also, the roof of the caves is flat enough to make the perfect floor for a superstructure of wood, which would be sufficiently big enough to hold five men, Locheill, Cluny MacPherson, Lochgarry, Dr. Cameron and the Prince, with five servants lodging somewhere below. (Dr. Cameron was arrested on Loch Katrine in 1752 and executed at Tyburn.)

The loch has been raised 26 ft since Prince Charlie's time and the big dam impinges on the natural scene, but Alder Bay is still beautiful, and anyone who is here should try to go to the top of Ben Alder which has the remains of a bothy on it, built by the military engineers who triangulated the Highlands to make an accurate map of the north, the first step in the Government's plans to ensure against any future outbreaks of trouble with the Jacobites.

Loch Ericht was dug out by glacial action along the line of a fault, and its very steep shores are due to the rapid flow of the ice being forced through a narrow passage, breaching the watershed. The deepest part of the loch however is the broad part, just opposite Cluny's Cage, approximately 538 ft if hydro-electric calculations are correct, since originally the maximum was 512 ft at this point.

Some of the water which raises it comes from Loch Garry at Dalnaspidal, the highest railway station in Britain, on the main Inverness line. A five-mile tunnel leads the water to a remote-controlled power-house about half-way up the east shore of Loch Ericht to utilise the difference in height level of 180 ft between the lochs. Output is about 11 million units of electricity annually.

The shallowest part of Loch Ericht is the narrowest part, just out from Loch Ericht Lodge, where the bottom is less than 100 ft, thus dividing the two deep basins. Notice should be taken of the boulders scattered by the ice all the way along the loch and into Glen Truim as far as Kingussie in the Spey Valley. The blocks are particularly obvious at the Dalwhinnie end of the loch—deposited by the moving mass of ice as it breached the valley now occupied by the loch.

These blocks are scattered as far as 3,000 ft up on the hills, proof of the enormous depth of the glacier ice which spilled over the watershed. Man has now reversed the flow by diverting the Spey catchment from Loch an-t Seilich and Loch Quaich by aqueducts to Loch Ericht, via a power-house to become part of the Tummel Valley catchment, harnessing nine power stations to produce 640 million units of electricity annually.

The elevated part of bleak Rannoch Moor is the most westerly part of this catchment where a chain of shallow lochs straggles through the raised platform of heather and bouldery peat. The spongy mattress of Rannoch Moor is relieved of monotonous bleakness by the lochs, and the remnants of the great forest which protrude like skeletons from bits of the bog, evidence that the peat is wasting away.

Rannoch Moor, once a great reservoir of ice sending tributaries in all directions, was probably covered by pine forest in Roman times—woods which gave shelter to wild boar, northern lynx, caribou, elk, brown bears, beavers and wolves.

The trees were destroyed partly by man but mainly by nature as the climate became more moist.

Shallow and with wriggling shorelines, these Rannoch lochs are best explored by canoe, and with very little portage the whole moor can be traversed from west to east, by linking Loch Ba and Loch Laidon, from the Glen Coe road to Rannoch Station.

Lochan na h-Achlaise and Loch Ba are the best known of the Rannoch lochs, because the main Glen Coe road passes between them, and a man with binoculars may easily pick up a goosander or a black-throated diver, or see the greenshank streaking across on fast beating wings, white rump flashing. Herons nest on scrubby islands, and short-eared owls lay eggs amongst the heather, with red grouse, and snipe and sandpipers.

These two lochs are favourites with weekend fishermen, as they are with photographers trying to capture the snowy peaks of Coire Ba reflected in the shallow depths. Lochan na h-Achlaise is only 28 ft at its deepest. Loch Ba is only 30 ft. The adjacent smaller lochs are even shallower; Loch Buidhe is a mere 3 ft deep, Lochan na Stainge 14 ft.

Loch Laidon which runs out of Argyllshire into Perthshire, with the boundary running through the northern fork of its tail and bisecting the body half-way, is much deeper, 128 ft, and is one of the best trouting lochs in Scotland. Stretching $5\frac{1}{3}$ miles north-east, the tail-piece which forks west extends $1\frac{1}{2}$ miles, but is a mere 17 ft deep.

Loch Laidon at the westerly fork of the tail, and at its southern end, has a floor of boulders and is peppered with islands, but the main basin is simple, dropping to its deepest part in the middle of the loch where for over three-quarters of a mile it is over 100 ft, though 53 per cent of the floor is covered by less than 25 ft. Salmon rarely get into it nowadays unfortunately, due to hydro-electricity developments further east, but perch have been introduced and the *Salma ferox* are large.

It is on the cards that Loch Laidon itself may be impounded by the building of a dam across its outlet stream, the Gaur, thus raising the level of the loch by 30 ft and inundating many of the delightful bays. Meantime the scheme has been held-over, so the wanderer along Loch Laidonside can still enjoy the feeling of untamed wilderness, almost like being in a vast saucer with high peaks projecting on every side.

The eastern end of the loch falls within Rannoch Moor National Nature Reserve which totals 3,704 acres, on some of which has been planted thousands of Scots pine seedlings from the Black Mount together with birch and rowan and alder. The Forestry Commission are planting on this eastern end too; also on the west margin above Loch Ba. With modern drainage tools it is pretty certain that most of Rannoch Moor could be made to grow forest again, but its primary interest to the conservationist lies in its being a shallow blanket bog, dating from about 500–700 BC when the climate became cooler and wetter with a build-up of peat which killed much of the forest, though much remained to shelter wolves and criminals, until it was burned out by man.

The mysteries of Rannoch and its lochs have still to be unravelled. Why, for example, does the rush *Scheuchzeria palustris* grow here and nowhere else in Scotland though it occurs in Ireland, a six-petalled yellow-green flowered plant of the bog pools whose common name is the Rannoch Rush? Look for it as you explore the moor, and note the red deer, which are tending to become more numerous as they are fenced out of the forests further east.

The West Highland Railway almost touches the north-eastern end of Loch Laidon, where road and railway meet at Rannoch Station and the line is carried over morainic mounds, peat-filled hollows and streams on bridges and viaducts, one of them with nine clear spans running for 684 yds over a hollow. The bogs of the moor were made passable only by collecting tree roots of the primeval forest and overlaying them with a cover of brushwood, then building a foundation of rocks and excavated material. On this floating mass there was added thousands of tons of ashes to take the permanent way.

The route finally chosen across the moor follows almost exactly the line for a road proposed by the great Thomas Telford, though Charles Foreman, the railway engineer responsible, did not know this when he put his own plan down on paper. Both of these men appreciated the particular problem of Rannoch Moor, which is its even height. It is so level that it cannot be satisfactorily drained, so its interior has remained a great vacuity with only foot-tracks between Rannoch Station and the Glen Coe road. But its isolation may be ended if present proposals to build a road across it materialise.

The railway line is a godsend to fishermen, who by rising early in the morning can catch the West Highland train from Glasgow or Edinburgh and have six hours or so on Loch Laidon before they need leave Rannoch. This train is also the best way of seeing the moor, especially the north part to Corrour and Loch Treig with glimpses of Loch Ossian on the way; regions unspanned by any road in the no-man's-land between Ben Alder and Ben Nevis.

The name 'Rannoch' comes from the Gaelic 'Ratheanach', meaning 'watery', which could not be improved upon in terms of description with one loch virtually connecting to another over eleven miles where the height differential between west and east is less than 60 ft. Strange when you think of it that all this water should flow east, when it rises only twenty miles from the Atlantic. The first capture of it for electricity is made just after the fast flowing Garbh Ghaour emerges from Loch Laidon, flowing into Loch Eigheach to be impounded by a dam, beneath which is an automatically-controlled power-house.

This is the most recent addition to the Tummel Valley catchment using the ribbon lochs which stretch to Pitlochry. Hydro-electric generation in this area goes back to 1930, to the time when the Grampian Electrical Supply Company were responsible for the generation of public supplies. Then in 1943 the North of Scotland Hydro-Electric Board took over development of water power resources with the additional duty of distributing electricity to three-quarters of the land area of Scotland.

The big push of new constructions began in 1947, and within one year twelve new schemes were under construction, with a total capacity of 432 megawatts. The Tummel and its tributaries which we are examining now has a capacity of 250 megawatts with an average output of about 640 million units of electricity. Loch Eigheach, the most westerly reservoir, was originally no more than an expansion of the River Ghaour $\frac{9}{10}$ of a mile long and much covered by reeds. Its maximum depth was 28 ft, and in breadth the loch was less than $\frac{1}{4}$ of a mile. Raised 30 ft it is now

$1\frac{3}{4}$ miles long by 1 mile broad, and three miles downstream is Loch Rannoch.

The drop between the lochs is 178 ft, and an odd thing here is that where we would expect to find Kinloch Rannoch at the head of the loch—which is what Kinloch means—we have to travel ten miles to the foot of the loch to find that village. With roads running along both sides you can travel along its north or south shores—indeed each must be travelled if you would begin to understand the topography of this exciting loch.

The quick change of scene from bleak Rannoch to the wooded loch in that short drop eastward is best appreciated on the southern shore which rises in a magnificent sweep of pine forest known as the Black Wood of Rannoch, reaching up the heathery hillsides and stretching along the loch for miles. It is no dark and monotonous plantation, but a natural open forest of Caledonian pines, with much birch, alder and juniper—home of the Rannoch looper moth, which is small and chestnut coloured.

Fine paths offer contouring routes through the forest, and one of the best is from Camghouran up to Loch Finnart and Loch Monaghan, popular with brown trout fishermen. From this wood timber used to be floated down the chain of lochs to the Tay. Today, the gnarled old veterans are being cared for by the Forestry Commission, by fencing and planting-out seedlings grown from locally gathered seeds adapted to their environment. This conservation of the Black Wood goes on alongside normal commercial plantations.

Caledonian pine wood is still the best that can be grown in many parts of Scotland, and in the past was used for the timbers and masts of ships, though senselessly squandered from the fifteenth century onwards and exploited more recently in two great wars for ammunition boxes.

The lower rainfall of the Tummel Valley from Rannoch east makes it one of the best tree growing areas in the Central Highlands and is seen in the quality of the birches along the loch shore, shining silver and shimmering green in early summer or brilliant gold in autumn. Wild cat, badger, fox, roe deer, red deer, red squirrel, stoat, weasel and fox live here. Bird-life includes the Scottish crossbill.

Loch Rannoch was the HQ of the heroic men who produced

the classic work on Scottish lochs, the *Bathymetrical Survey of the Fresh-water Lochs of Scotland* in six volumes under the direction of Sir John Murray, K.C.B., F.R.S. and Laurence Pullar, F.R.S.E. They spent from 20 March to 10 July 1902 here, taking soundings, temperatures, studying the biology, and the rise and fall of the surface of the loch—as they did for almost every loch in Scotland. Theirs is the definitive work, undertaken privately and occupying the best part of seven years hard labour.

Their thoroughness can be gauged from a few facts taken from Vol. 2 dealing with Loch Rannoch:

'The loch contains many small trout, and is famed for large *Salma ferox*. It is nearly 9¾ miles in length, considerably over a mile in maximum breadth, the mean breadth being about three-quarters of a mile, or about 8 per cent of the length. Its waters cover an area of over 4,700 acres, or nearly 7½ square miles, and it drains directly an area of 130 square miles, but, since it receives

Loch Rannoch and the peak of Schiehallion

the outflow of Loch Ericht, Loch Eigheach, Loch Laidon, Loch Ba, etc., its total drainage area is about 243½ square miles, or thirty-three times the area of the loch.

'Over 800 soundings were taken in Loch Rannoch, the maximum depth observed being 440 feet, or 20 feet deeper than the maximum depth recorded by Mr. Grant-Wilson during his survey in the year 1888, when he took about 320 soundings. The volume of water contained in the loch is estimated at about 34,387,131,000 cubic feet, or less than a quarter of a cubic mile, and the mean depth at 167½ feet, or 38 per cent of the maximum depth. The length of the loch is 116 times the maximum depth, and 306 times the mean depth. The loch is widest and deepest in its eastern half, narrowing and shallowing towards the west on approaching the island Eilean nam Faoileag, then deepening again to the west of that island. It consists of one large main basin, with two subsidiary small basins over 50 feet in depth towards the west end, separated from the main basin by the shallow water in the neighbourhood of Eilean nam Faoileag.'

Under 'Biology' they state: 'The plankton of Loch Rannoch may be fairly taken as the type of all the large Scottish lochs. Almost every one of the species included in the list of the lacustrine organisms was found in it, and there was nothing in it not found in the list. Of the Entomostraca, Bosimna was the most abundant. Skeletons of the Rhizopod Clathrulina elegans, though this is not a pelagic animal, were always found in it . . .'

There is also *Notes on the Geology of the Tay Basin* by B. N. Peach and J. Horne, both Fellows of the Royal Society, which reveals that Loch Rannoch would be longer but for the mass of glacial material damming its outlet, while Loch Tummel had been reduced to half its area by deposition—a state of affairs now rectified by the North of Scotland Hydro-Electric Board by the building of a dam at the eastern end since these notes were written.

Man has changed the rivers and lochs of the Tay Basin since the *Bathymetrical Survey* was written. Building dams has flooded new areas, resulting in a spectacular growth of brown trout, due to the bonanza of earthworms, the scientists think, lasting through the year of flooding and the one after. The Freshwater Fisheries Laboratory, formerly the Brown Trout Research

Station, have studied this in detail, and by marking fish and studying migrations have produced some remarkable information on the 'homing' instinct of trout, returning to spawn.

Of 3,000 trout marked, only one fish could be classed as having strayed from the predicted spawning stream which was their nursery. Once dispersed from the redds the fry tended to move along the streams in which they were hatched—51 per cent spending two years there, 27 per cent three years, 15 per cent one year and 7 per cent four years—moving down eventually in autumn to the loch, and returning upstream as ripe fish to spawn in small gravelly streams with suitable gravel for constructing a redd. The fish may also use a loch if there is no suitable stream. The story of the work done in the Tummel Valley lochs should be read in the booklet *Trout in Scotland* by K. A. Pyefinch, officer in charge of the Freshwater Fisheries Laboratory at Pitlochry.

The small reservoir of Dunalastair, just east of Loch Rannoch, is one of the flooded areas where much of this fish-research has been done, and the construction of the valley near the dam is due to a belt of quartzite. A keen eye will detect boulders from Rannoch Moor down the valley, even on the top of Schiehallion, for these boulders have ribs of darker material on their grey surface, each an inch or so wide—carried along the valley and over the high tops by the moving glaciers whose irresistible force enabled them to go uphill when required.

This shallow reservoir is good for birds—I have seen a Slavonian grebe on it—and a good cross-section of ducks on its three mile surface. The power station is at Tummel Bridge, at the entrance to Loch Tummel, where there is a large caravan park. The station just across the loch on Loch Tummel is powered from a new loch created 1,000 ft in the hills to the north called Loch Errochty, and a convenient public road leads up to it connecting to the main Inverness A9 route.

Loch Errochty, 3½ miles long and with a maximum breadth of over half a mile is impounded behind a diamond-headed dam on moorland which resounds with golden plover in summer, and where the short-eared owl hunts. The loch itself was created by building 1,164 ft of buttressed concrete 162 ft high, and diverting water from the River Garry by twelve miles of tunnels. So we have a reservoir in the hills discharging into 6 miles of tunnel to the power station on the Loch Tummel shore, the station being faced with stone taken from the tunnel.

In the *Bathymetrical Survey* Loch Tummel is given as 2¾ miles in length with a maximum breadth of ½ a mile. Today it is 7 miles long and nearly 1 mile in maximum breadth, but what has not changed is the general description. 'Loch Tummel is situated amid beautiful scenery, rock, wood and water being combined in such a way as to present pictures of rare loveliness, the crests of Farragan, Meall Tarruinn Chon, and Schiehallion rising to great heights to the south and south west. It contains large trout and many pike.'

Loch Tummel when it was a natural loch had a maximum depth of 128 ft on an irregular floor falling into three deep basins, the greatest depth being near the western end. The building of the Clunie dam two miles downstream from the natural outlet raised it by about 17 ft. Set with delightful birch woods and grassy shores spattered with fine camp and caravan sites it is one of the most popular lochs in Scotland, yet is not despoiled.

The famous viewpoint from a height on the road overlooking the windings of the loch stretching to Schiehallion has a large car-park now and is marked 'Queen's View'. Much of the charm of the drive along the north shore is due to the road being set high enough above the loch to provide panoramic views, each framed by a different composition of trees in a shimmer of greens and blues and browns.

The ridge north of the Queen's View extending to the end of the loch is apt to be forgotten because of the near attractions of the loch but it is of very great interest because of a number of Pictish forts and ancient worship stones and stone circles. They are shown on the one-inch Ordnance Survey map as 'Duns'—relics of fortified villages of a people who left no written language but a treasury of sculptured stones in various parts of Scotland, but not here.

The 'Duns' stretch from Cisteal Dubh, on the wooded ridge just above the east end of the loch to more than half-way up its length on the north side, while east of the hill loch above

Tressait, in a walk of less than two miles you can see Na Clachan Aoraidh—four stones of worship. Further east up Glen Fincastle on the fine old track to Blair Atholl is a big limekiln, dating from the industrious times when the crofters of the past spread the locally-quarried lime on the fields. Only ruins tell of these people today.

Loch Faskally lies just to the south, winding like a broad river to Pitlochry where the dam and the salmon-ladder are one of the attractions of this tourist town. The power station here has an exhibition hall open to visitors, with maps, diagrams, photographs and models of the underwater machinery which drives the turbines. From this you will grasp the earthmoving engineering involved, to rob hill-lochs of the Spey and divert them to Loch Ericht by tunnel and aqueduct and boring through the mountains west of Loch Garry to add another tipple, to complete a hat-trick of power stations by tunnelling from Loch Ericht through to Rannoch. Then to a new tack with Dunalastair linked to Tummel Bridge by open aqueduct, while Loch Errochty in the hills powers a station just across the road from the Bridge. A cocktail indeed, with Clunie and Faskally further east to end the complicated story.

Loch Faskally evens out the irregularities in the water flow occasioned by the varying discharges of the stations upstream. How do the migrating salmon fare in all this? There is a ladder, and an inspection-window at Pitlochry where you may see the big fish swimming as they are elevated into the loch. There is also a hatchery in the basement, where the eggs of fish which have been cut off from their spawning grounds are hatched and returned to their places of origin as fry or smoults.

The Freshwater Fisheries Laboratory at Pitlochry are concentrating on the problems of salmon and sea trout biology whose migrations to the sea and subsequent return for spawning are so important to the economy of Scotland. Much has still to be learned about the effects of hydro-electricity on the movements of salmon, but the method of stripping hen fish by hand and fertilising them with milt from cock fish for hatching in the laboratory is having fair results.

This is what happens in Glen Lyon now due to a series of impassable hydro-electric dams, so the fish are hand-stripped and transferred to Pitlochry for hatching to alevin and rearing to fry before being returned to the river. These Glen Lyon lochs lie across the hills south of Loch Rannoch, but to reach them means crossing the shoulder of Schiehallion from the end of Loch Rannoch, or by Loch Tummel, since the only public road is by Fortingall.

Glen Lyon, even if there were no lochs, is a place to visit for its twisting beauty of river and woods, compressed amongst rocks with 3,000 ft peaks on each side, or opening delightfully to grassy flats, only to close in again and present some new vista as side-glen follows side-glen and the oaks and beeches give way to bluffs of birches then to Caledonian pines.

Sheep and cattle, white houses on both sides of the fine river, take away the feeling of wilderness but do not diminish the magnificence of the setting. The lochs, lying high, seem bleak and featureless after the delights of Bridge of Balgie where I think the beauty of Glen Lyon reaches its climax, especially in late autumn as the colours reach their peak before the onset of the first big gales.

Loch Daimh lies up the steep road which branches right. It is marked Loch Giorra on Bartholomew's half-inch map, but the discrepancy springs from the fact that there used to be two lochs here, Loch Daimh and Loch Giorra with a farm between them beneath a wood. The big dam which faces you as you climb blocked the outlet and caused the two lochs to become one behind the 1,540 ft wall of concrete, and the former outlet stream is dry. Water now rushes along 3½ miles of tunnel and 1,680 ft of pipe-line south to Cashlie Power Station in Glen Lyon.

Loch Daimh is 3¼ miles long with a maximum breadth of just over ½ a mile, and has a very marked bend near the spot where there used to be dry land. The original Loch Daimh was the westerly portion, which was 1 mile in length and only ⅓ of a mile in breadth, with a maximum depth of 95 ft. Loch Giorra was approximately the same size but its maximum depth was only 49 ft, which possibly accounts for Loch Daimh being given the honour of the name.

Stronuich headpond behind a dam lies beside the power station at Cashlie. The headpond provides the compensation water for the river. The power station uses the water from Loch

Daimh descending from 1,421 ft to 959 ft by the tunnel and pipe-line described earlier. The annual output is 23 million units of electricity on average. The discharged water which keeps up the level of Stronuich is tunnelled through the mountains then along four and a half miles by surface pipe-line to Glen Lochay giving an operating head of 592 ft to the power station producing 160 million units of electricity.

Now we come to Loch Lyon whose big dam, 1,740 ft long, doubled the size of a remote loch by raising it from 100 to 170 ft, thus inundating shepherds' cottages and causing a hamlet called Pubil to be built just east of the dam to house them. They are not so cut off as it appears, since they possess keys for the private

Loch Daimh from Stuic an Lochan looking to the wide space of Rannoch Moor

road which crosses the hill into Glen Lochay, thus Killin is within easy range.

The traps and ponds near the power station tail-race are for stripping the salmon of their eggs and milt since there is no way for them to reach their old spawning grounds. Once stripped of their eggs and milt the spent fish are put back in the river. The young fish reared from the eggs at Pitlochry are returned here for release. Local opinion is that control of the river has had an adverse effect on the salmon and salmon fishing.

Loch Lyon is kept topped up by water from Glen Lochay, sent by aqueduct and tunnel north through the mountains, to be returned again from Stronuich to the Lochay Power Station. This means that the latter generating station gets its power from three lochs of different heights in the Glen Lyon region, from Loch Daimh at 1,421 ft above sea-level, Loch Lyon at 1,127 ft and Stronuich at 959 ft. The engineers have had their fun here.

It is not the whole story in a development that comprises eight dams, eight power stations and sixty miles of tunnels. The other major work in the Breadalbane scheme is the harnessing of the Ben Lawers catchment, using the Lochan na Lairige over 1,700 ft on the hill to Finlarig Power Station on Loch Tay near Killin—the difference in height between them being 1,362 ft, the highest differential of any of the North of Scotland Hydro-Electric Board stations.

The massive buttresses of the 1,100 ft long dam raised the once small and shallow loch 90 ft giving it a storage capacity of 560 million cu. ft. The 130 ft high wall of concrete occupies a glacial breach, and when you look down its tilting ramps you see the low pressure pipe-lines disappearing underground. The water is then conveyed by tunnel for two miles, to be carried above ground by high pressure pipe-line for the last plunge to the power station.

Just a mile or two down the road is the Ben Lawers Car Park and Information Centre, operated by the National Trust for Scotland. It is a good place to halt and take a walk on the marked nature trail, with fine views of Loch Tay. Better still you might climb Ben Ghlas if it is a fine day for a better look at a loch that needs a book to itself to do it justice—situated as it is in the natural corridor between the Kingdom of the Picts and the Kingdom of the Scots in the west.

Loch Tay is a classic example of a ribbon loch, long and narrow, like most of the larger Scottish lochs. Note where it begins, precisely where Glen Lochay and Glen Dochart join, where the former glaciers came together and caused over-deepening of the channel. The Dochart is really the River Tay, which begins as a small stream on Ben Lui near Tyndrum and flows past Ben More, gathering strength and foaming into Killin as a cataract among the whitewashed cottages perched beside the rocks and narrow bridge below the knobbly Tarmachans.

Killin, with hotels and a fine caravan site, makes a good base for exploration, as does Kenmore at the far end of the loch with similar attractions of amenities and picturesque situation. Kenmore is climatically better, since there is a decrease by one inch of rainfall for each mile you go east along Loch Tay. Kenmore can be reached on a fast road through Killin along the north shore, or by a narrower and more twisty road on the south side giving striking views of the high Ben Lawers range above wooded shores.

The charming feature of Loch Tay, on either side, is the pattern of settlement round it, in little fields, farms, stone walls and coppices, with alas, too many ruins. Stone circles, ruined castles and old millwheels speak strongly of the past. Finlarig Power Station at the west end takes its name from the hulk of a castle near it, where if you thread your way among the undergrowth you may see the beheading block and the pit where the Black Duncan Campbell carried out his judgements for himself and King James VI at the beginning of the seventeenth century. And just across the water from it, at Kinnell near a stone circle, is the home of the chief of the clan MacNab, whose family crest is the head of an enemy killed on Loch Earn.

History and natural history are all about you here, for it was at Taymouth Castle that the Marquis of Breadalbane reintroduced the capercaillie to Scotland in 1837 and 1838, the native stock having died out with the destruction of the pine woods. Much planting had been done in the seventy years since its extinction however, and the new stock were able to thrive, dispersing along the Tummel and the Tay into much of Scotland.

The woods around Taymouth are still the most impressive on the lochside, spreading over Drummond Hill in a vast mat of larches in contrast to the natural oaks on the south side. Close under Drummond Hill is Eilean nam Bannomh—Isle of the Female Saints—which as you might expect has priory ruins on it. Apparently it was held by the monks of Scone at first, in the twelfth century, by charter from King Alexander I whose Queen is buried there. Then in time it became a nunnery, and eventually a castle of the Campbells. Montrose fired cannon balls on it, and Cromwell's forces held it for a time. It lies close to Kenmore, a little wooded speck—easy to visit but seldom visited.

Loch Tay is a compound of tamed shores backed by wild hills. There are golf courses at each end, good hotels and well-surfaced roads along its shores, yet on the south side you cannot break across the hills anywhere except on footpaths leading to Comrie and Crieff. You have to go to Kenmore to break south-east by car, by a rough track that zigs and zags to 1,600 ft, leading into Glen Quaich and by Loch Freuchie to Anulree by a route for adventurous motorists only.

From Fearnan on the north side, the road leads north to Fortingall in a couple of miles, and well worth a visit for its attractive thatched cottages and churchyard containing the oldest piece of living vegetation in Europe—the Fortingall yew tree which dates back 3,000 years. Pontius Pilate is alleged to have been born here when Fortingall was a Roman Camp. The earthworks may be seen just south of the road as you enter the village, where the Glen Lyon road forks.

Loch Tay is one of the great salmon fishing lochs of Scotland, and if you want to witness a whisky bottle, full, being broken over the bows of a boat to the tune of the bagpipes you have to come in January when the season opens. Covering over 10 sq. miles Loch Tay is 14½ miles long with a mean breadth of ¾ of a mile, with a maximum depth of 508 ft occurring roughly in the middle. It is also good for trout, as is the Lochan na Lairige and Lochan Breaclaich, opposite each other on different sides of Loch Tay.

Lochan Breaclaich, like Lochan na Lairige is no longer natural, but is impounded by a hydro-electric dam 1,300 ft long and 80 ft high raising it from a maximum depth of 41 ft to roughly 100 ft. Four miles of tunnel and aqueduct leads the water eastwards through the hills to a power station and a new reservoir called Loch Lednock—2 miles long and contained by a 950 ft dam 130 ft high. Design of this dam was tricky, because this Comrie region is a noted centre of earth tremors—like the Great Glen. The waters of Loch Lednock, which includes the catchment of the River Almond, are fed by tunnel to St. Fillans power station on Loch Earn.

Loch Earn is one of the most popular lochs in Scotland, lying as it does on the roads leading from Callander, Perth and Killin, at a convenient driving distance from Glasgow and Edinburgh or Stirling. Lochearnhead is in fact a main centre for water ski-ing in Scotland. Championships are held there. There is a good dinghy sailing school, and the current problem at the moment is a conflict of interests between power boat users, dinghy sailors, water skiers and fishermen. Clearly, some form of zoning is necessary.

A trout and salmon loch noted for its *Salma ferox*, it used to be thought that it was 600 ft deep until Mr. Grant-Wilson in 1888 and the *Bathymetrical Survey* in 1902 proved it to be no more than 288 ft maximum, both parties measuring to within one foot of each other. They showed it to be a simple basin with a floor sinking gradually to its greatest depth in a total length of 6½ miles with the deep spot in the middle. It is ⅘ of a mile at its broadest and 317.2 ft above sea-level, the latter height was exactly the height determined by the Ordnance Survey—accuracy indeed.

Dundurn at the eastern end of Loch Earn is a Pictish fort sited as a guard-point against invaders to the Pictish kingdom. It would be fascinating to know how much use these mysterious people made of boats in getting about the country—very much, I would think, with ribbon lochs like the Earn and the Tay to hand. Loch Earn is said to be derived in name from Loch Eireann—the men of Ireland whom the Picts were no doubt trying to keep out, unsuccessfully. The Celtic Picts who were of Welsh, Cornish and Breton types were superseded by the Irish whose early Christian missionaries had such a civilising influence on Scotland generally. St. Fillans commemorates one of these ‘saints’.

Just west of St. Fillans is Neish Island—Eilean nan Nadiseach which has ancient ruins on its tiny area—relics of the Neish clan who lived here until the Chief had his head cut off and taken to MacNab on Loch Tay as vengeance for a piece of impudence. This is the head which is symbolised on the family crest of the MacNabs.

The story is briefly this: It was Christmas time in the reign of James V, and MacNab had sent some of his men south-east across the hills to Crieff or Perth to buy victuals and have a celebration. The Neishs robbed them on the way back to Loch Tay, and the furious MacNab called a conference of his twelve sons who took instant action. They carried a boat across the hills, launched it on Loch Earn and came to Neish Island in the dark. Forcing the door they caught the Neish chieftain and his retainers helpless, for they had eaten and drunk too freely of the Christmas fare. So they were put to the sword, and the head carried back to Loch Tay. The MacNab who cut off the head of Neish was a supporter of Montrose and was himself killed in 1651 at the Battle of Worcester. He was Iain Min MacNab, the eldest son.

North-west of Loch Earn are the two most westerly lochs of the Tay river system, Loch Dochart and Loch Iubhair which could be called expansions of the Fillan hemmed north and south by 3,000 ft peaks. Shallow and reedy, Dochart is $\frac{2}{3}$ of a mile long and $\frac{1}{6}$ of a mile in maximum breadth with a maximum depth of 11 ft, but it has an island with a ruined castle which gives it character—a former stronghold of the Macgregors.

Loch Iubhair—Loch of the yew trees—is $1\frac{1}{3}$ miles long, $\frac{1}{3}$ in maximum breadth and is 65 ft in maximum depth with a mean depth of 25 ft, whereas Dochart is covered by no more than 5 ft on average. Trout fishing is fair. The glacier which flowed along this valley to Loch Tay is thought to have been 600 ft thick. You can see the glacial debris spread up the hills. Loch Essan is cradled nearly a thousand feet above Loch Iubhair on the north side and contains dark trout in its $\frac{1}{2}$ mile-long shallow waters, worth the climb for the views alone.

In discussing the Tay lochs the problem is to know where to stop when there are so many minor lochs of considerable interest in the hills, many of them accessible only by private roads or by walking. The forgotten country east of the Dunkeld-Ballinluig stretch of the A9 is particularly attractive, with fine woods and an attractive network of paths leading to fine fishing lochs, some of them preserved.

Loch Broom to the north-east of Ballinluig and Loch Ordie north of Dunkeld are only two of these. Both have sluices on them, so to some degree are artificial. Broom is really a depression in the heathery bog, $\frac{3}{4}$ of a mile long, $\frac{1}{3}$ of a mile broad and only 9 ft deep. Loch Ordie is $\frac{2}{3}$ of a mile long, $\frac{1}{2}$ a mile broad and 69 ft deep, with some attractive fishing cottages on its shore.

North and south of Strath Tay are similar hill-lochs: Loch Derculich, $\frac{1}{2}$ a mile in length and breadth and 70 ft deep below the steep slopes of Farragon; while south across the road lies Loch Scoly, Loch Skiach, Loch Kennard and Loch na Craige—the latter being on the A826 about four miles south of Aberfeldy.

The highest of the Tay lochs is Loch nan Eun at 2,575 ft, lying west of the Cairnwell below the peak of Beinn Iutharn Beag in a high bare country of remote tops. The *Bathymetrical Survey* states that 'the trout are said to be as fine as in any river or loch in Scotland'. It is $\frac{1}{2}$ a mile long, $\frac{3}{4}$ of a mile broad and 50 ft in maximum depth, draining into Glen Shee by Glen Taitneach, and an angler could have fun fishing all the way from the Spital up to the high loch. These hills are rich in wildlife—ptarmigan for example have a higher density here than in the Arctic. Also of interest are the moles, which reach a higher elevation than elsewhere in Scotland.

Another remote loch worthy of pilgrimage lies to the south-west, in Glen Tilt, but is most easily reached from Blair Atholl. It has the odd name of Loch Loch, a narrow slit of water impounded among gravelly morainic material beneath the dark cliffs of Ben-y-Gloe. It too is a good trout loch, and also contains char. The burn which drains from it into the Tilt just south of the Bedford Memorial Bridge makes a good line of ascent.

It is a thin snake of a loch, $1\frac{1}{4}$ miles long by only $\frac{1}{6}$ of a mile broad, cut into a north and south portion by a shallow which divided them at the time of survey. The south portion is $\frac{1}{2}$ a mile, the north $\frac{3}{4}$ of a mile. The greatest depth occurs where the loch is widest in the northern part, reaching 81 ft. The *Bathymetrical Survey* reports: 'Loch Loch is peculiar in outline and in conformation. Besides the principal central constriction, which cuts the loch into two approximate halves, there are three minor constrictions, each accompanied by a shoaling of the bottom. . . .'

Another mountain loch worthy of mention drains directly into Loch Tay but is rarely visited, nor has its depth been surveyed. This is the Lochan nan Cat in the darkest recess of Ben Lawers, shaped like a bottle with its neck tilted to its outlet stream. Hung round with broken cliffs where the snow tends to linger, it is an impressive place which can be reached in a walk of just over three miles north from Lawers Hotel. The loch is $\frac{1}{2}$ a mile long and less than $\frac{1}{4}$ of a mile broad at maximum.

East of Dunkeld the Highland country falls away to fertile Strathmore which is a well-drained sand and gravel plain with kettle-hole lochs, sometimes connected to each other by artificial channels or millades where man has put them to use. Lochs Craiglush, Lowes, Butterstone, Clunie, Drumellie, Rae, Fingask,

Loch of the Lowes and Loch of Lush seen from Birnam Hill, breeding haunt of ospreys

White, Black and the Stormont lochs flow away from the Tay, but join it by the Lunan burn and the River Isla south of Meikleour. Loch of the Lowes has the special interest of being a Scottish Wildlife Trust Reserve, with an observation hide for visitors and a ranger to point out the tree where the ospreys nest, and help identify the rich variety of water and marsh birds, from great crested grebes to goosander. The whole south shore is open to the public.

Lochs Craiglush, Lowes and Butterstone lie just outside Dunkeld, to the north-east. With weedy shores and ringed by trees, Craiglush is ½ a mile long, ¼ of a mile broad, with a maximum depth of 44 ft. Lowes is just over 1 mile long by ½ a mile broad and is 53 ft in maximum depth, and is connected by an artificial channel to Craiglush. Butterstone is roughly circular with a diameter of ⅗ of a mile and is 25 ft deep. Loch of Clunie further east has an island with a castle said to have been the birthplace of the Admirable Crichton. It lies below the road to Blairgowrie, like the Loch of Drumellie. Both are less than 1 mile long, and are 69 ft and 58 ft deep respectively.

All these low-ground lochs have perch, pike and trout in them, and all have ornithological interest as breeding grounds of duck and grebes, swans, coots and waterhens. Rae Loch is a mile west of Blairgowrie and is only 16 ft deep, and it flows into Fingask which is smaller but is 48 ft deep. White Loch is 32 ft in maximum depth but the Black Loch is a mere 7 ft.

East of Coupar Angus in the Sidlaw Hills there is the Long Loch and Thrieply Loch, more usually known as the Round Loch. The Long Loch is ¾ of a mile by ¼ of a mile, with a maximum depth of 42 ft. The Round Loch is ⅕ of a mile in diameter and is 19 ft in maximum depth.

Loch Benachally supplies water to Blairgowrie from the Forest of Clunie to the north-west of the town and is just over 1 mile long by ½ a mile broad, with a maximum depth of 64 ft. Lintrathen Loch due north of Alyth, a little east of the B954, supplies Dundee with water and is a great gathering ground for winter geese and duck, when thousands may be seen together. This loch is 1½ miles long and ¾ of a mile broad sloping down to 70 ft at its deepest.

Forfar Loch also drains into the Tay and lies near the town, handy for fishing permits which are issued by the Town Clerk. It is 1 mile long by ¼ of a mile broad, with a maximum depth of 29 ft. Its outlet is by the Dean Water and the River Isla.

The Tay, it will be seen, not only drains some of the most attractively wooded country but also some of the wildest mountain and moorland in Scotland, with a cross-section of every kind of loch, from peat holes and reedy meres to rock-hemmed mountain tarns and large ribbon lochs as different from each other as the sylvan Tay and the bleak Ericht. To explore them all sets a mighty challenge along the greatest river systems Tummel, Garry, Tay and Earn.

Lochs Awe, Avich, Nant, Tulla, Dochard

Loch Awe has a unique distinction. It is the longest loch in Scotland, 25.47 miles compared to 24.23 for Loch Ness and 22.64 for Loch Lomond. Conversely the mean breadth of a ½ a mile is only 2.3 per cent of the total length, the smallest percentage recorded for any mainland loch. It is also peculiar in that the top has become the bottom, nature having carved a new outlet for it by the Pass of Brander to the north-west, whereas in pre-glacial times it emptied into the sea from the south.

It has yet another distinction which it shares with Loch Lomond. Both were surveyed by the Navy as long ago as 1861—the only Scottish freshwater lochs to be sounded in detail 'in the interests of navigation'. Murray and Pullar resurveyed it in 1903, finding general agreement with the Admiralty Chart, getting a maximum depth of 307 ft compared to 306 ft in the earlier survey. Only four lochs contain more water, Ness, Lomond, Morar and Tay.

All these four are making some contribution to hydro-electricity generation in some way or another but none on such a scale as Loch Awe, which nature had already made topsy-turvy before engineers devised the grand plan of pumping water into a corrie of Ben Cruachan only to bring it down again by the methods known as pumped storage.

You get a very good impression of how this works if you go to Cladich and look across the island-speckled loch to the great horseshoe of the Cruachan peaks. The obvious feature is a high dam nearly half-way up the mountain. This is where the water is stored, and inside the mountain are the reversable pump/turbines, the tunnels and the great cavern of the machine hall which is 300 ft long, 77 ft wide and 120 ft high.

The huge pylon-lines bring in power as well as take it out. Striding over forest, hills and moors the cables bring power from Hunterston Nuclear Power Station on the Clyde to pump the water into the dam 1,200 ft above. This is done at night and weekends where there is a surplus of power. The water is brought down again when the peak demand is high. The operating head is the highest in the world for this kind of plant, and it has not been without its troubles.

Like Loch Lomond, Loch Awe is virtually two lochs, broad in the base with a sprinkling of wooded islands and castles, and narrowing rapidly to become a ribbon for most of its length. The basic difference here is that Loch Awe does not become broad until it reaches the peaks which terminate it, which is the reverse of Loch Lomond.

How did it come about that the outlet from Loch Awe managed to carve a way through the Pass of Brander when its outlet used to be where Ford is situated now, at the southern end of the loch? An examination shows Loch Ederline below Ford to be a kettle-hole, once occupied by ice, and that the melt-water escaped through two melt-water channels.

The north end of Loch Awe spanned by the Oban railway. Ben Lui distant

At the same time, there was pressure of ice in the north, spilling down from Rannoch Moor and forcing its way westwards towards where Loch Etive is situated. The ice found a fault, a line of weakness in the lava and breached a gap at right-angles to the general southward trend of the ice. Had this weakness not been present in the rocks it is certain that the pressure of the ice southward would have scoured away the mere 30 ft of material which impounds the loch at present.

So the most dramatic scenery of Loch Awe is from Dalmally westwards to the dark ravine of the pass, which is one of the great journeys of Scotland where road and rail run parallel because they have nowhere else to go. This is Campbell country whose fortunes flourished in alliance with Bruce and Wallace. They expanded out of their original stronghold on the tiny island of Innischonnail into Kilchurn Castle in the fifteenth century.

Kilchurn on its marshy headland has a stage-setting gauntness, ruined and turreted with seventeenth-century additions, the old part is the square tower which was built by Sir Colin Campbell of Glenorchy, founder of the acquisitive Breadalbane family. It is now in the care of the Department of the Environment and there is no admission to enter. The drama of its situation is best appreciated from afar. Situated where the River Orchy enters the loch, access is easy, but it has to be walked, and is all the better for that.

Ruined piers are mementoes of the days when tourist steamers used to ply on the loch before they were outmoded by the motor car and improved roads on both sides of the loch. You can drive right round it now, except for the portion immediately opposite Ben Cruachan where there is no breach on the frowning Pass of Brander cliffs. To explore the north-west triangle you have to go in from Kilchrenan.

This means motoring almost to Taynuilt, under Creag an Aonaidh where Robert the Bruce won his battle against John of Lorn in 1308 by raining down arrows on the Argyll men from the flank when they thought they had only a frontal attack to deal with. They were routed forever.

The outlet of the Awe is now controlled by a hydro-electric dam, connected by three miles of tunnel to a power station situated where the river discharges into Loch Etive, below

Taynuilt. This is where you have to do an about turn and take the Glen Nant road which is single-track and winding, but well-surfaced—Taycreggan Hotel makes a fine base for exploration—and there is plenty to explore, for this is the best wildlife area of all Loch Awe.

A walk should be taken to the top of the crags from this side, for the sake of looking through the remarkable defile where Loch Awe becomes a snake of black river to the curving sea loch. Two miles eastward on the broad loch are scattered the tiny islands of ruined castles and graveyards: Inishail—'The Isle of Rest' with its fine carved stones, ruined convent and chapel; Fraoch Eilean—'The Heather Island' on whose twelfth-century castle the Campbells built bits and pieces over the centuries; Innis Chonnan—'The Island of St. Connan'. Much has been written on the history of these islands. The naturalist will find special interest in the natural woods and scrub growing on them, representing vegetation uncontaminated by grazing or burning. It is an easy enough matter to hire a boat to explore these islands.

Indeed hire a boat and you can fish Loch Awe for salmon, trout and sea trout for it is open water and no permits are required. The naturalist should certainly make a stop at Inverinan and visit the Forestry Office where an interesting experiment in public relations is having great success. It began by marking the network of forest tracks and publishing a little guide book to them. Then a wildlife exhibit was staged, using photographs and specimens to describe the abundant wildlife of the hills and forests.

The effect of timber planting on a large scale increases the breeding success of predators, notably hen harriers, sparrow-hawks and buzzards. Jays and woodpeckers also benefit, though moorland birds become scarce. On this side of Loch Awe the blanket plantations of Sitka spruce have been described as 'monotonous'. This is true. On the other hand they grow faster in western Scotland than anywhere else in the world, and the best are now being cut for saw-logs. The smaller ones go for pulp to the paper mill near Fort William. It is the most productive use that has been found so far for a combination of high rainfall and acid ground.

Ford at the head of the loch takes its name from the days

before there was any bridge. The old name is Alt nan Cho—the 'Ford of the Hazel Nuts' where between Loch Awe and Loch Ederline there was an easy passage for cattle in the droving days. It has an air of great peace about it as if basking in its history of Picts and Scots when this was Dalriada, and the sway of battle leaned to the Irish who gave their name and religion to Scotland. Down there only a few miles lies Dunadd, just a fortified rock which was the capital of the contested kingdom. Everywhere around it to Loch Awe are ancient relics, cairns, circles, sculptured stones, hill forts, earthworks, chapels. It is an archaeological treasure-house.

The old 'Ford of the Hazel Nuts' was a shallow stretch of river south of the present road-bridge. There used to be stepping stones there, but locals will tell you that they were swept away in a cloudburst on the day that the Second World War was declared. It was hereabouts, at Inverliever, the Office of the Woods, later to become the Forestry Commission, purchased their first property, 9,000 acres which until 1968 was their proudest possession, until one January night a hurricane blew up and destroyed the magnificent sixty-year-old timber. The 100 ft trees, 3 ft thick, were woven like a wreath round the hill above the village. The productivity of the Loch Awe woods is over 100,000 tons of timber a year.

Working north up the east side of the loch you are in more open country with wider views since there are no large plantations. Leave your car and climb the 1,000 ft hills and you will find yourself in an upland country of small lochs, dozens of them stretching to Loch Fyne, rock basins excavated by the passage of the ice, and now the haunt of black-throated divers. Loch Awe cannot be discovered in a rapid drive. It has to be explored bit by bit, and Port Sonnachan on this side is the perfect compliment to Kilchrenan on the other side for doing so.

In point of detail, the most interesting thing about Loch Awe is its shallowness, more than half of it being under 100 ft deep. Only 1.2 per cent of its 9,505 acres is over 300 ft, and only 10.7 per cent is over 200 ft, while 30.5 per cent is over 100 ft deep. The deepest water is at the south end, out from Braevallich about five miles north of Ford, where the glaciers dredged deepest. The arm extending towards the Pass of Brander has a maximum depth of

249 ft. The 12 mile middle portion of the loch between Portinnisherrich and Inistrynich is less than 200 ft for 12 miles in length. This sinuous topsy-turvy loch is irregular.

Loch Avich is the biggest of the lochs which drain into Loch Awe and is situated one mile west of the central part, and is most easily reached from Inverinan by a through-road to Kilmelfort, though its outlet stream is nearer Dalavich. This loch is 3½ miles long with a maximum breadth of ½ a mile and is a simple basin dropping to 188 ft towards the eastern end. The evidence of a melt-water channel and outwash terraces show that in Ice Age times the drainage was westward. The basin exhibits a classical 'U' section typical of a glacially eroded rock-basin and all but 30 per cent is over 50 ft deep. There is no salmon in the loch but good trout. Permits can be had from Inverinan Lodge Hotel four miles distant.

The flow of Loch Nant has also been reversed, not by nature but by man. A dam at the northern outlet prevents it from spilling over exclusively to Loch Etive. Now the water flows to Loch Awe, by tunnel to a power-house near Kilchrenan, with an estimated output of 27 million units. The discharged water helps to keep Loch Awe topped-up.

Loch Nant is a bit more than two miles north-west of Kilchrenan, and in its natural state was 1 mile long and ⅓ of a mile broad, 92 ft at its deepest and of irregular outline. Its volume was estimated at 148 million cu. ft. Its volume now is 920 million cu. ft, due to aqueducts which have doubled its natural catchment. The effect on its shape is to make it much more irregular. It looks on the map like a man with outstretched arms. The height above sea-level is approximately 700 ft.

Loch Tulla was the birthplace of Duncan Ban McIntyre and before taking the narrow road up through wild Glen Orchy to this splendid loch on the edge of Rannoch Moor it is worth going up to the monument to the bard situated to command the finest view of the loch and Glen Orchy beyond Dalmally. The poet, who was born in 1724 and died in 1812, saw the terrible changes that followed the '45. His poetry should be read for his vision of the Highlands. To his sorrow he fought on the wrong side—against the Prince.

The fast Glen Coe road passes along the east side of Loch

Tulla, tempting fast cars to go faster, but anyone with an eye for country will not pass on if the weather be clear and the high peaks ringing the loch westward are free of cloud. Ben Starav, Stob Coire an Albannaich, Stob Ghabhar are the aristocrats, forming a block of summits stretching to the wild head of Loch Etive penetrated only by paths. There are no driving roads. The foreground is bare, but the connoisseur will note the Caledonian pines clustering round the west end of the loch.

There is a hotel there called Inveroran, reached by crossing the old humpback bridge from Bridge of Orchy and much beloved of fishermen and mountaineers. The track to it is the old Glen Coe

Loch Tulla below peaks of the Black Mount

road which is closed to cars beyond the Forest Lodge due to ruts, vegetation and decay. Yet it was in use until the early 'thirties when the new road closed the old cattle-droving route and opened a way round the east end of the loch, climbing smoothly to thread the Rannoch lochs.

Duncan Ban the poet was born in a little crofting township that occupied a slope just west of the hotel, in Glen Fuar—the 'Cold Glen'—only a short walk up a track to the ruins of two houses. This was the place where he was so happy. The inspiration that Robert Burns got from the fields, McIntyre got from the hills stretching round Druimliaghart—as the ruin is marked on the map.

'Duncan of the songs' never wrote a line of poetry. He memorised 6,000 lines, perhaps more. He got his education not in school but from life, and from Mary McNicol, the Inveroran innkeeper's daughter whom he married—Mari Bhan Og—fair young Mary. Forester, gamekeeper, soldier, a City Guard in Edinburgh, he is buried in Greyfriars. That his 'songs' still lived on after him is clear from the fact that the monument above Loch Awe was not erected until forty-seven years after his death—by public subscription. Fortunately he dictated his poetry, which still lives on, but the English language is a poor substitute for the Gaelic of it. There is no mark of remembrance here on Loch Tulla.

Yet this is not entirely true. There is Ben Dorain, the subject of some of his best poetry, just across the loch, and this is the finest viewpoint for it. Ringed by mountains you have the feeling of being in an oasis of woods and water and sky, because you are not shut in. Even the little island—Eilean an Stalcair—has character, flagged with a Caledonian pine or two, and situated almost in the middle of the loch. The deepest sounding of 84 ft is $\frac{1}{4}$ of a mile north-east of it.

The loch is $2\frac{1}{2}$ miles long, with a mean breadth of about $\frac{1}{2}$ a mile and in 1963 it was so hard-frozen that the postman was walking over it for a week or two, this being the easiest way of delivering his letters to the shooting lodge on the south side. Loch Tulla is 542 ft above sea-level—the lowest point of Rannoch Moor—so it is hardly surprising that like all the other Rannoch lochs it is shallow, 70 per cent is 50 ft or under. What distinguishes it from the others are the remnants of the old forest and the infinitely richer wildlife and scenery.

Loch Dochard is the perfect compliment to Loch Tulla and lies just three miles west of it by a rough private track which is a right-of-way for walkers. It is only $\frac{2}{3}$ of a mile long and 42 ft deep in the centre, but few lochs have such a feeling of grandeur and absolute remoteness about them. The loud streams tumbling down from the slabby mountains show that it receives a considerable drainage.

Its height above sea-level is 735 ft. It is intriguing to discover that the Water of Tulla should be the only other place in Scotland which has 'parallel roads' similar to those in Glen Roy, indicating that there was a loch whose waters fell in four levels marked by roads at 1,041 ft, 1,030 ft, 1,020 ft and 816 ft, with indications that the lowest waters spilled over the watershed beyond Loch Dochard, which would seem to indicate that at one time Loch Tulla and Loch Dochard were continuous, spilling into Glen Kinglass over the present watershed.

Any man interested in walking exciting paths should consider continuing westward over the watershed in Glen Kinglass, then south by Loch Etive to Taynuilt. With a little planning it can be fitted into bus timetables, or better still you could arrange to be picked up by a friend with a car.

Anyone who has travelled the road to the isles from Fort William to Mallaig will remember narrow Loch Shiel, hardly more than a slit in a gorge of mountains shoulder upon shoulder. From the high viaduct of the West Highland Railway the diesel passenger gets a vision of loneliness, emphasised by the small figure of the Highlander standing forlornly on his stone plinth, dwarfed by the surroundings.

At road-level the monument on the marshy flat at the head of the loch is imposing. Note however that it looks away from the water, to the infinitely wilder hills of Knoydart, for the monument commemorates the Highlanders who fought and died

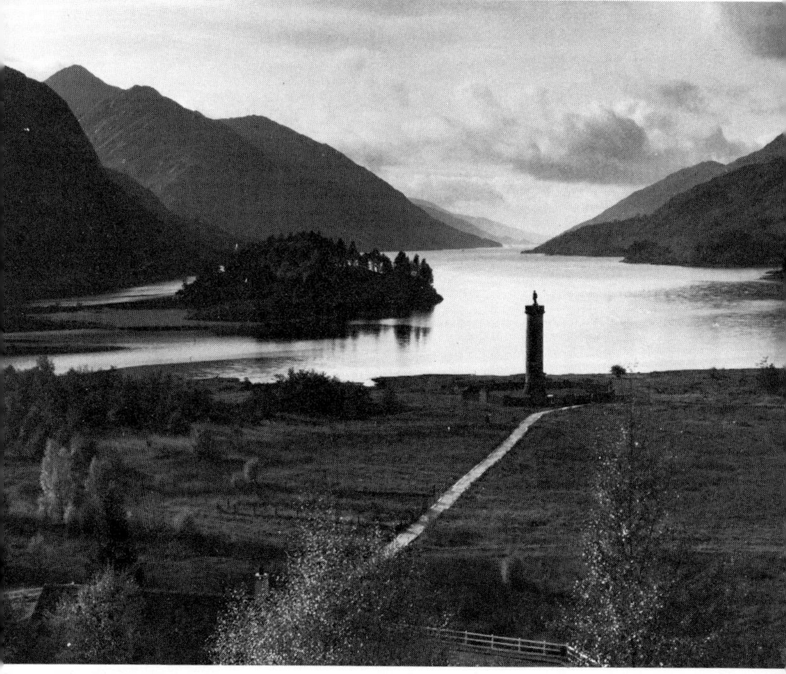

The Highlanders' Monument, Loch Shiel, where the clans gathered to march with Prince Charlie

in the Jacobite rising of 1745, and not merely the Bonny Prince and the place where Charlie landed by rowing boat at noon on 19 August.

Here at Glenfinnan the standard was raised, and on the 21st they marched away to easy victory and final mortifying defeat. In less than a year the brave men were dead, maimed, in prison, or on the run like the Prince himself. The Highlanders got the Prince safely away, but the Highlands never recovered. Nobody lives in these wild hills to the north now, and to the south in Moidart lies some of the most depopulated countryside in Britain. There is not even a regular boat service on the loch any longer.

This is MacDonald country, and the monument was erected by Alexander MacDonald of Glenaladale, a descendant of the Glenaladale who was with the Prince in the thick of his troubles, not least on 18 July 1746 when they lay on the top of Fraoch Bheinn immediately above the loch, hemmed by redcoats with nothing except local knowledge to see them through. Disastrous as it all turned out, at least it did this much good, it revealed to the world the noble character of the ordinary Highlander, people who by their loyalty and selflessness were the real heroes of the '45.

Not that this land could ever support a vast population—the country round Loch Shiel is too rough, and even the bed of the loch is so irregular that it alternates between being deep and shallow. About four miles from the monument the maximum depth of 420 ft is reached, yet more than half the loch floor is covered by less than 100 ft of water. But there is no regularity. Deep water occurs close inshore in places, while at the widest part of the loch there is a stretch in the middle which is covered by only 2 or 3 ft of water.

To explore Loch Shiel or fish its waters, it is best to base yourself at Acharacle, driving in from Loch Ailort by the picturesque coast road which winds by Loch Moidart to Dalelia and Acharacle village, where you can go for a sail or hire a boat on the river-like stretches of loch which are notable for salmon, grilse and sea trout. You can see here how nearly Loch Shiel missed being a sea-loch like Sunart and Ailort north and south of it. However it is cut off from the sea by a huge fan of material deposited by the glacier which scooped out the fault-guided basin, leaving 12 ft between its lip and sea-level.

Of the islands on the loch, Eilean Glean Fhianin is the largest and lies close to Glen Finnan. But the island of Eilean Fhianin at the seaward end is more interesting being the burial place of the Clanranald, with the remains of Finnan's church. A canoeist with a tent could have an exciting time on Loch Shiel, exploring its numerous small islands and climbing some of the remoter peaks. And in May and June the weather is usually drier than at other times in this wet area.

Loch Morar, over the hills north of Loch Shiel, is the most remarkable example of down-cutting by ice in Scotland, for it is 1,077 ft deep and was once covered by glacier ice 4,000 ft deep. The easiest access is from Morar, near Mallaig, but the loch itself is hidden until you get up past the little power station where the

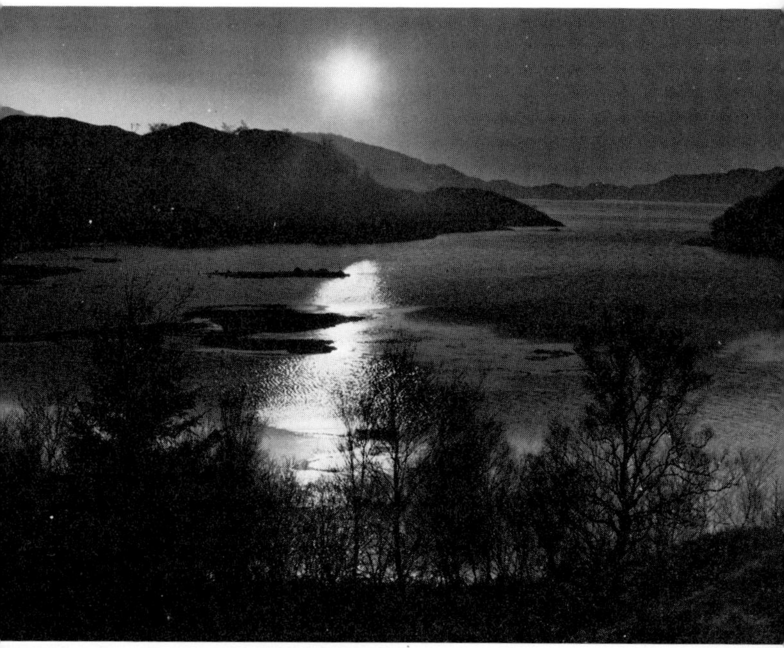

The broadest part of Loch Shiel at Polloch

river is harnessed. Then you look over the broadest part and its scatter of islands, and you might reflect on history and natural history, for the islands are covered with native scrub. The trees have disappeared from over-grazing by sheep and deer on the shores. And it was on an island here that Lovat of the '45 was captured hiding in a hollow tree and subsequently beheaded in London—a sad end for an intriguer of his calibre.

Loch Morar does not disclose its wilderness from this aspect however. That lies far beyond the five miles of road of its rather gentle western end. You need a boat to penetrate further west, or walk from Loch Arkaig by Glen Pean—along the route taken by the Prince after Culloden on that night of 19 April 1746 when he arrived at Meoble at a 'small sheal house near a wood utterly tired out'.

You can still see the ruins of the clansmen's houses if you walk this way today, past the Lochan Leum an-t-Sagairt into a wild ravine, then over Coir' a' Bheigh with walls of rock rising from tangled blocks. Beyond the pass lies grey Loch Morar, a wild slit in the mountains like Loch Shiel. Alas, the houses round the lonely head are empty, though the one marked 'Oban' is used as a summerhouse.

The nearest inhabited houses are at Meoble, almost half-way down the 11½ mile long loch, where the rock basin goes down over a thousand feet below sea-level, in a basically simple floor, quite without the irregularity of Loch Shiel, with its mixed-up shallows. They share the same peculiarity however that both narrowly missed being sea-lochs, due to the litter of glacial debris separating them from the ocean so close to their mouths.

Meoble is well worth a visit, and there is a fine walking route over the hills on a reasonable footpath about seven miles from the head of Loch Shiel by the stream of the Allt na Criche, with magnificent views of narrow Loch Beoraid and the high hills of Knoydart on the way. Meoble lies in an oasis of green amongst these hills, with dots of white houses beneath stands of larch and spruce.

The gravel road extends only four miles to the fishing lochs, so this is a sporting estate and farm of cattle and sheep with complete privacy, marching with Locheil's estate to the east which is similarly remote, but before taking you there, it is worth mentioning an easier walk to appreciate the remarkable situation of Loch Morar.

This involves motoring up from Morar to the end of the road at Bracorina, and climbing north on the footpath which leads to the rocky crest of 1,000 ft hills separating Loch Nevis from Loch Morar, so you have freshwater on one side and salt on the other, and all Knoydart and its 'Rough Bounds' to the east. Think of yourself as an outlaw, blockaded from the sea on the west side, and hemmed in by searching soldiers from the south, north and east, and you know the position that Charlie was in, facing hunger and death.

It is across that bristly backbone of drowned valleys we shall go in another chapter to Loch Arkaig.

Lochs of the Spey Basin

Lochs Spey, Crunachdan, Insh, Alvie, Eilein, Na Gamhna, Morlich, Pityoulish

Reedy Loch Spey is the source of the 100 mile long river which is the fastest flowing in Scotland next to the 85 miles of the Dee which rises at 4,000 ft on Braeriach and reaches the sea at Aberdeen in that distance. The Spey does not have such an impressive beginning, rising in boggy ground close to the col which separates the catchment from Glen Roy.

The situation is of particular interest, for the drainage of Glen Roy and the drainage of the Spey are separated by only a 9 ft difference in height. So a short walk westwards takes you to what was once the shore of the ice-imprisoned lake which left the 'parallel roads' to mark its declining levels.

The Wade road from Laggan, past the barracks at Garvamore, is the best way of getting there. The grey stones of the former barracks are just across from the Wade bridge. Nowadays the pylons of the North of Scotland Hydro-Electric Board cross the Corrieyairack, and with them as your signpost you can follow the road for nine miles to Melgarve. Then you must take the lower pass by leaving the Corrieyairack. Leave your car too and follow boggy ground to reach Loch Spey 1,142 ft above sea-level.

This is the haunt of the 'Phantom Piper', and it has nothing to do with the events of the '45 or General Wade. It is the name given to a signalling system from a remote-control weather station in a refuge hut on the very summit of the Corrieyairack at 2,543 ft on the highest pylon line in Britain. Because the route is often blocked by snow and the wires endangered by thick ice building up on them, an ingenious system to cope with these problems was worked out.

The 'Phantom Piper' gets its 'puff' from batteries charged by a wind-driven generator, and according to whether it sends out a high note, a medium or a low note, the North of Scotland Hydro-Electric Board control room in Elgin reads the danger to the wires from icing. The message can also be picked up by radios in the vehicles of the service engineers.

The control room in Elgin can interrogate the instruments on the pass by dialling a number on a private telephone system to get from them coded information about wind direction and strength, temperature, tension on the wires and the thickness of the ice on them.

If the bagpipe music plays a pibroch of 'ICE' at dangerous thickness, then it is time for the engineers to go into action. They cut off the current from the Spey side of the pass, in Glen Truim, and switch in a heavy current from a generator in Glen Garry. This causes the wires to heat up and the ice to drop off. The lines lying horizontally instead of vertically overcome the problem of chunks of falling ice causing the wires to clash against each other as they bounce with the action of melting. The summit lines were reconstructed in 1967 to bring into being the present effective system.

Returning along the river it is worth taking a brief look at Loch Crunachdan situated amongst woods and making a fine foreground for the Creag Meagaidh massif. This $\frac{2}{3}$ of a mile long loch was impounded in 1943 to boost Loch Laggan. The effect has been to reduce the power of the Spey to cause widespread flooding, while putting the water to better use for aluminium smelting. Even so, the marshes of Ruthven Barracks at Kingussie may sometimes become a lake, extending to Loch Insh.

I would advocate that the traveller following the Spey should take the road rightward out of Kingussie and follow its delightful windings through knolls of pine and birch above the marshes of the gaunt barracks which saw the end of the Jacobite army. Here the beaten men assembled after Culloden eager to carry on the fight, but their leader had gone, and the message he sent, 'Let everyone seek his own safety in the best way he can', was the end of the cause.

Ruthven on the marshes, loud with the wailing cries of gulls and curlews, echoes something of its historical desolation—the failure to fight until proper peace-terms were ensured. Here was the last gathering of the clans, in MacPherson country, and over there is Creag Dubh where Cluny lived for nine years in a cave amongst the rocks with a large price on his head, and although every member of the clan knew where their chief was hidden, none gave the secret away.

Loch Insh is partly hidden by crowns of trees on the attractive knolls which hem its green banks. It is 1 mile long, and not quite as much broad, with a maximum depth of 100 ft. The bottom is irregular, one half of the total area being covered by no more than 25 ft. Its shores have to be explored on foot, and they are full of secret corners and ornithological delights.

Gaggles of wild geese and droves of fieldfares and redwings use the valley as a migration route. A fine herd of whooper swans winters here. The western rampart of the Cairngorms provides a bold front of thrusting rock shoulders hung with Caledonian pines and heather reaching back to snowy corries. The thermals are used by the local gliding club in Glen Feshie, just east of the loch shore, where a few enthusiasts meet every weekend, sharing the sky with eagle and buzzard.

Loch Insh at Kincraig. The loch combines a sailing school and RSPB Nature Reserve

Kincraig is the village for Loch Insh and is on the railway at the north end of the loch which contains the only migratory char in Scotland. Scientists tell us that the char, *genus Salvelinus*, is a relic of our Ice Age past. But it is strange that of the various sub-species found in other lochs only the Loch Insh variety migrates like salmon. Insh incidentally contains both trout and salmon.

The next two lochs are very different. Loch Alvie belongs to the gentle slopes of the Monadhliath—Loch an Eilein to the rugged Cairngorms. And between the two is Tor Alvie crowned by a slender monument to the fifth and last Duke of Gordon. Kinrara lies at the base of it and this is where the famous Duchess lies buried, she who raised the Gordon Highlanders with the reward of a shilling and a kiss—and she had beauty enough it seems to make any man eager to go and be a soldier.

Loch Alvie to the west of the main road lies under the great heather slope of Geal Charn Mor, and often enough its summit snow-ribbon is mirrored in the oval waters of the loch which is 1 mile long and ½ a mile wide. The depth is mostly 25 ft, but the maximum is 70 ft, and the trout fishing is good. The little church on the green shore has great charm, and if you go to the burial ground beside it you may read on a stone:

'Buried here are the remains of 150 human bodies, found, October 1880, beneath the floor of this church. Who they were, when they lived, how they died tradition notes not.
Their bones are dust, their good swords rust.
Their souls are with the saints, we trust.'

Loch an Eilein reached most easily from Aviemore, has become something of a tourist 'draw' now, but it remains an unspoiled gem of Scotland, ringed by natural pine forest and birches, crystallising the finest in scenery and wildlife that the Spey has to offer. To make it more interesting for the visitor its circuit on a gravel track has been given the status of 'Nature Trail'.

You park your car at the north end, pick up a Nature Trail pamphlet and by reading the paragraphs corresponding to the numbered posts you can learn about the distinctive features of each spot, for this is part of the second biggest Nature Reserve in Europe noted for its primeval forest, its animal and bird life.

It is open forest, spreading up the hills from the loch shores in superb birches and Caledonian pines, with much juniper. Rainfall is less than a third of what is normal in the west, so there is much more heather and associated vegetation, crowberry and blaeberry. Special birds are the crested tits, which usually announce their barred presence with quivering calls; and Scottish crossbills which have a sub-specific rank, and experts believe to have different calls. This reserve was formed to protect them, and the habitats which extend to the arctic-alpine zone, in a region of corries, glens, lochs and tundra unique in Britain.

This vast area is meant to be enjoyed, but not developed for tourism like nearby Cairn Gorm which has ski-tows, chair-lifts

Loch an Eilein, a moraine dammed loch close to the Spey Valley

and restaurants. The management aim here is to keep the wild truly wild. A pamphlet costing 5p and telling you things to do and see within the reserve is available from the Nature Conservancy.

Loch an Eilein is a little over 1 mile in length with a maximum breadth of ½ a mile and a maximum depth of 66 ft—towards the western end. The ruined castle on the island just out from the north-western shore, usually chuckling with jackdaws, is the distinctive feature of the loch. 'Eilein' is the Gaelic for island, so the loch takes its name from the island—'The Loch of the Island'.

The castle dates from the fifteenth century, it is thought, and maybe as far back as the time of Bruce. Certainly it was a ruin in the sixteenth century until restored for defence by the Grants of

Loch an Eilein, ringed by primeval pine-wood and backed by the Cairngorm plateau

Rothiemurchus. It proved useful in 1690 against attacks following the Battle of Cromdale. A fragment of history from the early castle tells of three murderers imprisoned there for several years before being given their punishment, which included beheading, quartering, torturing and hanging. The victims were a trio of murderers who paid retribution for destroying Macintosh who was their Chief.

The castle was famous for another piece of destruction—the destruction of the Loch an Eilein ospreys which nested on the castle tower until systematic robbing year after year exterminated the fish-hawks in the early twentieth century. The inspiring ornithological success story of Speyside today is that the great birds have returned—but not to the castle—though they sometimes fish the waters of the loch from time to time.

The recolonisation began in the 1950s when a pair of birds built a nest in a pine tree not so far from Loch an Eilein, and reared two young. Other nesting attempts ended in failure or robbery, until 1959 when teams of wardens mounted a round-the-clock watch to make the Loch Garten birds the most closely watched pair of ospreys in the world.

Publicity brought a stream of watchers to the nesting area, and the RSPB built an observation post to allow members of the public to view the nest through powerful binoculars screened at a safe distance. 'Seeing the ospreys' has become one of the attractions of Speyside, and money collected from visitors is doing much to assist the general work of bird protection. The birds are now breeding on several other sites, but this is the most likely area of Britain to see ospreys hunting.

The walk round Loch na Gamhna should be included with a circuit of Loch an Eilein. This loch is only $\frac{1}{5}$ of a mile broad and less than $\frac{1}{2}$ a mile long. The walking is a little marshy in places but the track is fair, below the Cat's Den, a small rocky hill worth climbing for the view over Rothiemurchus to Glen More, and the windings of the Spey between the Cairngorms and the Monadhliath. The margin of the reedy loch is a great place for greenshank, and I have often flushed a goosander on my walk round. The loch itself is only 41 ft deep.

Loch Morlich lies not far to the east, and if a man can arrange a lift at the far end he should consider following the tracks through Rothiemurchus forest to it, passing *en route* the entrance to Glen Einich and the Lairig Ghru. From this great forest logs used to be floated down the Spey to the boat-building yards at the mouth of the river. You can still see the remains of the sluices on the Luineag at the western end of Loch Morlich. Some logs went only as far as the sawmills at Inverdruie. Other logs were formed into rafts and taken downriver by 'floaters', men who took them all the way to the sea.

Walk east along Loch Morlich to the little sandy bay amongst the pines at the far end, have a seat and take stock of the setting of this forest loch backed by 4,000 ft mountains whose long-lying snows are being put to such good use by skiers. There is a camp-site just beyond the bay, and whatever the weather there are few weekends in the year when there are no campers, for the Cairngorms have become the 'Little Switzerland' of Scotland.

The loch itself is a kettle-hole, like the other lochs of the Spey Valley, just a large hollow surrounded by glacial drift, its outlet carved through a natural dam of morainic material. The whole place is a fluvio-glacial museum of outwash terraces and erratic blocks. The loch is just over 1 mile long and $\frac{2}{3}$ of a mile broad, but 60 per cent is less than 10 ft deep, so although it is larger in superficial area than Loch Insh it contains less water. The maximum depth is 49 ft.

Loch Morlich is within the Glenmore National Forest Park, and apart from the Youth Hostel and the fine lodge built by the Glasgow Education Department as Glenmore Adventure Centre, the timber buildings are those of the Forestry Commission. The emphasis is on trees and tourism, which has meant a decline in natural history interest.

Unfortunately the margins of Loch Morlich are nothing to what they were in pre-development days. You cannot have drainage and disturbance and make a Mecca for outdoor folk without something suffering. Loch Morlich is the take-off place for the ski-road and chair-lifts to the peak of Cairn Gorm which has brought traffic throughout all seasons of the year. The visitor who likes his scenery undefiled should make his way two miles east up the 'Robber's Pass' to the Green Loch, no more than a pool of aquarium-green clarity trapped in boulder-fields. The green is attributed to the fairies washing their clothes here. The special point about this green loch is that it is only 1,174 ft above sea-level, whereas you have to go up over the 2,000 ft level before you see the other 'green lochs' or Lochan Uaines as the Gaelic has it.

Loch Pityoulish is not far from Aviemore, on the B970, but is easily missed for the road only touches the north end of it. Leave your car and go across to the grassy knolls forming the west shore for a mighty view of the Cairngorms over the ½ mile long loch. The whole granite mass stands before you, cleft by the Lairig Ghru Pass, the corries of Braeriach to the right, those of Cairn Gorm to the left. The pass itself leads through from the Spey to the Dee and is one of the finest cross-country walks in Scotland. Even from here you can see the pink colour of the screes which give the Gaelic name Monadh Ruadh to the range—'The Red Hills' as distinct from the Monadhliaths on the other side of the Spey which appropriately are 'The Grey Hills'.

Despite its small size, roughly ½ a mile long by a ¼ of a mile broad, Loch Pityoulish is 74 ft deep, and like many another Highland loch there is a tradition that a water horse lived in it. Of greater historical truth is the hollow below the larches of the east end, where the Shaws of Rothiemurchus ambushed and slaughtered a party of the Cummings clan—just another reminder of the good old days.

Loch Garten lies only a short distance away, just east of Boat of Garten, in semi-natural woods of the Abernethy Forest, and this of course is where the osprey observation post is set up. The birds have been remarkably faithful to this eyrie since 1959, returning about mid-April or slightly earlier and laying usually a fortnight later. Hatched in late May or early June, the birds are fledged and on the wing from mid-July or early August. So don't miss the chance of viewing the birds if you happen to be here at these times.

Lochs of the Ness Basin

Lochs Oich, Quoich, Garry, Ness, Tarff, Knockie, nan Lann, Kemp, Killin, Mhor, Ruthven, Ashie, Cluanie, Loyne, Meiklie

When James Watt surveyed the chain of lochs in the Great Glen with the object of linking them to form a semi-natural passageway for ships between the Atlantic and the North Sea he saw the practicability of it at once. The watershed between the seas was no more than 115 ft. Of the total distance of sixty miles only one-third would require cutting. True there would be delays in the thirty-two locks he envisaged, and the wind could be dangerous in the open lochs, but there were many advantages. Sailing ships would be able to avoid the tide-races and storms of the Pentland Firth. Trade between the Baltic and the west coast ports would be speeded up, as would vessels plying between the West Indies and the east coast. His estimate of cost was £164,032—a very precise figure.

No doubt the Greenock engineer wrote out his report with scientific zeal. But for twenty-nine years nothing was started until 1803 when Thomas Telford began what was considered to be the engineering marvel of the world. Unfortunately he began to build just as Watt's steam engine was being harnessed for the propulsion of ships. The Canal had been outmoded by a new form of transport even before it was begun.

Telford estimated that it would take him seven years to build a 20 ft deep canal. It took nineteen years by which time ninety-five steamships had been built in Scotland and the menace of the Pentland Firth was vanishing. The Canal when it was opened to traffic in 1822 was too late for the age of sail and too early for the age of steam.

Nor did it remain open very long. Crumbling masonry on the rock walls caused it to be closed. The cost after repair work, and including all the earlier outlays amounted to £1,400,000. So when the Canal reopened in 1847 the sum expended had been more than three times Telford's estimated cost of £350,000. The more modest figure quoted by Watt had been based on a 10 ft deep canal.

Loch Oich on the summit was to prove troublesome, not only because of the problems of dredging and constructing an outlet, but because Glengarry, the clan chief who lived beside

Invergarry Castle, opposed the intrusion of his privacy. It was no mere passive protest. Arriving with an armed band one September morning in 1816 he routed the workmen and seized their boat. Nor was any action ever taken against him. But the steam-bucket dredgers continued their work on Loch Oich, even though Glengarry was still holding up the work two years later. Apparently he was not satisfied with the £10,000 compensation which had been fixed.

South of Invergarry Castle ruins, where Loch Oich begins, there is a grim memorial associated with Glengarry. Seven sculptured heads on the top of it on the site of where there used to be a well give it the name 'The Well of the Seven Heads'—the stone heads are symbolic of the human heads which were washed in the well and presented to Glengarry as retribution for murder. The story is told on the monument. The cousins who murdered their kinsmen paid the full price.

Loch Oich has an intimate beauty denied the two bigger lochs in the Great Glen. There is good salmon and trout fishing in its narrow waters, and Invergarry is a good centre of exploration, since it also opens up the great lochs to the west draining into Loch Oich. Narrow and straight for 4 miles, Loch Oich has a mean breadth of only $\frac{1}{5}$ of a mile and as the shallowest part is the centre, it accounts for the high cost of dredging during the construction of the Canal. The maximum depth is 133 ft, but 68 per cent is less than 50 ft, and opposite the mouth of the River Garry the maximum depth is 20 ft due to material brought down. The narrow islands are an attractive feature. Through the mountains to the east runs the Corrieyairack Pass to Speyside, with westward Glen Garry and the wild hills of Knoydart.

Loch Quoich has the unique distinction in a wet country of having an exceptionally high rainfall. Over 10 in. of rain fell in $22\frac{1}{2}$ hours one December day in 1954, and the North of Scotland Hydro-Electric Board quote the annual average as 135.6 in. So it is not surprising to find that Loch Quoich is now a reservoir contained behind a thousand feet of rockfill dam. The reservoir holds 12,500 million cu. ft compared to 8,345 cu. ft in pre-hydro-electric days. The rise of 100 ft in level made the loch 9 miles long where it used to be only 7, doubling its maximum breadth to make it $1\frac{1}{2}$ miles. Two small dams at the western end prevent spillage to the Atlantic watershed.

It is bleak and desolate today compared to what it was in pre-hydro-electric days, when it had natural woodlands and cottages at Kinlochquoich. These are now beneath the waters of the enlarged loch. Nobody lives here now. The country westward containing narrow glens hemmed by high ridges is amongst the most inaccessible regions of Scotland.

It was a hard country even for clansmen, containing few habitations, grazed by deer and a few head of cattle. This is where the Prince came closest to capture and death by misadventure. The Hanoverian troops had their net drawn tight round from Loch Shiel to Loch Hourn. Troops had been marched in from the Great Glen, and landed by sea from the

Loch Quoich

west. The fugitives had somehow to break through and find food on the way.

Look up to the peak of Sgurr na Ciche from Loch Quoich and you see the great hollow of Coire nan Gall where the hunted men lay up, waiting for darkness, while one of them rustled around the deserted shielings until he found a clansman who gave him two small cheeses for the hungry party. He also brought the worrying information that the enemy were searching very close. They could do nothing but sit tight, and trust to luck. It held.

Come gathering darkness they descended on the enemy fires and the sound of voices. Choosing their place, they slipped through the cordon and began the steep climb over the next ridge, steering east by Meall an Spardain. On top they looked down on other fires and began a difficult traverse to avoid them.

It was on the slippery traverse, picking a way above rocks that the Prince nearly lost his life. He had been warned to take care in a specially difficult place when he lost his footing and shot down the slope, to be caught up in a small bush just long enough for a companion to make a grab and hold him from falling down the cliff. Safely through they were now confronted by the main chain of sentry-posts stretching from Loch Hourn all the way along Glen Garry.

They broke out at Loch Coire Shubh about a mile from Kinlochourn, an exciting spot in a lively scenery of tumbling waterfalls and rocky peaks with trees in the gullies. They actually passed between the sentries here, and took cover immediately afterwards, passing the day in a clump of birches and keeping an eye on the redcoats moving about searching for them. They moved north across the mountains when darkness came.

Loch Quoich discharges into a tunnel which leads the water three miles east to a power station discharging to an enlarged Loch Garry. There are some points of interest for the technically minded. The 1,050 ft rock-fill dam is the largest of its kind in the country, 126 ft high and 300 ft in width at the base. A 12 in. facing of concrete on the upstream end makes it watertight.

Another interesting feature is a small generating station within the dam to produce 2.6 million units of electricity per annum from the compensation water. The capacity of the main station is 22 megawatts, operating under a head of 312 ft. Loch Quoich is good for trout and fly-fishers may hire a boat at £1 per day by applying at the power station.

Loch Garry has salmon, which get into the loch by means of a Borland fish lift in the narrow dam across the eastern end of the gorge impounding the loch. This loch was once a place of fine natural woodlands, much of it oak, but little enough of it remains now, though the Forestry Commission are active and have preserved some by fencing.

The new Loch Garry is 280 ft above sea-level, which is a rise of 23 ft on the old level. The deepest part, around 236 ft, is near the middle of the 7-mile long loch. Just 1 mile at its broadest, it tapers away west into Loch Poulary which is still attractively wooded. The salmon and trout fishing is good. There is an important hatchery at the eastern end of the loch, where salmon and trout are reared from the egg stage and fed on liver until they are big enough to be put back in the rivers.

Invergarry power station lies 2¾ miles distant from Loch Garry, discharged by tunnel to empty into Loch Oich, which in turn discharges into Loch Ness by the River Oich which is also the Caledonian Canal emptying at Fort Augustus.

Everything about Loch Ness is unusual, its great depth for the whole 22¾ miles of its length; its narrowness and the darkness of its water; the uniformity of its straight-cut sides which drop so steeply that the wave-action prevents plants from taking hold on the gravelly shores; its capacity assessed at 263,000 million cu. ft which is more than three times that of Loch Morar and more than 2½ times that of Loch Lomond; its modest 53 ft above sea-level though trenched by hills of a thousand to two thousand feet; the fact that the mean breadth is only 4 per cent of its length; and not least the fair certainty that it is the home of a frightening creature which for want of a better name has become known to the world as 'The Loch Ness Monster'—though the evidence is building up that there is more than one.

The first mention of a strange water beast in Loch Ness goes back to the time of St. Columba about AD 565. It is told in *The Life of St. Columba* by St. Adamnan, Abbot of Iona in Book 2, Chapter 27. Unfortunately there is no description of the monster, only of the miracle wrought by St. Columba when he drove it back with prayer as it roared with open mouth to attack a swimming man. The incident is reported to have taken place in the River Ness, and the Pictish heathens present '. . . constrained by the miracle, which they themselves had seen, glorified the God of the Christians'.

The neighbourhood of Urquhart Castle has proved a rich sighting area in the recent history of the monster. The explanation may be that the modern road to Inverness is at a much higher elevation than the castle, therefore giving a much better panoramic view of Urquhart Bay where the loch becomes 2 miles wide, and the maximum depth of 754 ft is reached one mile south in the middle of the loch. Urquhart Bay, curiously enough, has a water-edge flora which is unusual for Loch Ness.

What does the monster look like? One of the earliest

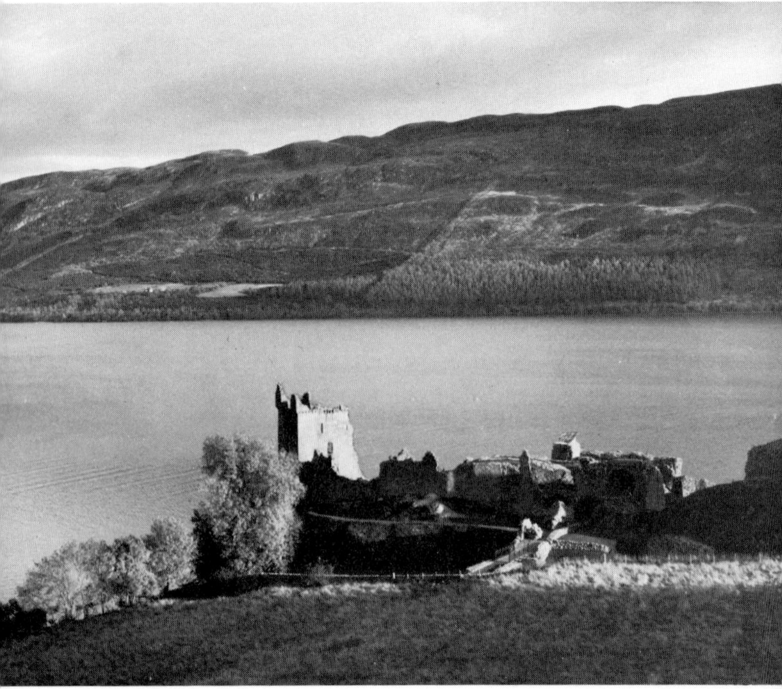

Castle Urquhart on Loch Ness

descriptions by Mr. and Mrs. Spicer in 1933 likened it to '. . . a huge snail with a long neck'. Other accounts spoke of an animal with a head like a snail. The Spicers saw it on dry land in the act of crossing the road. 'It was horrible—an abomination. First we saw an undulating sort of neck, a little thicker than an elephant's trunk. It did not move in the usual reptilian fashion but, with three arches in its neck, it shot across the road until a ponderous body about four feet high came into view.'

Professor F. W. Holiday in his book *The Great Orme of Loch Ness* has given a well reasoned case for the monster being a huge worm capable of changing its shape in the elastic manner of worms, hence its ability to make humps, and narrow its neck. He relates it to the 'Tully Monster' discovered near Chicago in 1958.

The American fossils however are of a creature no more than 14 in. in size, some of them considerably smaller, whereas the Loch Ness monster is thought to be as much as 100 ft long. The fossils were given the name *Tullimonstrum gregarium* in 1966—'*gregarium*' because so many of them were found. The Coal Age of 280 million years ago had yielded up a rare find of enormous importance to anyone interested in the Loch Ness monster, because as Professor Holiday points out, 'It was the first proof that animals of such worm-like shape existed.'

The American 'Tully Monster' is described thus by Dr. E. S. Richardson Jr. of the Chicago Field Museum: 'At one end of a dirigible-like body was a spade-shaped tail; from the other end extended a long thin proboscis with a gaping claw; across the body near the base of the proboscis was a transverse bar with a little round swelling at each end, outside the body.'

In drawings of the 'Tully Monster' frisking about as in life in the sea Dr. Richardson says: 'The spade-tail suggests that they could swim and guide themselves; the segmented body, clearly seen on many fossil specimens, must have been flexible as in the body of an earthworm. We know from many specimens that the proboscis was flexible, and since the claw at the end was armed with eight tiny sharp teeth, it must have been used for grasping prey.' There was no indication of a throat within the proboscis. In the case of the Loch Ness monster the proboscis ties up with the long neck. Professor Holiday suggests that 'the Orme' may have to put its neck straight out of the water in order to swallow a fish, if like the Tully Monster it has no means of chewing food.

It must be a fish eater since the deep floor of the loch is without plants, and Loch Ness is good for trout, pike, eels, lampreys, sea trout and salmon. Seven members of 'The Loch Ness Investigation Bureau' keeping watch have seen salmon panicking before an unexplained object following them. Some film was taken successfully, but it proves nothing conclusive. However there is a piece of film in existence which shows a triangular object moving which the foremost experts have decided is 'probably animate'.

A good way of seeing the loch is to take the Caledonian Canal ship *Scot II* from Muirtown outside Inverness and sail down the full 24¼ miles of water between Loch Dochfour and Fort Augustus. On this sail you can appreciate that you are on a big water, yet the hills and trees are always close in views that are never the same for five minutes, and although the straight shores and lack of islands account for some monotony, the possibility of a sight of the monster is adequate compensation.

The little village of Foyers on the east shore has a unique distinction, since it was here the first aluminium was produced in Britain in a factory set up as long ago as 1896. And it was powered by the first hydro-electric scheme in Britain which produced a large part of the world demand for the new metal. The factory operated for seventy-one years and only closed down in 1967.

A modern pumped-storage hydro-electric scheme has been operating at Foyers since 1974, using reversible pump turbines to raise water from Loch Ness 589 ft into Loch Mhor with off-peak power. Brought back down through the turbines, its output is 300 megawatts.

Urquhart Castle on its peninsula, backed by the green fields and woods of Drumnadrochit is the most picturesque part of Loch Ness, having both intimate charm and great dignity. The bay is just the feature that Loch Ness needs to break the monotony of straight sides, and the roofless ruin is a good place to view its widest waters.

It is important to realise that Loch Ness was raised by the building of the Caledonian Canal, before which the castle must have been more imposing than it is now. As a strongpoint it began its life as a vitrified fort, evolved to a motte with a double bailey, and was reinforced with stone defences in the fourteenth century. Robert the Bruce held it. Edward III of England tried to take it from Robert de Lauder and failed. Then in 1509 it passed to the Grants who held it for 400 years of strife and trouble until the Jacobite rising of 1689 when it was blown up.

Interesting things have been found, medieval brooches and an Edward I penny, but the treasure in the dungeons remains protected, they say, by plague. The vault containing the treasure is as much a mystery as the monster. It was the Grants who raised the great square tower and most of the buildings around it. Captain James Grant held it with three companies in 1689. Gunpowder and weather destroyed it.

Loch Ness was chosen by the racing motorist John Cobb for an attempt on the world speedboat record. He died when his jet speedboat capsized and sank, and the memorial to his death may be seen by the side of the road between Invermoriston and Drumnadrochit. It is a simple cairn with an inset plaque. It is curious that bodies of people drowned in Loch Ness are seldom recovered. Divers who went down to look for such a body a few years ago refused to go down again, nor would they give a reason.

Fort Augustus at the head of the loch was where many a Jacobite was taken to be shot in the '45. Built by General Wade in 1715 it became a garrison for hunting down the clansmen and pillaging their homes after Culloden. Some of the buildings of that fort are now incorporated in the Benedictine abbey. The name Fort Augustus remains, but it should more properly be called Kilchumein, after Cummein, Abbot of Iona, for whom it was originally named.

The Great Glen was to prove too handy a route for subduing the belligerent Highlanders on each side of the low-lying lochs. General Wade not only built Fort Augustus, but launched an armoured ship on Loch Ness for transporting men and provisions from Inverness. Not that this was an original idea, for Cromwell's forces had done the same seventy years earlier, in 1651. The later ship held sixty men and carried four cannons.

It was General Wade who drove the roads from Fort Augustus across the high Corrieyairack to the Spey, over a summit at

2,507 ft; and north through the hills east of Loch Ness to Inverness where lie some fine lochs of high natural interest. These should be explored, even though some of them lie off the road in a country of strange little lumpy hills.

Loch Tarff is by the roadside, 956 ft above sea-level and three miles north-east of Fort Augustus. Covering ½ a mile at its broadest and shaped like a triangle it has fine character, due to its speckling of islands and fine views westward, and to the Monadhliath. It is a shallow loch. The mean depth is only 24 ft, though the maximum is 89 ft.

Loch Knockie, Loch nan Lann and Loch Kemp are situated to the north of Loch Tarff, but are out of sight, west of the main road. They lie in unfrequented country but have great charm, with wooded or rocky shores. Details are briefly as follows:

Loch Knockie is 1¼ miles long by ½ a mile broad and has some wooded islands. Indented by numerous bays the shore lines are attractive. It is shallow, the mean depth being 24½ ft, the maximum being 75 ft.

Loch nan Lann lying west of the southern end of Loch Knockie is only ¾ of a mile long by ⅓ of a mile in maximum breadth and is deep for its size, attaining 109 ft near the centre. Woodlands give it charm on the east side.

Loch Kemp lies slightly further north with rocky shores among low hills. It is ½ a mile long and ¾ of a mile at broadest, and reaches 51 ft deep close to the south-east corner. The mean depth is 26 ft.

Loch Killin lies up the River Fechlin from the Wade Bridge at Whitebridge, and its catchment has been diverted to Loch Mhor as part of the Foyers project utilising pumped storage. Loch Killin is 1,044 ft above sea-level with a fine crag rising above it. It is 1¼ miles long and ¼ of a mile at its broadest, the maximum depth is 67 ft, though half the loch is covered by less than 25 ft of water. It contains an interesting form of char known as 'the haddy'.

Loch Mhor lies along the Strath Errick road among hills farms and woodland copses. This was the road which Prince Charlie galloped along in defeat, riding away from Culloden to the west coast. The house of Gorthleck where he stopped to break the bad news of the battle to Lord Lovat still stands, beneath farm steadings.

Loch Mhor was given its name when Loch Gart and Loch Farraline were combined to provide a head of water for the Foyers aluminium works, which made it 5 miles long with a breadth of $\frac{1}{3}$ of a mile. Maximum depth was 91 ft, and the mean 24 ft. Today it is a pumped-storage upper reservoir.

Loch Ruthven lies between Strath Errick and Strath Nairn just north-east of Loch Mhor and is a narrow curved loch among wooded hills and little crags. Length $2\frac{1}{4}$ miles with a maximum breadth of $\frac{1}{2}$ a mile, it is shallow, with a mean depth of only 11 ft, but there is one hole of 42 ft three-quarters of a mile from the top.

Loch Ashie lies parallel with the north tip of Loch Ness and is a reservoir for the town. Length $2\frac{1}{2}$ miles and $\frac{1}{2}$ a mile at broadest it is a simple basin with a maximum depth of 51 ft. Height above

Loch Ruthven, high above Loch Ness on the old Inverness road

sea-level is 718 ft. There is good brown trout fishing at low cost. A boat and two rods is only 75p per day, permits obtainable at Dochfour Estate Office, Dochgarroch.

The lochs of the eastern side of Loch Ness are larger than any of the hill lochs on the western flanks, but they are eclipsed by those draining into Glen Moriston near the watershed between the Atlantic and the North Sea. The road running west from Invermoriston is comparable only to that through Glen Coe for transformation of scene. In both cases an open beginning closes to a narrow trough of mountain peaks linked peak upon peak, with the road following the river, threading through tumbled moraines and steep rocky slopes.

Loch Cluanie, draining into Loch Ness, sits almost on the watershed, bleaker than it used to be because of enlargement behind a 2,215 ft long and 133 ft high dam. The old Loch Cluanie was 123 ft deep. Flooding behind the dam raised it almost a hundred feet and lengthened it from 4¼ miles to 7½, though its maximum breadth has scarcely changed. A tunnel and a pressure shaft take the water to Ceannacroc to an underground power station, one of the first of its kind to be built in Britain. The output is 20 megawatts.

Loch Cluanie is 702 ft above sea-level, 43 ft lower than Loch Loyne which discharges water into it by tunnel. Once upon a time the Kyle of Lochalsh road passed between two straggling lochs known as West Loch Loyne and East Loch Loyne in its climb from Tomdown to Cluanie Bridge Inn. This road was inundated by the building of an 1,800 ft long and 27 ft high dam at the eastern end which raised the capacity of the hill lochs from 163 million cu. ft to 1,520 million cu. ft. Its waters reach Loch Cluanie by 1¾ miles of tunnel.

The dam, easily seen from the new Kyle of Lochalsh road between Invergarry and Glen Moriston, has historic interest for it was the first to be built with blast-furnace slag, using a process which saved 40,000 tons of cement. Curved like a boomerang, the greatly enlarged loch has nothing of the charm of the old winding lochs. The new road however is a much finer viewpoint, especially on the early stages of the climb out of Glen Garry where the hills of Knoydart rise in a jumble of summits over Loch Quoich. Down at the western end of Loch Cluanie the old road may still be seen winding narrowly uphill. North above Loch Cluanie are the remains of a much older highway, General Wade's military road beneath Sgurr nan Conbhairean, 3,634 ft, on whose top Prince Charlie spent a miserable night of rain. But the mountain was to provide a cave which is still one of the most secret places in Scotland. It was here he met up with the Seven Men of Glen Moriston, without whom it is possible he could not have survived the next vital weeks.

The only other loch of importance draining into Loch Ness is Loch Meiklie, halfway along Glen Urquhart amongst woods and cultivation. The loch is just over 1 mile long by ½ a mile in maximum breadth and 45 ft at its deepest, though half the floor is covered by less than 20 ft. It discharges into Urquhart Bay by the River Enrick.

In the hills just west of Loch Ness, between Glen Urquhart and Glen Moriston behind Mealfuarvounie lie many small lochans, some of them of high wildlife interest but none of them very accessible.

Loch Cluanie, between Glen Shiel and Glen Moriston

Hill-Lochs and Lochans of the High Cairngorms 126

Lochs Einich, Coire an Lochain, Avon, Etchachan, Lochan Buidhe, the three Uaines, The Pools of Dee

Of these superbly wild lochs, lochans and 'pools' only Loch Einich can be reached on wheels—and that by bicycle, which is the best way to go from Aviemore on a rough but ridable track beginning at Coylum Bridge. Your direction is Glen Einich, past Tullochgrue, and taking care not to get into the Lairig Ghru across the river. You cross no bridges, but follow the glen opening before you under the conical peak of Carn Elrig which is a useful guide. That distinctive peaklet should be on your left.

Even if there was no Loch Einich, the glen opening before you repays any effort of getting to it, with the river tumbling through knolls of Caledonian pines and the wild corries of Braeriach drawing nearer above vast heather slopes. It is no hardship to be wheeling your bicycle at this point over steep little rises, for there is usually much in the way of wildlife, crested tits, crossbills, siskins, redstarts, redpolls, a glimpse of a merlin or a goosander, a dipper or a grey wagtail by the river.

Then the pines become more stunted, thin out, and you are among old river terraces, moraines and glacial rubble characteristic of the Spey Valley, where the glaciers did not reach the sea but deposited their debris with less erosive effect. But there is green ground higher up, where in the days of not so long ago the crofters brought their cattle and lived with them through the summer.

Maybe it was one of them, the 'son of a thin fellow', who was killed hereabouts in a fight with cattle thieves. His name is given to posterity in Gaelic at Loch Mhic Ghille-choile, an oval sheet of water hidden by a ridge just west across the river from the site of the lower bothy. It is beyond here that the contours begin to close in to the trench of narrow Loch Einich stretching $1\frac{1}{4}$ miles beneath Sgoran Dubh's cliffs to the headwall of Coire Odhar and its tumbling waterfalls. On the easier slopes of Braeriach eastwards a track climbs up Coire Dhondail breaking out onto the Braeriach plateau in a steep 2,000 ft lift. There is also a route up from the west shore ascending to easy ground in Coire Odhar, so the ground is neither so precipitous or as dangerous as it looks, though the face of Sgoran Dubh is for rock climbers.

There are char in Loch Einich, and plenty of trout, but the convenient bothy which used to be situated at the outlet is gone, and so have the sluice gate remains, more reminders of the timber-floating days when a flood of water could be sent down to carry the logs to the sawmill. The loch is shallow near its outlet, but deepens to 160 ft where it becomes a rock basin gouged out by glacial action in a confined space. It is the debris of that glacier at its mouth acting as a dam which holds it in position.

From the end of the loch it is worth the labour of climbing eastward up the heathery slopes of high angle and going over the lip into a dramatically different scene, the great hollow of Loch Coire an Lochain, an oval of loch clasped in a horseshoe of rock and scree at 3,267 ft, the highest corrie-lochan in the Cairngorms, and often enough floating little icebergs in mid-summer.

The $\frac{1}{4}$ mile oval of this exceptional corrie-lochan was not excavated by the enormous pressure of a glacier as in the excavation of Loch Einich which is a major trough. Loch Coire an Lochain is shallow, and the whole wide corrie was initially no more than a depression at the head of a stream where accumulations of snow built up, with a bergschrund between it and the rock bordering the snow. It was frost shattering at the lip which ate into the mountain, together with a plucking action at the sides of the little glacier where the same process of freezing and melting was going on. The present loch occupied the hollow when the ice disappeared.

That is the story of all the high corrie-lochs of the Cairngorms, except for Loch Etchachan which is partly glacier-excavated and partly the result of frost-shattering action. But this takes us into the region of the River Dee drainage, so we might as well go over the top of Braeriach, easily done by following the south shoulder of the corrie, and doing the highest-level walk in Scotland past the 'Wells of Dee', which is the most elevated source of any river in Britain.

Braeriach is 4,284 ft and an enormous hunk of pink gravelly plateau with miles of cliffs biting deeply into it on the north-eastern side, not a place to go without careful watching of your whereabouts on the map and having a compass handy as a check against retreat. You can walk here for nearly three miles without dropping below 4,000 ft where the horseshoes of corries swing one after another to Cairn Toul.

The 'Wells' are about the mid-way point on the walk, a spring of icy cold water often surrounded by snow patches in June, made all the more charming if the moss campion is in pink clumps on other parts of the plateau. Other springs close by add to its volume, but in a short distance it leaps from the plateau into the corrie to begin among snowfields its eighty-five miles to Aberdeen and the sea.

And just across the Allt a Garbh-Choire, between two projecting spurs, is clasped Lochan Uaine of Cairn Toul, its little oval facing north with a white cataract of outlet stream foaming over rock-slabs to join up with the Dee in its first rush to the glen. This 'green lochan' is 3,042 ft above sea-level. And it lives up to its name even more than the other corrie-lochs of the same name, especially when little icebergs are floating about its clear green water.

'The Pools of Dee' are in the Lairig Ghru, trapped in the boulder-fields near the summit at the foot of the bright pink screes shooting down from the mountains on both sides. The 'Pools' are three little lochs, fragments of an underground stream, which are bright mirrors of blue sky, green grass, pink stones and snow-patched peaks. They lie close in the high angle of Inverness-shire, Aberdeenshire and Banffshire, and are part of the source of the Dee.

Very close to them is the March burn which foams down from the Ben Macdui plateau—often with a big snowbridge at its top—and if we follow it up we come to tiny Lochan Buidhe whose outlet stream descends a vastness of stones appropriate to the voices of wailing golden plover and 'creaking' ptarmigan which are its sounds.

Then suddenly the stones become precipitous crag where you have to pick your way carefully, and down below the great waterslide lies Loch Avon, a long narrow trench of water between ramparts of stone. And below the sheerest face of crag on the south side lies the Shelter Stone—one of the most inaccessible places in Britain but visited by Queen Victoria who was Scotland's greatest advertiser.

This is what she wrote after being there on 28 September 1861. 'Nothing could be grander and wilder; the rocks are so grand

and precipitous, and the snow on Ben Macdui has such fine effect.' The easiest way of visiting it today is of course to go to Glenmore, and take the chair-lift up Cairn Gorm and descend the grassy slopes south into Coire Raibeirt, but anyone who does this must remember that there is no easy way out should the weather turn bad, so careful judgement is necessary.

The height of the loch above sea-level is 2,377 ft, but it is so sandwiched between high enclosing walls that you cannot see it until you are well on the way down to it. It is a major glacial trough like Loch Einich, gouged out by ice and the maximum depth is 115 ft in a length of 1½ miles by just over a ¼ of a mile broad, and there is no path round it. The walking is hard, and at

The glacial trough of Loch Avon between Cairn Gorm, left, and Ben Macdui, right

the eastern end of it there is a marvellous tangle of mounds, ridges and erratic blocks.

Loch Avon ends where the easy pass called 'The Saddle' breaks north into Strathnethy. A glacier flowed over here in the Ice Age, acting as a stopper for the mass of ice that flowed east from where the head of the loch is now situated, so the bulldozing effect which created the bed for Loch Avon was forced to an end, hence the rubble of sand and gravel mounds hereabouts.

Loch Etchachan, 3,058 ft, lies due south of the west end of Loch Avon and is more like a corrie-lochan in shape, but it is the biggest loch of its height in Britain. I have walked across it and skied across it in March, once inadvertently in a blizzard when I was unaware of what I was doing until I came to its outlet into Coire Etchachan which leads into Glen Derry. Trout live in it despite its arctic character, for it is usually frozen for half the year.

Ben Macdui, the highest summit in the Cairngorms rises 4,296 ft just south-west of it, and up here under the Sron Riach is the other Lochan Uaine at a height of 3,142 ft, a hundred feet higher than the one on Cairn Toul near the source of the Dee. The only corrie-loch in Scotland higher is the one we saw on Braeriach, Loch Coire an Lochain, height 3,267 ft.

There is yet another Lochan Uaine, above Glen Derry, at a height of 2,497 ft beneath Derry Cairngorm, but this one is fed by a cascading mountain stream, so is a more cheerful sort of place, without the sombre character of the others. And it has been humanised by the song of a poacher who liked to live up here and hunt the deer in defiance of the owners. The song is 'Allt an Lochain Uaine'—the burn of the loch, the words by William Smith the poacher, sung to the tune 'Gu ma slan a chi mi'—a fine Highland melody.

Recent scientific investigation in some of these highest corries in Scotland reveals a likelihood that they carried little glaciers as recently as the mid-eighteenth century. Reports of these times certainly indicate larger summer snowfields than any we get today, and the most recent moraines have been dated at 1810 and 1740. The dating was done by measuring the growth of the lichen *Rhizocapon geographicum* on the stones deposited by the ice.

It is in these regions where the snowfields linger longest in the high corries that our only snow buntings breed in certain years. It has all been written down in Desmond Nethersole Thompson's classic monograph 'The Snow Bunting', which should be read for its feeling for this unique piece of country.

From the top of Braeriach a climber looks out to where there used to be a corrie glacier, now it is occupied by Lochan Uaine

Lochs of the Dee Basin

Lochs Builg, Muick, Lochnagar, Coire an Dubh Lochain, Callater, Davan, Kinord

This varied assortment of lochs belong to the Dee Basin, with the exception of Loch Builg which shares its water with the Spey for it lies in the hollow of a glacial breach, its main flow discharging into the Avon to the north, while at the south end there is leakage into the Gairn. The breach is of the same kind that separated the Avon from the Don which were originally one river, until the down-cutting of ice created a new southerly valley into which the Avon was directed.

Loch Builg is six miles north-west of Balmoral, but the public road is available for only two miles north of Crathie, beyond which there is a private track, for which one must get permission to take a car. The loch, at 1,586 ft above sea-level, is 1 mile long, ¼ of a mile in maximum breadth, with a maximum depth of 86 ft in the middle. Its chief interest, apart from its unusual characteristic of being on a watershed, are its arctic char, and plentiful trout. Also, the warty peak of Ben Avon can be climbed in a rise of less than 2,000 ft, or you could be diverted by the thought of gold in the lochans at the southern end, for the name, Lochan Óir refers to the tradition of gold here, 'Óir' being the Gaelic word for it. However another tradition of a water-kelpie guarding it may put you off. An outcrop of limestone rich in flowers is a more tangible reward for a bleak place.

Loch Muick lies eight miles south of Ballater and is easily reached by a good road up a wooded glen, becoming wilder as the hills close in on the rock basin cut from the Lochnagar granite, a place beloved of Queen Victoria who built the house at the far end because she loved this wild loch-head so much. She built it in 1869 and today there is a fine plantation beside the mountain torrent descending steeply from the hill above.

The loch is 2¼ miles long, ½ a mile in maximum breadth, with a maximum depth of 256 ft in the centre. Good for trout, and in the midst of some of the rockiest hills in the Cairngorms it is classic deer stalking country, with the bonus of a second loch 800 ft higher up in a fine walk of less than two miles following the stream which feeds into Loch Muick.

Dubh-Loch is a good name for this dark little ribbon of water lying under a wall of granite nearly a thousand feet high. The word 'Dubh' is the Gaelic for 'black', of course, but I have seen it deep blue, with the reeds at its edge emerald. Nor is it even bleak, thanks to the birches which grow high and soften this tremendous scoop. On the tops of these hills, only a thousand feet above, there is a higher density of ptarmigan than in the Arctic.

The corrie of Lochnagar with its little loch under a mighty cirque of cliffs is an absolute 'must' for a lover of mountain and loch scenery, for this is the ultimate perfection of corrie form, and the best way to it is from the Spital of Glen Muick. The path crosses to the west bank of the river here, and leads to a shooting lodge which is the true beginning of the route to the summit.

As an alternative to going to the top and looking down into the corrie, I recommend leaving the track just beyond the Foxes'

The climber on Lochnagar is on the edge of a drop plunging 700 ft to the water from which the mountain takes its name

Well and crossing the gap between Meikle Pap and Cuidhe Crom, where there is a plaque and an outline sketch of the cliffs. A bouldery descent from here leads you into the corrie floor at 2,575 ft with the mountain wall rising 1,200 ft above you, half of it precipice.

That cirque of cliffs extends nearly a mile, and may be heavily armoured with snow and ice when the rest of the mountain is clear, hence its challenge to mountaineers who find some of the finest sport in Britain here, by ridge and gully and pinnacle. Indeed there is only one corrie with loch and cliffs which have any similarity to it, and that is Coire Ardair of Creag Meagaidh above Loch Laggan.

Surprisingly enough for a coarse-grained granite formation on an acid mountain, this corrie is noted for alpine plants, with brook saxifrage, alpine speedwell, blue sow-thistle, highland cudweed and a variety of rare sedges. Botanists were in fact among the first explorers of this corrie, not to mention the quartz hunters looking for semi-precious 'Cairngorms' stones. It was the searchers for gems who used the term 'spout' to describe a gully among the rocks, hence Red Spout and Black Spout on Lochnagar, two of the most conspicuous features on the face.

Coire an Dubh Lochain on Beinn a Bhuird must be mentioned before we leave the subject of corrie-lochans. Facing east and 3,080 ft above sea-level there is no easy way into its splendid recess beneath 600 ft cliffs. The best way is from Invercauld near Braemar, by path up Gleann an t-Slugain. The naturalist will particularly rejoice in the expedition, especially if he comes back over the tops of the mountain and descends by Glen Quoich to Mar Lodge. On that long expedition he will have a cross-section of everything that is best about the Cairngorms in birds, animals, and scenery.

Loch Callater, 1,627 ft above sea-level, lies south of Braemar, but a car is useful only for the first two miles of the Cairnwell, for the track up the east-branching glen is not only very rough, but has a locked gate on it. A bicycle is the answer, unless you are doing the cross-country trip over Jock's Road by Glen Doll across the 2,800 ft headwall.

Like the Dubh Loch above Loch Muick, which is due east just over the hill, Loch Callater has been trenched deep into the hill with the same glacial tools, and even if it lacks the grandeur of the other two it is an impressive place, especially looking down on it from above. Nearly 1 mile long and $\frac{1}{5}$ of a mile broad, and with a maximum depth of 30 ft it contains trout, pike, eels and is noted for its small salmon, about 8 lb. in weight. The ice did not gouge its rock basin very deeply, for half the loch is covered by no more than 10 ft of water.

Loch Davan and Loch Kinord. These two kettle-hole lochs lie close to each other, about five miles north-east of Ballater and are classic examples of hollows left by slowly melting lobes of dead ice. Loch Davan, $\frac{3}{4}$ of a mile long with a maximum breadth of $\frac{2}{3}$ of a mile has a maximum depth of only 9 ft. Loch Kinord at 1 mile with a maximum breadth of $\frac{1}{4}$ of a mile has a maximum depth of 12 ft. Both are charming sheets of water fringed by trees.

More interesting than either of them however is the Burn o'Vat above and west of them, where a tiny stream cleaves a remarkable rock-cauldron between vertical granite walls. Obviously this tiny stream could never have carved this ravine. It is of course a melt-water channel, which was carved when there was an ice-cap discharging a mighty cataract of water into it, and as the ice wasted away, so did the stream dry up, until today there is no more than a trickle.

Climb up to the top of the Burn o'Vat, which is a spur of the peak of Morven, and look across to the 'U' cleft of the Pass of Ballater. That cutting is not the work of the Dee but was excavated by another ice-tongue which found a weakness in the granite. This glaciation seems obvious, like the explanation of Loch Davan and Loch Kinord just below, yet it had not even been guessed at 150 years ago, when men of science put forward theories to account for the immense variety of highland landscape.

Notice the similarity between the Spey lochs and the Dee lochs, where the home-bred glaciers were spent before they reached the sea. They deposited their litter in the valley. They did not carry it far out to sea as in the west where the ice over-ran what is now the Western Isles, laying bare the most ancient rocks and excavating the grandest features of the Highlands as well as denuding them of good soil.

Lochs of Lochy Basin

Lochs Arkaig, Lochy, Treig, Laggan, na h-Earba, Ossian, Ghuilbinn, Pattack.

Fort William is the pivot of this group of lochs draining west and east into Loch Lochy, the most southerly of the freshwater lochs forming the Great Glen of Scotland—a mighty fault extending from the Atlantic to the North Sea where earthquakes still occur along the line of dislocation. The line of cleavage is less dramatic than the Highland Boundary Fault on Loch Lomond where the mountains suddenly rise from the Lowlands. The situation is reversed here because the landscape drops vertically as you go north.

Loch Lochy provides the most scenic fireworks, because it is a mere 93 ft above sea-level while Ben Nevis rising immediately south is 4,406 ft, no mere grassy hill but an alpine peak, ice-bound into early summer and solid rock for nearly half its height. Some of the hardest climbs in Scotland may be found here on the enormous fretwork of the north-eastern face. Here on Loch Lochy the scenery is gentle, tree-clad, and low-lying while the mountains are too often in storm.

The delightful Bay of Bunarkaig, where my photograph of the Nevis range was taken from, is a good place to begin an exploration of the Lochy Basin, by turning west along the 'Dark Mile' to Loch Arkaig. A good way to reach this point is by Banavie, up past the system of locks known as Neptune's Staircase, now fully mechanised to speed ships through this almost natural waterway linking Loch Lochy, Loch Oich and Loch Ness to provide an inland passage through the Caledonian Canal.

Loch Arkaig is a mere 140 ft above sea-level, and Achnacarry House, home of Cameron of Locheil is just across the river near the start of the narrow loch, on the site of the original home of the chief, laid ruin after Culloden when the redcoats were on the prowl ravaging the country as they hunted for the Prince.

From the battlefield the Prince rode across the hills, dropping into the Great Glen where two salmon found in a stake-net provided a much needed breakfast after sixteen hours in the saddle. Then from Invergarry he followed down the west side of Loch Lochy and along the Dark Mile to Loch Arkaig. He was so tired by the time he reached the far end that he had to be helped out of his clothes, stretching out after a meal of curds and butter and milk. The trickle of stones, across the River Pean, are all that is left of the house of Donald Cameron, who rose from his bed in the dark to admit the Prince. One of the greatest man-hunts in history was just beginning. And it was by Loch Arkaig he finally escaped across the hills to Loch nan Uamh to take ship for France.

So there is history all along the twelve miles of Loch Arkaig winding narrowly to lose itself in the roadless no-man's-land of high peaks and wild glens traversed only by footpaths. The mean breadth of the loch is only ½ a mile, and driving along it requires care on a single-track with blind bumps, sharp gradients and

Loch Lochy, with behind it the range of peaks known as the Grey Corries

difficult bends. The road gets worse the further west you go, but the rather tame scenery gets wilder as 'The Rough Bounds' close in.

There was a magnificent Caledonian pine forest here until the war, when Achnacarry House was being used as a training base by Commandos, and they accidentally set the wood alight. The blackened skeletons along the south shore are the remains of the Locheil Old Forest. New forests are being planted along the shores now. Campers are still welcome, and catered for in neat sites along the roadside. Each little site is numbered and permits are available at the entrance to the Dark Mile. The main users are fishermen after the large trout for which the loch is noted.

The osprey was nesting on the island at the east end of the loch when the *Bathymetrical Survey* sounded the loch between 28 April and 1 May 1903. The last breeding record is 1908, though a single bird frequented the site until 1913. Cormorants roost there today on trout fishing excursions from the sea. Measurement shows Loch Arkaig to be a fairly simple basin with the deepest sounding of 359 ft occurring about the middle of the loch. There is no well-marked 'U' section however, normal to glacial lochs. The broadest part, where it is nearly a mile, occurs in the central part.

Loch Lochy drains to the Atlantic and is just under 10 miles long with an average width of $\frac{3}{5}$ of a mile, though at the Bay of Bunarkaig where it is most beautiful it is $1\frac{1}{4}$ miles wide. This hamlet inhabited by shepherds and forestry workers is the main settlement. The hill slopes dropping steeply into the loch are blanketed in fine timber, so there is a certain straight-sided monotony in the upper reaches of Loch Lochy as the more open views drop behind.

Broad at the base compared to its extreme narrowness at the top, Loch Lochy can be regarded as a simple basin with its deepest part in the centre at 531 ft and a mean depth of 229 ft. Containing 37,726 million cu. ft it holds twice as much water as Loch Arkaig due to the comparatively large area covered by more than 300 ft of water, roughly a third of the whole loch.

The little bottle-neck at the top, called the Ceann Loch, is shallow, the entrance to it being a mere 40 ft though it deepens to 66 ft. There are no important feeder-streams at this top end. The main inflow is from the River Arkaig and Glen Gloy. Only a little spillage enters Loch Lochy from Loch Oich via the Caledonian Canal. The lochs which I shall deal with now drain into the Spean and into the River Lochy at the Mucomer Falls now harnessed for water power.

The bridge at Mucomer where the Lochy thunders through its wooded trench is a good place to stop before heading east along the Spean. There was a marvellous salmon-leap here in the pre-hydro-electricity days. Anglers still find it an exciting spot. Eastwards along the Spean lies Loch Treig and it is worth pausing at Spean Bridge and Roy Bridge to examine the hillsides hemming the glen, for this was the site of a huge glacial lake.

The evidence is in the 'parallel-roads' which wind round the hillsides like man-made constructions. Some maps show where the ice-barrier formed a great dam just east of Spean Bridge completely blocking the valley. Behind it was a wall of water over 600 ft deep before the different falls in level and the creation of new shorelines. Each 'road' is a shoreline and they extend far up Glen Gloy and Glen Roy.

Glen Roy is the best place to see them, and a short excursion should be made north from Roy Bridge on the good road to a large car-park. The topography clicks into place when you look across to Ben Nevis and the great wall of high peaks rising above Glen Spean and draining across its mouth. High precipitation creating large glaciers in Ice Age times would be slow to melt even in the time of the waters following the amelioration of climate.

There must have been something like a cross-roads of glaciers here, with ice-pressures from the mountains west of Loch Lochy and glaciers debouching from the Nevis massif. The water was imprisoned by the ice at three distinct levels, 1,149 ft, 1,068 ft and 857 ft. The 'roads' showing the different shorelines are 10–30 yds broad and slope towards the glens. They are more distinctive at a distance than close-up.

The explanation that the 'parallel roads' result from having been the shorelines of ice-dammed lakes seems obvious today, yet the explanation had not been guessed at until the middle of the last century. Now we know for certain that it was the glaciers advancing and retreating which laid bare the ancient rocks by removing newer deposits; that it was the sheer volume of moving ice which excavated rock basins like Loch Morar to a depth of over a thousand feet and exploiting faults to breach glens and scoop out hanging valleys. The two periods of maximum glaciation seem to have been 55,000 years ago, and 15,000–20,000 years ago.

Louis Agassiz from Switzerland read the evidence in 1840. Travelling in Scotland he saw signs everywhere of former glaciation and postulated the theory of ice-dammed lakes in Glen Roy. He believed that Scotland had been over-ridden by a great ice-cap submerging most of the mountains, where other scientists of his time favoured 'submergence' by floods or high sea-level. Even Geikie favoured deep submergence, but was swung over about 1863 after T. F. Jamieson had shown that Agassiz's theory of the origin of the Glen Roy roads was correct.

Loch Treig, just east of Roy Bridge and south of Glen Spean is also of high glaciological interest because it is at right-angles to the watershed, in a north-south direction where the normal is east to west. The 6-mile long loch which occupies a trough between 3,000 ft peaks has been scooped out by ice forced through a line of faulting and shattering. There may have been a col between the hills here, which was deepened by the ice being forced rapidly through the narrow passage. Loch Ericht is an example of the same sort of action, and so is the breach by the Lochan na Lairige.

The ice-mass which excavated Loch Treig is thought to have been 1,500 to 1,800 ft thick, resulting in a rock basin whose floor is 3,000 ft beneath the summits above it. The actual depth of water is between 200 and 300 ft for most of its length. Shaped like a thin triangle, the maximum width is $\frac{3}{4}$ of a mile.

The waters of Loch Treig have been put to work to power the aluminium factory at Fort William, a scheme which involved the drilling of a tunnel through a portion of Ben Nevis. This tunnel is 15 miles long and 15 ft in diameter and in 1929 was longer than any other of its kind in the world. To use Loch Treig as a reservoir meant raising its level, which was done by conveying water by tunnel from the Laggan Reservoir further east.

In order to carry out these works the West Highland Railway had to be shifted $1\frac{1}{2}$ miles when the level of Loch Treig was raised by the building of a dam across its northern end. The rubbly shorelines of the altered loch cannot be called beautiful, but few people ever see them for no road traverses them. The only way to see Loch Treig is to take a railway ticket on the West Highland Line or view the north end of the loch from the little road that goes to Fersit Halt.

In the Spean Valley just east of Loch Treig man has copied nature by building a barrier to impound Loch Laggan which feeds Loch Treig. By doing so he has made history repeat itself, since the man-adjusted loch is almost the same size as the ice-dammed lake which occupied this region in glacial times, i.e. 12 miles long. The Glen Spean loch of that far away time drained into the Spey.

The western part of the reservoir formed behind the dam is too bleak to be beautiful, but Loch Laggan itself remains grand, especially as you go east where the forest thickens, giving sylvan

Loch Laggan, a hydro-electric reservoir with remote high country on north and south

character to the hills on each side which are amongst the wildest in Scotland.

Ardverikie Lodge on the south side has the showpiece setting of a hunting lodge, with crags and shaggy pinewoods, mountain paths and the kind of remoteness which won the heart of Queen Victoria who seems to have swithered between Speyside and Balmoral for her Scottish seat. Apart from the good fishing and excellent deer stalking, it had the advantage of easy access from Glen Truim on the main railway line to Inverness. It is a rather jealous preserve today.

There are no problems of access on the north side of Loch Laggan however, and walkers who love dramatic mountain scenery should take a walk from Aberarder into the great recess of Coire Ardair where the cliffs rise 1,500 ft from a tiny lochan. Just to the right of these cliffs lies 'The Window', the most likely pass to be used by the Prince when he crossed from Loch Arkaig to the head of Glen Roy and came over here to enter the mountains south of Ardverikie and reach Cluny's Cage on Ben Alder.

Immediately across the loch from Aberarder lie two interesting hill-lochs with the single name of Lochan na h-Earba, but the best way to them is to retreat west beyond Moy Lodge and strike uphill to an estate road leading to the lochs, which are dominated by a magnificent escarpment of rock, 500 ft sheer, superb for climbing.

Lying parallel to Loch Laggan, the twin lochans are thought to have been one until an alluvial fan built up between them, the West Loch being higher by 10 ft than the East Loch. The respective heights above sea-level are 1,152 ft and 1,142 ft. They occupy the line of a fault, and being situated in a trench are extremely narrow.

The measurements are: West Loch, length 1¾ miles and ¼ of a mile in mean breadth, the greatest depth being 81 ft, with a mean depth of 35½ ft. It is a simple 'U' shaped basin whose outflow is to the East Loch, some half a mile distant.

Details of the East Loch are: length 1¼ miles and ⅕ of a mile in mean breadth. The maximum depth is 69 ft and the mean depth 31 ft. As might be expected the deep water is at the western end. The eastern end is extremely shallow. The pine marten was introduced to this region in 1935 and seems to have spread southward.

It is near Moy Lodge that the drainage from Loch Ossian comes in from the south reinforcing the catchment of the reservoir which makes the western extension of Loch Laggan. Loch Ossian is well worth a visit, but there is no easy way to it from here. Lying south-east of Lochtreighead, the best way of reaching it is from Corrour Halt on Rannoch Moor which lies only a mile from the west shore. Its bleakness is mitigated by its woods, which contrast with the absolute sterility of this highest part of Rannoch Moor.

Ringed by 3,000 ft peaks and within walking distance of much magnificent country, the only accommodation is a Youth Hostel on the west shore of the loch. Tracks lead through the hills to Glen Spean and Loch Treig, but all the high ground is deer forest with consequent restrictions in the sporting season which is roughly from August until January. The shooting lodge is at the eastern end of Loch Ossian.

Like Loch Treig, Loch Ossian occupies a glacial breach scooped out of high hills by the rapid passage of ice. Ossian is 1,269 ft above sea-level as compared to 784 ft for Treig, and unlike the latter is uncontaminated by engineering works spoiling its shoreline.

Loch Ossian has a maximum depth of 132 ft but the mean depth is only 43 ft, due to 68 per cent of its 3¾ miles length and ⅓ of a mile mean breadth being 50 ft and considerably less. Only 5 per cent is over 100 ft. The bottom of the loch is uneven and undulates much. A shoal in the middle of the loch is covered by only 11 ft. Much of the forestry round the loch represents pioneer work by the late Sir John Stirling Maxwell, who built the lodge.

Loch Ossian drains into Loch Ghuilbinn, a little oval sheet of water ¾ of a mile long and ½ a mile at its broadest, though the mean breadth is only ¼ of a mile. Maximum depth is 49 ft and the mean depth 13 ft. It is a simple basin, 1,160 ft above sea-level in an amphitheatre of fine mountains.

Loch Pattack further east is roughly similar in size and characteristic. Reinforced by the drainage from three other hill-lochs, the stream which issues from it provides the main volume of water entering Loch Laggan. Pike have managed to nose their way from Loch Pattack into Loch Treig, using the system of tunnels and aqueducts built to power the aluminium factory at Fort William. The fishing is good in all the lochs described.

The Blackwater Reservoir

In 1901 the British Aluminium Company obtained permission to harness power from the hills north of Glen Coe for large works at Kinlochleven, so the small lochs, Loch a'Bhaillidh, Lochan na Salach and Lochan Inbhir were combined in a $7\frac{1}{2}$ mile reservoir by the building of 1,100 ft of dam across the drainage of the River Leven. The capacity of the reservoir has been given at 4 million cu. ft, with giant pipes descending westward to the generating station.

The easiest way to see it is from the Glen Coe road, by taking the steep zig-zags of the Devil's Staircase three miles west of Kinghouse Inn. This became the 'Navvies' Road' in 1904 when 3,000 men moved into Kinlochleven to build the smelter and the Blackwater dam. Hard drinking and hard fighting tales have been told of these Irishmen and Highlanders. A whole new complex of houses, works and roads had to be built, yet within three years aluminium was being produced in a temporary smelter before the main one in 1909 when it was going full-blast.

Lochs of the Findhorn Basin

Lochs Moy, Lochindorb, Allan, Lochan Tutach, Dallas, Blairs

That grand and most mysterious of great Scottish rivers, the Findhorn, which rises in the Monadhliath and enters the Moray Firth below Forres, has few lochs draining into it. Of the six named above, only Loch Moy and Lochindorb are of any importance, the others being small and shallow, but notable in the north-easterly bulge of Scotland which has few lochs.

Loch Moy is on the Inverness road, a few miles north of the slatted concrete bridge and big railway viaduct over the Findhorn. Culloden Moor lies to the north of it, over the River Nairn, so we are back to dramatic incidents of the '45 since these wooded shores and the house at the north end is the seat of the Clan Mackintosh, and the monument visible on the larger of the two islands is to Sir Aeneas Mackintosh. The ruins of the castle beside it are the relics of the earliest seat of the clan, which goes back certainly to the early fifteenth century. The smaller island was used as a prison.

Loch Moy, nine miles south-east of Inverness is just over 1 mile long and ½ a mile in maximum breadth, with a maximum depth of 50 ft, and it contains a lot of char as well as trout. Shallow for ⅔ of its area, covered by less than 20 ft of water, there is an early record of an attempt to raise its level—by the enemy Comyns.

The Mackintoshs were in their castle on the island and found themselves in danger of being drowned by the ingenious Comyns who had dammed the outlet but unwisely camped on the flat ground below the stream. And while they waited for the loch level to swamp their enemies one brave clansman swam from the castle under cover of darkness and broke the dam. The enemy were routed by the force of water rushing down on them, and the Mackintosh who had released the flood was likewise swept to his doom.

There is a record going back to 1422 that the island castle then contained 400 men. The more modern castle was built in 1655 by the twentieth chieftain. Unlucky was the man imprisoned on the small island, for if the loch level rose in heavy rain he was soon underwater.

The most famous event on these shores dates to the '45 in what has become known as the 'Rout of Moy', when Lord Loudoun and 1,500 Government troops marched through the night from Inverness in the hope of taking the Prince in bed at Moy. But a smart boy of fifteen, Lachlan Mackintosh, outflanked the advancing troops and gave the alarm. The Prince promptly withdrew from the loch with his small bodyguard to await events. Lady Mackintosh took command. She stationed five men on the Inverness road to await the Government troops, and when they hove in sight they let crack with their muskets and shouted battle cries of advance as if they were in command of the much feared Jacobite army. The strong attacking force turned about, back to Inverness, leaving only one casualty, Donald Ban MacCrimmon, the finest piper in Scotland, alas, on the Government side.

The 'rout' took place on 16 February, during a Sunday night of thunder and lightning, and it was bad luck that it was the Macleods of Skye who should be in the Government advance guard. Bad luck for them also that they mistook a lot of peat stacks for an advancing Jacobite army when the Mackintoshs began firing and urging on an imaginary force. The four-poster bed in which the Prince slept is still to be seen in Moy, though not in the original house which was replaced in 1957 by the present mansion.

Lochindorb lies six miles north-west of Grantown-on-Spey and it too has an island with a famous castle-ruin which goes back to the fourteenth century and further. This dark loch is the one depicted in Maurice Walsh's novel *The Key Above The Door*, and its bleak setting on Dava Moor fits its history and the temperament of the Wolf of Badenoch, who made the island his stronghold.

Just over 2 miles long, with a maximum breadth of $\frac{2}{3}$ of a mile, half of Lochindorb is covered by less than 10 ft of water, though the maximum depth is 51 ft. It was a suitable lair for the 'Wolf' who burned the town of Forres and sacked the Cathedral of Elgin in 1390. Illegitimate son of King Robert II, the 'Wolf', Alexander Stewart, Earl of Buchan, perpetrated these infamies because he had been excommunicated by the Bishop of Moray for preferring a mistress to his wife. His effigy in armour can be seen in Dunkeld Cathedral, a strange finish for a rascal.

Read a bit of local history if you intend to fish for salmon, sea trout or brown trout on this loch. And from your boat you may land on the island and ponder awhile. The two nearby lochs, Loch Allan and Lochan Tutach are also trouting lochs. Loch Allan is a mile and a half north of Lochindorb, and has a crook in it like a swan's neck. It is only $\frac{1}{2}$ a mile long and 29 ft deep at maximum, but its bed is in three distinct basins.

Lochan Tutach is a mile north-west of Loch Allan, and is rather a smelly lochan with a maximum depth of 16 ft and a diameter of $\frac{1}{4}$ of a mile.

Loch of Blairs lies two miles south of Forres and contains rainbow trout as well as brown trout. It is only a $\frac{1}{3}$ of a mile long with a superficial area of 28 acres. The maximum depth is 5 ft,

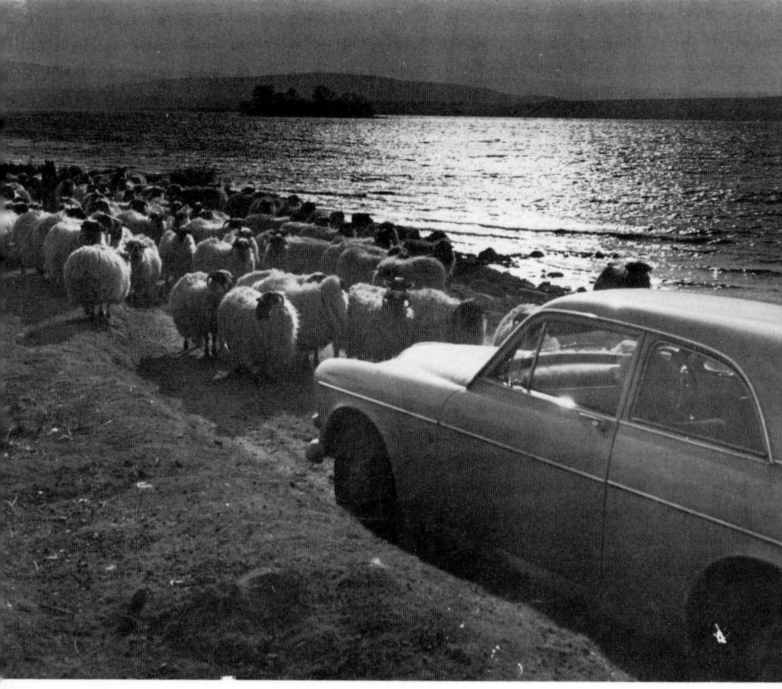

Road to Lochindorb in its bleak setting. The island is walled with the castle ruins of the Wolf of Badenoch

but the mean depth is only half as much. In the country where it is situated they claim to have forty days more of summer than the rcst of Scotland.

Loch Dallas is a hill-loch 1,000 ft above sea-level, ½ a mile long, ¼ of a mile broad, with a maximum depth of 8 ft, but the mean depth of the brown water is less than 4 ft.

No loch in this district can compare with interest to the River Findhorn, which should be explored piece by piece, which means a fair amount of walking, since so much is hidden from any road. Because of its birth in the mountains it is liable to rise very suddenly, and anglers of experience watch carefully for signs of flood, lest they be caught in some narrow gorge where they cannot readily escape. Unharnessed for hydro-electric power, it remains as yet one of the great free rivers.

Lochs of the Beauly Basin
Lochs Affric, Benevean, Mullardoch, Monar, Beannacharan

It is a truism that whereas hydro-electric dams may improve a moorland or bleak landscape by the creation of reservoirs, they cannot improve on natural lochs hemmed by high mountains and natural woods. In Glen Affric, Glen Cannich and Glen Strathfarrar there was, before electrification, the finest integration of river, loch, mountain and woodland scenery in Scotland—each offering a unique cross-country walking route from the North Sea to the Atlantic across Scotland, through the highest mountains standing north-west of the Great Glen.

The whole area was scheduled as a National Park in 1947–8, but no National Park in Scotland came to pass. The North of

Approach to Loch Affric by the river which flows into Loch Benevean

Scotland Hydro-Electric Board moved in, and of the lochs shown above, only Loch Affric remains 'natural', while Loch Mullardoch has been ruined, and Loch Monar robbed of its charm. Yet Glen Affric remains a magical place, still containing most of its former glory because of the Hydro-Electric Board decision to use Loch Mullardoch for water storage, and cut Affric workings to a minimum.

The way to Glen Affric is from Strath Glass, south-west from Beauly or due west from Drumnadrochit on Loch Ness by Glen Urquhart. Cannich Village, built since the power scheme, stands below the point where the River Cannich meets the Glass whose main source is the Affric.

The open river valley soon begins to close in as you go into groves of birch and Caledonian pines clinging to the steep bluffs—a place of fantastic yellow and bronze in autumn. The warm-sandstone power house at Fasnakyle does not jar, nor does the dam three miles upstream containing behind it the narrow waters of Loch Benevean.

Much of this is Caledonian pine-wood reserve, reflecting the sterling work of the Forestry Commission who in the 1960s committed themselves to a vast programme of fencing-out deer and sheep to protect seedlings from the hungry mouths which made regeneration impossible.

Loch Benevean is the English form of Mheadoin, stemming from the peak of that name above it. When the dam was built, the 2½-mile-long loch was doubled in length and the charming old road which wound through the pines was inundated. The new road seemed an ugly scar and people who knew and loved Glen Affric were bitter about the alterations and the felling of so many noble trees.

Twenty years on we can look with pride at how the fight to save the native pines is being won, and we can marvel too at how nature has clothed the shore line of the new Loch Benevean with graceful birches. Access now is more generous than before. The visitor can drive further into the glen, and for their delectation two short nature-trail walks have been laid out, one at the Dog Falls and another at the car-park where the public road ends. Westward the track continues as a right-of-way to Kintail, passing Affric Lodge set amongst green meadows on the edge of

Loch Affric, backed by the highest mountains north of the Great Glen.

Here is a comparison between it and Loch Affric: Loch Affric is 3¼ miles long, with a maximum breadth of ½ a mile and a maximum depth of 221 ft. Loch Benevean is 5 miles with a maximum breadth of ½ mile and a maximum depth of 167 ft. The main difference between the lochs is that there is an ugly tide-mark round the shore of Benevean, though the hydro board did their best to avoid fluctuations in level which would cause this.

Before leaving Glen Affric it is worth having a close look at the dam which is tucked away in a gorge, downstream from the original outlet of Loch Benevean, the concrete span being only 516 ft long and 86 ft high. But the water which rushes through a tunnel 3¼ miles long to the power-house at Fasnakyle comes not

Loch Affric

so much from Loch Benevean as from Loch Mullardoch across the mountains in Glen Cannich.

To see this main reservoir you have to start out from Cannich on the narrow road twisting west, as delightful as Glen Affric at first. Alas, the upper glen was sacrificed in order to save Glen Affric, by the building of the longest dam in Scotland, 2,385 ft in its entirety, with an apex pointing downstream, and a height of 116 ft. Benula Lodge, with cottages and woods, now lies beneath waters which swamped the paths to the west and absorbed Loch Lungard into Loch Mullardoch.

Loch Mullardoch is now 9 miles long, and its waters are tunnelled to Loch Benevean from the eastern end of the dam $3\frac{3}{4}$ miles through a mountain. The storage capacity of this reservoir is 6,830 million cu. ft, just over double the combined volume of Loch Lungard and Loch Mullardoch before the dam was built. There is a small power station in the tunnel at Mullardoch, but the main generating station is the one at Fasnakyle mentioned earlier, with an annual output of 240 million units of electricity.

Glen Strathfarrar is the next parallel glen to the north, and the new Loch Monar is a monotonous sheet of water like Loch Mullardoch. The way to it is from Struy in Strath Glass, and thanks to hydro-electric works the one-time bad road is good, but there is a locked gate to stop unauthorized entry. Permission to drive up may be obtained by application to the Nature Conservancy Council, Inverness, or by asking at the house beside the gate. Glen Strathfarrar should not be missed. Much of its forest was burned 150 years ago to make grazings for sheep. It is to be regretted that this superb glen should have been hydro-electrified.

It had everything, a sylvan beginning, a magnificent river, roaring waterfalls and the cataract of the Garbh Uisage tumbling through a gorge where Caledonian pines stood askew on the rocks, backed by the wild peaks of Loch Monar. The lodges, the trees, the loch, with the path along its north shore to the shepherd's house, had the aura of ultimate remoteness.

But the gorge is now spanned by a wall of concrete 113 ft high and 528 ft long, in a double-curvature arch, behind which is a great reservoir which has swallowed up houses, lodges and path . . . and trees. The previously 4-mile long loch is now 8 miles, and the maximum depth of 260 ft was raised another 75 ft, to provide a capacity of about 5,000 million cu. ft of water passing through four power stations to provide 59 million units of electricity.

The first of the power stations is underground, at Deanie, 5¾ miles by tunnel from Loch Monar, near the west end of Loch Beannacharan. This lower loch which receives discharged water has been further heightened by a dam at its other end, raising the 113 ft maximum depth by another 8 ft. From the dam on Loch Beannacharan there leads another 3½ miles of tunnel to another underground power station below the Culligran Falls. These power stations generate 94 and 57 million units of electricity respectively, which is a considerable annual output.

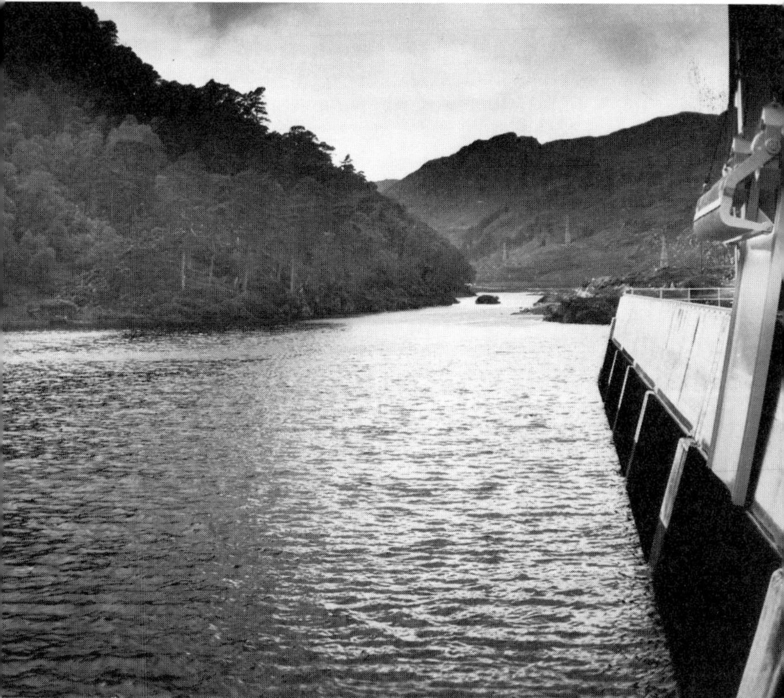

Pylons and hydro-electric workings in Glen Strathfarrar, where two shooting lodges now lie under an enlarged Loch Monar

Yet it is not the whole story, for at Aigus and Kilmorack there are two more dams, each with a power station. The Aigus dam is 270 ft long, and the Kilmorack 400 ft. Both are 64 ft high, and both have provisions for passing compensation water to enable fish to migrate, and Boreland fish passes to enable them to surmount the dams.

These hydro-electric schemes were completed in 1963 and have massively altered the wilderness feeling of what used to be a backwater of Scotland. Only Glen Affric retains anything of the original feeling of 'wilderness', and only it offers the attractions of an ancient track west through the hills to Loch Duich, with a Youth Hostel at Altbeath in the remotest stretch of the glen.

On the credit side, there are well-surfaced roads where there were only narrow tracks to the shooting lodges. Also, there is the village of Cannich which did not exist before large scale forestry and hydro-electric operations. There is nowadays a fair emphasis on cattle ranching in Glen Strathfarrar by Lord Lovat, the wartime Commando leader, whose name of course is Simon Fraser, 22nd Mac Shimi, and whose ancestor was captured on the island on Loch Morar for his part in the '45 and beheaded on Tower Hill, London in 1747.

It was another forebear, Col. Archibald Fraser of Lovat, who helped restore the kilt after it had been banned as an article of war. Yet another raised the Lovat Scouts which began their great service to the country in the Boer War and served it again in two successive wars. Many of the men of these glens were trained in the Canadian Rockies, and fought in Italy afterwards.

Lochs of the Ewe Basin

Lochs Maree, Tollaidh, Fada, Clair, Coulin, Kernsary, Ghiuragarstidh, a' Bhaid Luachriach, Mhic Ille Riabhaich, nan Dailthean, an t' Slagain, Sguod, an Drainc

It is almost a cliché to compare Loch Lomond and Loch Maree. But the 'Bonny Banks' would not be right for the Ross-shire loch. It does not have that kind of sylvan charm. The slopes are altogether steeper, rockier, wetter, more heathery. Loch Maree is more the embodiment of what is called 'Highland grandeur', a rough description appropriate to such a shaggy tumble of crag and water.

It is the largest loch north of the Great Glen but has less than half the area of Loch Lomond, 11.03 sq. miles as against the 27.45 for Scotland's biggest loch, and defeats it on only one measurement. Loch Maree has a bigger proportionate area of

Loch Maree, east shore where there are no roads, only tracks

islands to water surface than Loch Lomond. This is known as the insulosity factor, which is 0.09 as against 0.08. But Loch Maree has recently acquired a more unique distinction. It is now the largest entirely natural loch remaining in Scotland, Loch Lomond having been reduced to the status of reservoir and Loch Ness and Loch Awe harnessed for hydro-electric pumping stations.

The immediate similarity between Loch Lomond and Loch Maree is one of impact. You are presented with the whole rather than the part. The aura is immediate. You respond to it as to music. But whereas Loch Lomond is Mozart, Loch Maree is Beethoven, more sombre, more profound, casting you more back into yourself. On Loch Maree you have the feeling of a primeval landscape.

Slioch above Loch Maree

The very woods above you on Ben Eighe are fragments of the Caledonian pine forest dating back 8,000 years. Across the loch on Slioch the bare bones of the peak thrust up to a summit, with more strength and force than Ben Lomond. The colours are sombre, dun rather than emerald. The rocks swell out of the ground in grey bosses, ice-scored and polished, changing colour to pink where the layers of Torridonian sandstone have been heaved over the grey gneiss as on Slioch. Here it is no surprise to meet a wild cat, an otter, red and roe deer, or a pine marten. Eagle and peregrine falcon can appear in the sky any time. Man has not made much impact here yet.

However, there were iron-works here 350 years ago, consuming 20 acres of oaks daily for charcoal until 'the woods of it were all spent up and the lease expired'. That quotation came from Letterewe on the roadless shore of the loch, but it could have applied to Fasagh, Poolewe or Talladale, where there were other 'bloomeries', using bog-iron and charcoal from the oakwoods to make pig-iron for cannons, among other things.

The remains of the bloomery at Furnace can still be seen on Loch Maree. The charcoal from the burned woods was taken to the bloomery which was in two storeys, the charcoal and iron-ore being dropped from above into the closed furnace, then a set of bellows below would blow the fuel to the heat required to melt the iron from the slag. At five tons of timber to smelt one ton of pig-iron it was expensive in raw material, but the demand for iron was high, and it was met so long as the supply of oaks lasted.

All the more miraculous then that so much oak and pine forest should remain, especially when timber shortages in the last two wars made inroads on Coille na Glas Leitire—'Wood of the Grey Slope', which has been growing here for 8,000 years and since 1951 has been the object of intensive study by Nature Conservancy scientists trying to encourage and regenerate it. Beinn Eighe, appropriately enough, became Britain's first National Nature Reserve when the Conservancy was formed.

So the perfect way to begin exploring Loch Maree is to pay a visit to the Information Centre at the Field Station of Anancaun, talk to the Warden, and set out armed with a pamphlet on the Nature Trail which rises from the lochside picnic site about three miles north of Kinlochewe. Short-stay campers are allowed to put their tents down at Taagan, where the loch begins, and it is a convenient place on good grass with no charge for its use.

The farm lands between here and Kinlochewe are on alluvium built up by river action in a silting process that has pushed steadily forward thus shrinking gradually the size of Loch Maree. The rivers have a powerful flow here and can raise the loch nine feet when the rainfall is high. Six inches fell in 24 hours on one March day of 1968 bringing down a great deal of debris. Small wonder that the large alluvial cones on some of the streams where they enter the loch are more marked on Loch Maree than on the majority of lochs. Conversely, low water can cause separate islands to join up with each other.

Why the name Kinlochewe for a village removed fifteen miles from the sea loch of that name? The explanation seems to be that Loch Ewe was the old name of Loch Maree before Saint Maelrubha came to Eilean Maruighe in the seventh century and made the small island famous as a place of pilgrimage. So Maruighe became the name of the loch and was corrupted to Maree, which is the English form for the 12-mile loch aligned along a major fault. Murray and Pullar in the *Bathymetrical Survey of the Scottish Freshwater Lochs* made the length 13½ miles by taking in part of the so-called River Ewe, which they say more properly belongs to the loch because soundings of 30 ft were obtained.

It was Charles Darwin who said that every journey is made worthwhile if you pursue some kind of study on it. The chance to put this wise precept into action should not be missed on Loch Maree where the Nature Conservancy has made it easy for the tourist to see beyond the scenery. Armed with your pamphlet the circular Nature Trail takes only an hour, or you can turn it into a mountain walk that takes four hours.

The junction of the ways is a fine viewpoint at 350 ft crowned by a log cabin. Now you can look over the pink-barked pines to Slioch rising hugely above the deepest part of the loch where the bed digs down to 336 ft. Slioch—'The Spear'—is a pyramid of warm sandstone thrust on top of grey bosses of Lewisian gneiss whose lower gullies hang with oaks and birch, multi-coloured in autumn.

A geological plinth constructed like layers of a cake shows the succession of the rocks, enabling you to detect how the peaks are built up. That lower grey of Slioch is Lewisian gneiss—the very floor of the world whose age goes back some 2,000 million years and more. The darker Torridonian sandstone on top is only half as old, but is one of the most ancient of rocks, formed under the sea or exposed as desert before it was squeezed up and pushed over the older surface. The sparkling white rocks capping the tops is Cambrian quartzite, the only one of the three to have fossilised remains of life in it. Examine it in the plinth and you can see the tubular worm casts of the earliest organisms. The world was entirely lifeless when the gneiss and the sandstone were formed.

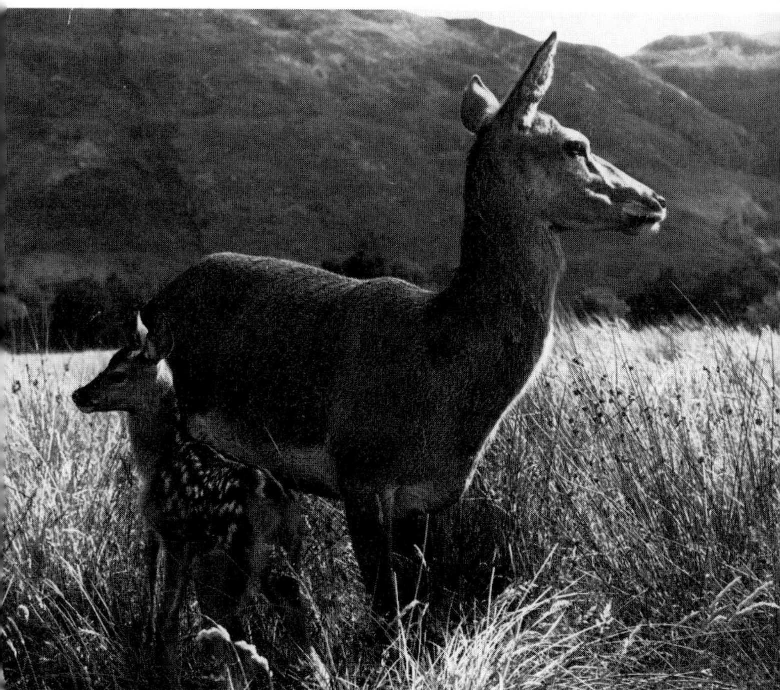

Loch Maree—red deer hind and calf

Loch Maree occupies the greatest of the west-north-west group of faults—weaknesses in the Earth's crust where great slipping movements have altered the lay of the rocks horizontally and vertically. The wooded islands of the loch are composed of Torridonian sandstone and grits, though the nearby shore rocks on the north-east are Lewisian gneiss rising to heights of 2,000 ft. Climb Slioch and you will find boulders of the oldest rock have been carried on ice as high as the Cambrian quartzite near the top of the peak—all part of the history of formation and glaciation.

As with Loch Lomond the score of islands are situated in a group, many of them covered in natural woodland. One of them—the largest—Eilean Subhainn, even has its own loch with little islands on it. The size of the island is only 292 acres but the loch is 250 yds by 70 yds, and the maximum depth goes down to 64 ft. As with Isle Maree, Eilean Grudididh and Eilean Ruaridh Bheag there is evidence of former habitation.

Isle Maree is the most famous island of any loch in Scotland, and much has been written about its sacred and Druidical associations. What St. Columba did for Iona, St. Maelrubha did for Isle Maree by setting up his cell here. Isle Maree was invested with special holy properties, well described by Thomas Pennant when he paid his visit in 1772 and wrote thus:

> Land on Inch-Maree, the favoured isle of the saint, the patron of all the coast from Applecross to Lochbroom. . . . The curiosity of the place is the well of the saint; of power unspeakable in cases of lunacy. The patient is brought to the sacred island, is made to kneel before the altar, where his attendants leave an offering in money; he is then brought to the well, and sips some of the holy water: a second offering is made; that done he is thrice dipped in the lake. The same operation is repeated every day for some weeks: and it often happens, by natural causes, the patient receives relief of which the saint receives credit.

From Isle Maree south-west to the head of the loch is known as the Grudie Basin, the deepest of the three basins into which the loch is subdivided, with the greatest depth of 367 ft where the loch is most constricted between Slioch and Meall Ghuibhais—

'The Hill of the Firs'—now spanned by Nature and Mountain Trails. In this basin the 200-ft depth extends for over six miles, deepening to 300 ft for two miles, and to 350 ft for one mile.

The Slattadale Basin is the island area, from west of Eilean Ruaridh Mor to south of Eilean Subhainn, where the 150-ft area has a depth of 2 miles by a $\frac{1}{4}$ of a mile. Deep channels extend round the islands and the 200-ft area stretches $1\frac{1}{2}$ miles by 150 yards broad south of Eilean Ruaridh, the greatest depth of 232 ft being in the north-west.

The Ardlair Basin is more irregular than the other two with a maximum depth of 285 ft where the floor of the loch is bumpy with small hills. But the 200-ft area runs for $2\frac{1}{2}$ miles and averages $\frac{1}{4}$ of a mile in breadth. North of the islands there is a remarkable shallowing to less than fifty feet. South of Isle Maree there is also a large sandflat covered by no more than a foot of water in times of low rainfall.

The salmon and sea trout are the pride of Loch Maree, and the hotel at Talladale is one of the most reputable fishing inns in Scotland, springtime for the salmon, summer to autumn for the big sea trout which run up to 20 lbs. The mail bus carries passengers up this west side of Loch Maree, but 120 years ago when there was no road, all the letters from Gairloch parish, plus those from Lewis and Harris, were carried in the leather bag of Iain Mor am Posda—Big John the Post. Correspondence must have been light in those days when Big John tramped to and from Dingwall with his bag.

The route he followed was the drove road on the other side of the loch and the track is a Right of Way, curling through oak and birch woods, climbing over rocky passes, then dropping again with constantly changing vistas as the ridges and tops of Ben Eighe and Liathach spike into view, powdered as if with snow, the quartzite emphasising the verticality of the great drops plunging downward in wall upon wall of precipice. Lots of wild goats on this side, superbly horned and hairy. Letterewe, the shooting lodge, stands in an oasis of lawns and gardens, at a crossroads of paths leading into the wildest hinterland in Scotland, to the Fionn Loch, to Lochan Fada and Loch na Sealga.

A fine walk has been opened up on the west shore where the

public highway swings away from the loch at Slattadale, but a footpath goes on to Tollie following through woods and climbing over a pass to a little peak called Creag Mhor Thollaidh less than 400 ft above the highest point of the path. This is a thrilling viewpoint, not only for the loch and its islands, but for Skye and the Hebrides and the monolithic peaks of Sutherland.

The Mountain Trail at the other end of the loch is slightly more strenuous. It was opened in 1970 after relays of voluntary workers had dug, drained, carried stones and built bridges over some of the most difficult rock and heather in the neighbourhood. Naval helicopters carried material and the Royal Highland Fusiliers helped load and unload it, a big combined operation resulting in perhaps the finest hill path to be built this century. It climbs to a Conservation Cairn and Indicator Viewpoint at 1,800 ft.

It begins at the highest point of the Nature Trail, following up the line of the Allt an Airidhe gorge where the trees gradually thin out as they become gnarled and dwarfed by wind. Green patches of good grass and flowers show where the soil is lime-rich. The demarcation is clear as long heather gives way to a sward of grasses dotted with globe flowers, chickweed wintergreen, moonwort, etc. High above the cleft of the gorge there is more startling change of scene, as you climb out to a plateau of quartzite cradling little saucer lochs. It has been well named a lunarscape.

A line of cairns makes route-finding easy. Arctic plants grow in the thin soil. Prostrate junipers, Alpine bearberry, mountain azaleas are only a few of the plants on this contrasty soil and vegetation. Scientific exploration since 1951 has revealed that the flora is richer than was suspected when Beinn Eighe became Britain's first Nature Reserve. The country all round Loch Maree is a reservoir of Highland wildlife. Black-throated and red-throated divers, greenshank, peregrine falcons, golden eagles, dunlin and golden plover are among the breeding birds. Otter, wild cat, roe and red deer, badger and pine marten range the loch shores. Alas, the ospreys which used to nest on Eilean Subhainn, and on a promontory opposite Isle Maree have not yet returned since the days when Osgood Mackenzie robbed their nests.

It was the potato famine of 1846–8 which caused the road to

be built along the west shore of Loch Maree. Osgood Mackenzie writes: 'But for the potato blight, when should we have got our roads made through the country? My mother never left Gairloch, not even for a day, for three long years when the famine was at its height.'

That resourceful lady put all the able-bodied men on her land to work, paying them a wage which enabled them to live. Little Osgood was allowed to cut the first turf, surrounded by starving Skyemen. In those bad times it was necessary to dole out oatmeal to keep the coastal crofters from starving, when their only standby was shellfish boiled in milk. Osgood's mother rode her horse everywhere at this time of desperation, acting as doctor, building nine or ten schools in which the Gaelic language had to come first, and influencing people to pull down their insanitary dwellings and build new ones with timbers which she provided.

Osgood himself forecast that more education would mean less cultivation and in his lifetime saw the crofts go back as people became less willing to spend all their time with crowbar and handplough. The croft lands lie mainly on the coastal fringes of Loch Ewe, and nowadays they do little more than feed a cow and provide some vegetables and potatoes. Like most people the crofters depend upon wage packets nowadays, and the boarding of summer visitors provides a good supplement to their income.

Loch Tollaidh

Not a notable loch, but an interesting one historically, for it was events sparked off on the artificial island, or crannog, which divested the Gairloch lands from the Macleods and passed them to the Mackenzies. This is the loch you pass on the drive over the moor between Gairloch and Poolewe, and it is worth pausing to look at the rocky setting and the peaks of the A'Mhaighdean wilderness which stretches behind.

Loch Tollaidh is a rock basin in sheared and folded Lewisian gneiss. Elliptical in shape it is just under a mile long, with a maximum breadth of 800 yds and a maximum depth in the centre of 86 ft. Once there was a dam at the outlet stream, to maintain the water at a higher level and release enough to power a mill-wheel as required.

If the day is fine you will be rewarded if you leave your car eastward of the loch, and take a walk down the farm track to Tollie Bay, or climb the nearest hillock for a view of Loch Maree, thc wild and beautiful hinterland which afforded the energetic Mackenzie such delight to the end of his days, though his living memorial is Inverewe Gardens which he created out of little more than rock and peat.

It was the creation of something out of nothing which was the basis of Mackenzie's philosophy. He loved craftsmanship, the skills of the hands, whether applied to building, agriculture, fishing or shooting, especially when it was a game of wits. And he was a patient man, waiting 20 years for the trees he planted to grow up, so that he could build a garden in their shelter, a garden that is a wonder of the world, growing sub-tropical and other plants on a barren peninsula of Torridonian sandstone swept by Atlantic winds.

It was when Mackenzie was excavating the foundations for his house on Am Ploc—The High Hump—he found that the ground was unexpectedly soft below. It was a former seabeach, three parts pebble, one part blackish earth, so he wheeled out thousands of barrow loads of stones, picking them like potatoes, dumped them in the sea, replacing them with cartloads of soil carried from long distances. Even the blue clay marl from the seashore, full of decayed oyster shells and crabs, was spread on his prepared ground.

He tells the story of how when cutting a 12-ft-deep bank above the garden to make a terrace he came across the deep holes of a former badger set, and from it came raspberry seedlings where none had grown before. He presumes the badgers had eaten the fruit and the seeds had been waiting centuries to germinate. It was a foretaste of what his remarkable garden was to produce once he had provided the sheltering trees.

He was eventually able to boast that anything that will grow in Britain will thrive here, yet all that was growing when he started were two dwarf willows. The Eucalyptus trees he planted are over 90 ft high now and the whole garden is the subject of a fine book, *Inverewe* by May Cowan.

See it in the rather colourless Highland spring if you would fully appreciate the miracle that Mackenzie wrought with sheltering shrubs and woods to provide micro-climates for early flowers from all over the world, dwarf daffodils from the Atlas Mountains, lustrous yellow beneath multi-coloured rhododendrons from the Himalayas, and above them both the great magnolia in flower overhead—all this on what used to be windswept headland—vivid with colour in contrast to the snow on the great wall of the Torridon peaks.

Mackenzie created it, but he also destroyed a great deal at the same time. Listen to his words as he gives the figures from his game book for one year, 1868. Grouse, 1313; black game, 33; partridges, 49; golden plover, 110; wild duck, 35; snipe, 53; rock pigeons, 91; hares, 184; a total of 1,900 head without mentioning geese, teal, ptarmigan and roe. He writes: 'What a big pile it would make if all the black game I shot between 1855 and 1900 were gathered in one heap. Now alas! there are none, and why, who can tell?'

Mackenzie did not appreciate that it was precisely because game was so plentiful that there was so much of what he called 'vermin' on his ground. Like all the shooting men of his time he thought that by poisoning and trapping golden eagles, foxes, badgers, otters, wildcats, pine martens and polecats he would see a big increase in birds. Even killing 34 golden eagles in four seasons had little effect however. All his long life he waged war on 'vermin' yet his game continued to decline. What had gone wrong was the total environment, due to the destruction of the woods and over-grazing by sheep. The rich capital of game had been expended.

Yet Mackenzie was himself a conservationist, for he deplored the misuse of land going on around him. Undoubtedly he loved wildlife, even when the smoke was puffing out of his gun as he dropped a whooper swan or a snipe. The general decline he saw around him was due to massive deforestation, soil impoverishment due to muirburn. He would be enthusiastic about the efforts of the Nature Conservancy if he were alive today, I am sure. And he would be forced to admit the truth that it is the prey which controls the predator, and not the other way round.

Lochan Fada

North-east of Loch Maree lies an interesting long loch with a contradictory name, Lochan Fada, contradictory because the word Lochan usually refers to a small loch, more in the nature of a tarn, whereas Fada means long. There are many Loch Fadas in Scotland, but this one happens to be the biggest of its name in the country. Length 3¾ miles, maximum breadth ⅔ of a mile, with a maximum depth of 248 ft, it could hardly be called small. It is a rock basin lying between 3,000-ft hills, deeper at the lower end where the glacier ice excavated a fault.

Seen from the top of Slioch you appreciate its setting in the jumble of peaks which thrust between here and Loch Broom, where only footpaths thread the wilderness. No other piece of undeveloped country like it remains in Scotland, and it is my hope that nothing will change it. No one lives permanently

Lochan Fada beneath the peaks of A'Mhaighdean and Ruadh Stac Mor

within it. It is deer forest and fishing country *par excellence*. The crags offer some of the finest climbing in Scotland. The walking routes are without compare.

The easiest way to see Lochan Fada is to walk from Kinlochewe on the old drove road to Loch Maree, as if you were going to climb Slioch, and branch right up Glen Bianasdail after crossing the stream. You can see the ruins of the ironworks building here, and the shore below is known to this day as Cladh nan Sussanach—the Englishman's graveyard. The glen you follow up is narrow and walled by steep crags on the right; it is a hanging valley where a corrie glacier continued to dig deep after Loch Maree had been formed. The stream drains out of Lochan Fada so all you have to do is follow up the good path.

The whole atmosphere is impressive, looking out from the defile, back to the grey peaks of Beinn Eighe and its Caledonian pines fronting Loch Maree. Then after climbing to 1,250 feet you drop to the rather bleak head of the lochan. The best of it lies west, and if you are a strong walker you should go along 3 miles and come back by a fine path which climbs to 1,750 ft, dropping by Loch Garbhaig and the Furnace Burn. True you have more than this distance to walk back along Loch Maree to regain your route of the morning, but the path winding through the natural oaks contouring up and down should not be missed.

Lochan Fada occupies a pre-Torridonian valley which has been re-exposed by the removal of great masses of sandstone by glacier action. The mixture revealed now is Lewisian gneiss with, on top of the bed rock, the remaining Torridonian sandstone. The narrow shape of the loch means that only a limited surface is exposed to heating agencies. This allied to its height above sea-level means it is colder at all depths than Loch Maree.

An attentive look east reveals that the natural drainage line from Lochan Fada was once eastwards, until down-cutting by the stream in Glen Bianasdail excavated a new outlet and lowered the level of the entire loch, leaving the old drainage line in Gleann na Muice without a head. The evidence can be read in the streams, especially if you return to your base via the Heights of Kinlochewe. The two little lochans immediately east of the Lochan Fada and at a slightly higher elevation were submerged in Lochan Fada, most probably, before the level was lowered. A track from here leads south-eastwards to the Heights of Kinlochewe. The total round by the routes described is about 14 miles.

A longer and better expedition however is to follow the south shore of Lochan Fada westwards where it ends below the spectacular cliffs of Ben Lair in narrow Gleann Tulacha—a wild and splendid place quite the opposite to the bleak eastern end. The most rewarding thing to do here is cross the stream north and climb a thousand feet to the ridge of Beinn Tarsuinn Chaol to look into the splendid rock basin of the Gorm Loch Mor beneath A'Mhaighdean.

The ridge is knife-edged, but without difficulty, though the slopes falling to the Gorm Loch are rocky. The savagery of the scene is heightened by the extreme loneliness of the country, no easy way out in any direction. The north face of Slioch rises in great ribs of pink sandstone, but all else around is gneiss, though the north-easterly peaks are capped with Cambrian quartzite. Even the head of Loch Coruisk in Skye has not more character.

After seeing the west end of Lochan Fada there is an exciting way back, by swinging away south-westwards just over one mile from the end of the loch on a good track which climbs to 1,800 ft. It leads you back to Loch Maree via Loch Garbhaig, whose outlet is the Furnace Burn dropping 1,000 ft to the oakwoods of the shore. The remains of the old ironworks are still visible.

Loch Garbhaig has a fishing bothy on the west shore and a large island half a mile from it. It is a bare loch, though evidence of tree stumps in the bogs show there must have been a fair amount of woodland on the southern approaches. The loch is just over 1 mile long with a maximum breadth of $\frac{1}{3}$ of a mile and a maximum depth of 93 ft. Despite being the same level as Lochan Fada it was found to be 4 degrees warmer.

Loch Clair and Loch Coulin

In the juxtaposition of Liathach with Loch Clair nature has excelled herself in providing a perfect mirror for a rock peak of impressive bulk rising '. . . from river bed to the sky, Grey courses of masonry tier on tier, And pinnacle riven on high'. Set amongst birches and Caledonian pines in Glen Torridon, said to be the oldest glen in the world, Loch Clair has great atmosphere. Loch Coulin is simply an appendage of it, on the walkers' track that runs over the Coulin Pass to Achnashellach. The drainage of the lochs is by the Allt Gharibhe into Loch Maree, and there is a direct footpath from Loch Coulin north to Kinlochewe.

This too is Mackenzie country, and of all their lands from Kintail to Loch Broom this is the most spectacular, and the most poverty stricken, for it has been well said that the noblest scenery makes the poorest agriculture. The exposure of rock to grass shows what a hard country this is, but compared with the rest of Glen Torridon, Lochs Clair and Coulin are sylvan, hence their impact—especially in winter when the summit ridges are snow capped and the rocks are bare, rising a full 3,000 ft above the low glen.

Loch Clair and the Peak of Liathach

The skyline of peaks lying north across Glen Torridon is the nearest thing we have in Scotland to a National Park, with the Nature Conservancy owning the easterly section and the National Trust for Scotland the westerly peaks including the summits of Liathach, Beinn Alligin, parts of Beinn Dearg and Beinn Eighe. With camping grounds, information centres and nature trails it means the minimum of restrictions in a wild country which used to be sacred to deer stalking.

Lochs Clair and Coulin are on private land and there is no right of way for cars on the narrow track to the Lodge. It is no hardship to walk in a place where there is so much to see of geological and naturalist interest, for this is classic country for Highland birds and mammals, where greenshank and black-throated divers nest, otters have their holts and pine martens their dens.

Loch Clair is only separated from Loch Coulin by an alluvial fan which has been built up by the stream coming in on the west, the Allt na Luib, otherwise they are one loch dammed by morainic drift, even the two small islands on Loch Clair are moraines. The depth of 93 ft maximum for Loch Clair occurs in the deeper water of the south-eastern portion, the total length being $1\frac{1}{3}$ miles, with a maximum breadth of 300 yds. The mean depth is 42 ft.

Loch Coulin lies 300 yds over alluvial ground and it too is $1\frac{1}{3}$ miles long, with a maximum breadth of $\frac{1}{3}$ of a mile, but with a maximum depth of only 49 ft. It is irregular in bottom compared to Clair, being cut into three basins, the deepest being in the broad south-eastern portion. The north-westerly basin is 32 ft in maximum depth, and the central basin 22 ft.

Going west down Glen Torridon a pause should be made opposite the small Lochan an Iasgaich to look at the sea of hummocky moraines above the climbers' cottage. It is called Coire a' Cheud-chnoic—'Corrie of the Hundred Hills', and it is well named. You could do worse than leave your car here, and walk north up the path signposted Coire Dhu to see the hidden face of Liathach which is even sheerer and more fretted than its other side.

Loch Kernsary

This loch drains into the bottom of Loch Maree opposite Tollie Bay, and is the most southerly of a whole scatter of good but bleak fishing lochs. This loch of many inlets is distinguished by having a crannog—an artificial island—near its south-western shore, but unlike the one in Loch Tollie it has no history. A track runs along its north side into the great wilderness behind Slioch, a place purring with dunlin and piping golden plover in summer.

Low lying, Loch Kernsary is roughly $1\frac{2}{3}$ miles long and $\frac{1}{2}$ a mile in maximum breadth, with a greatest depth of 93 ft in the north-west, 250 yds from the shore. Apart from its irregular shape it has four basins each deeper than 50 ft on a floor of mixed Lewisian gneiss and Torridonian sandstone. The ice markings on the rocks known as 'Striae' lie parallel to these 50-ft basins.

Loch Ghiuragarstidh drains into Loch Kernsary and lies half a mile to the north. Small as it is, only 1,200 yds long and 370 yds at its broadest, it has little islands with pine trees, and boulders and reefs in its southern half give a clue to its shallowness. In fact all but 4 per cent is covered by less than 25 ft of water. The maximum depth is 37 ft, in the northern part.

Loch a'Bhaid Luachriach. There is a path to this loch from Aultbea where it is known locally as the Goose Loch, and the local hotel has the brown trout fishing rights. Shaped like the wings of a butterfly, it is almost two lochs, with a little connected body-piece. The length is over $1\frac{1}{2}$ miles with a maximum breadth of over 1 mile. The north-east is a simple basin reaching a depth of 143 ft in its centre. The south-west is an irregular basin, with a maximum depth of 43 ft. The connection between the two is only 15 ft wide.

Loch Mhic' ille Riabhaich lies a mile or so south-east of the last named loch on a path climbing over a shoulder of low hill. Its main interest, apart from fishing, is the remains of a strong point on one of its little islands, nothing about which is known. Half a mile in length and just a bit less in breadth it is mostly shallow, the maximum depth being only 12 ft.

Loch nan Dailthean on the Poolewe–Aultbea road is even shallower though it is $\frac{1}{2}$ a mile long.

The northerly arms which enclose Loch Ewe have other

shallow lochs. The easterly arm has Loch an t'Slagain near Slaggan Bay which receives the outflow of several smaller lochs to the east and south. Its length is $\frac{2}{3}$ of a mile by $\frac{1}{3}$ of a mile, with a maximum depth of 55 ft to the south-east. Aultbea Hotel has the fishing rights, and the best brown trout season is from June until August.

Loch Sguod is on the other side of Loch Ewe, on the western arm and is shallow, reaching a maximum depth of no more than 14 ft. The length is $\frac{3}{4}$ of a mile and the breadth $\frac{1}{2}$ a mile. Right out north-west of it extending to the point are other lochs, the biggest of which is Loch an Drainc, length $\frac{3}{4}$ of a mile by $\frac{1}{3}$ of a mile in maximum breadth and with a maximum depth of 55 ft. Mixed woodlands, steep little knolls and moorland give great character to this interesting area right out on the tip of Loch Ewe.

Lochs of the Gruinard Basin

Fionn Loch, Dubh Loch, Lochs Beannach, na Moine Buige, Eileach Mhic'ille Riabhaich, Fada, na Beiste, na Sealga (Sheallag)

Fionn Loch means the White Loch and Osgood Mackenzie devotes a chapter of *A Hundred Years in the Highlands* to it. He calls it '. . . the best trout loch in Scotland', and supports the assertion with evidence of catches. He writes of a weighing-in. 'There were four beauties lying side by side on the table of the small drinking-room, and they turned the scale at 51 pounds. The total weight of the twelve fish caught that 12th April day by trolling was 87 pounds 12 ounces.' Osgood didn't catch them, but he missed 'The biggest fish I ever saw on that loch . . . I was casting with a light rod, and had on an ordinary cast with three small flies, just where the small burn flows into the loch at the Feith a Chaisgan sandy bay, when I hooked an enormous fish . . . double the size of any we had seen before. It jumped three times clean out of the water close to the boat, and we saw it as well as if we had landed it; but in spite of us all doing our very best to ease the tension on the line, it soon carried off everything. Without in the least wishing to exaggerate, I honestly declare that fish to have been a twenty-five pounder.'

Big fish are still plentiful in the Fionn Loch, and permission should be sought at Kernsary, a keeper's cottage approached by a private road out of Poolewe. A payment is demanded at Kernsary if you wish to leave a car. The track continues north-eastwards over the moor for another 3 miles to the strange world of the Fionn Loch.

You can walk from Kernsary on a footpath all the way to the head of the loch, but a much better way of letting the Fionn Loch make its impact is to walk from Letterewe on the east shore of Loch Maree, and cross the high Bealach Mheinnidh on the bridle path and suddenly come upon what is perhaps the most striking change of scene in Scotland, with the Fionn Loch laid out like a map before you, while on all sides of you there are wild cliffs. The path leads down to a little causeway separating Dubh Loch from the Fionn Loch. And over the other side lies the lonely white house of Carn More, no longer permanently occupied, but used as a shooting box in the stalking season.

The maximum width of the $5\frac{3}{8}$-mile-long Fionn Loch is $1\frac{1}{2}$ miles, and the maximum depth of 144 ft occurs in two places, near the south-eastern end, and in the central part opposite Lochan Beannach. The bottom is extremely irregular, and although boulders protrude, there may be deep water each side of them. The northerly fish tail reaches a depth of 97 ft, while its more westerly prolongation is 78 ft maximum.

The voice of this place in summer is the triple staccato of the greenshank, the piping of golden plover, the 'reeling' of dunlin, the singing of meadow pipits and the twittering of twites. Golden eagle, peregrine falcon and raven live on the crags. It is to be hoped that the motor car will never invade this sanctuary.

Dubh Loch: only the width of a man-made causeway separates the Fionn Loch and the Dubh Loch, and in very high

The Dubh Loch (left) and the Fionn Loch from A'Mhaighdean

water they may become one. Litigation in the court decided that these lochs were one, but the House of Lords overturned the decision, so Dubh Loch has the status of a separate loch. the mile-and-a-quarter dark loch has a character of its own, penetrating as it does into the rocks which rise steeply from its shore in places. Even the shape of the loch, at an angle to the Fionn Loch, gives it the feel of a corrie lochan in such stark surroundings. High above it, from the house of Carn More, contours the climbing path to the Strath na Sheallag. Ideally you should walk over it to Dundonnel on Little Loch Broom if you get this far.

The Dubh Loch is only $\frac{2}{5}$ of a mile in maximum breadth with a greatest depth of 88 ft in the centre. In contrast to the irregular Fionn Loch the Dubh Loch is a simple basin, though there is a bank of shallow water about 300 yds from the south-eastern end. At one point in this shoaling there is only 2 ft of water though it drops to 20 ft each side of it. There is a stalkers' path along the south side of the Dubh Loch leading into a wild recess below A'Mhaighdean. Follow this up and you are at the Gorm Loch Mor only a short distance from the Lochan Fada.

A strong walker could explore all of this from Kinlochewe, though the ideal is to carry food and a sleeping bag and have a night in the bothy at Carn More. But you have to be entirely self-supporting.

Loch Beannach, Loch na Moine Buige, Loch Eileach Mhic'ille Riabhaich, Loch Fada and Loch na Beiste are other lochs of the Gruinard Basin, the first four peppering the region of the Fionn Loch among many others. The last named lies north of Laide on the western arm of Gruinard Bay. Details are as follows.

Loch Beannach lies close to the western shore of the Fionn Loch at a point about half way along its length. It is an irregular and complicated loch with sinuosities which almost cut it in two. Measurement is difficult because of the shape but the surveyors gave the maximum depth as 27 feet. Islands and rocks show that it is very shallow, and in fact the mean depth is only $6\frac{1}{2}$ ft.

Loch na Moine Buige is almost part of the Fionn Loch westerly extremity, and has a depth of 60 ft maximum and a mean of $24\frac{1}{2}$ ft. Length $\frac{3}{4}$ of a mile, it is $\frac{1}{4}$ of a mile broad, so can be considered deep for its dimensions.

Loch Eileach Mhic'ille Riabhaich: this is where the Fionn Loch spills out and makes a small loch before becoming a river by dropping over two waterfalls. Length is $\frac{3}{4}$ of a mile and it is less than $\frac{1}{4}$ of a mile broad, with a maximum depth of 33 ft in its widest part.

Loch Fada: yet another loch of this name and a longish loch lying north-north-west of the Fionn Loch. Length $1\frac{1}{2}$ miles, it has a few good islands on it. Half a mile in maximum breadth it is 56 ft deep near the wide central portion, though the mean is only 17 ft.

Loch na Beiste: is situated on the Rubha Mor where there are many little lochs of its kind. This one gets the name from a beast which was thought to live there, but when the owner tried to

Loch na Sealga (Sheallag) fed by remote streams

drain the loch to reveal its secret he failed. The moon casting its shadow on two stones, giving it the shape of an animal, is thought to be the true explanation of the beast. It is a simple loch 35 ft at its deepest, and a $\frac{1}{3}$ of a mile long by $\frac{1}{4}$ of a mile broad.

Loch na Sealga: this superb loch spills into the Gruinard River but is fed by the streams from some of the remotest hills in Scotland. Dominated by the pinnacles of An Teallach on the north, and Ben Dearg Mor and Beag to the south, the problem of the traveller making his way against the grain of the country is to ford the broad feeder river, the Abhainn Strath na Sealga.

It should be waded where it is broadest, north-west of the join with Gelann na Muice Beag, and if the time of year is out with the deer stalking season, you can be sure of a roof over your head at Shenavall. It is no more than a bothy, so you need sleeping bag and food. A good track from here leads across the shoulder of An Teallach to the Dundonnel road.

The loch contains good fish, salmon, sea trout, brown trout and char but is preserved. The deepest part of the $3\frac{1}{8}$-mile loch is a mile from the inflow where it goes down to 217 ft and is flat bottomed over the wide south-eastern portion, getting shallower as the loch narrows, reaching less than 50 ft in its last mile.

Strath na Sealga, or Sheallag, 'The Valley of Hunting', is on the line of the cattle droving road from Gruinard Bay, swinging south by the Lochan an Nid to Loch a'Bhraoin and the Dirrie Mor to Garve.

Lochs of the Conon Basin 178

Lochs Droma, Glascarnoch, Vaich, Luichart, Orrin, Fannich, Loch á Chroisg, Gowan, Beannachan, Garve, Achilty, Glass Morie

Loch Droma on the Dirrie Mor on the heights between Ullapool and Garve belonged to the Loch Broom drainage until captured by the North of Scotland Hydro-Electric Board as part of their Conon Valley Scheme which harnesses the catchment of the Fannich Mountains and the lochs of Strath Bran, together with some completely new lochs like Glascarnoch and Vaich to the north of Garve by Altguish Inn.

Loch Droma occupies the glacial breach where the ice broke through to Loch Broom, but had been enlarged artificially even before Hydro-Electric Board alterations. It was less dreary in the old days when it had a good stand of firs on its north side. In those days the length was $1\frac{1}{4}$ miles by $\frac{1}{4}$ mile maximum breadth with the greatest depth 16 ft. It is smaller today, at a mile long by $\frac{1}{5}$ of a mile broad, the new area being 103 acres compared to the old of 116 acres. With a spillway level of 883 ft O.D., the maximum depth can hardly have changed.

Bleak as it is, with high peaks on each side, Loch Droma points west to An Teallach, and when this peak is mirrored in the loch at sunset the effect is of remarkable beauty. It is no longer the 'Destitution Road'. That name which still sticks was not given because of the scenic bleakness, but because it was the road taken by the destitute crofters driven out by hard times and political pressure.

The water from Droma, formerly outflowing to the north-west, now feeds eastward into what used to be the Glascarnoch River valley but is now occupied by a large reservoir called Loch Glascarnoch impounded by a big concrete dam above Altguish Inn. The spillway level here is 826 ft, and the length of the loch is nearly $4\frac{1}{2}$ miles by 1 mile greatest breadth, though the mean breadth is just over $\frac{1}{2}$ a mile. The capacity of the reservoir is 17,132,000,000 gallons.

Going north from Garve to Ullapool you motor along the south shore of this reservoir which is fed by tunnel from another new reservoir to the north called Loch Vaich, whose spillway is 840 ft and the highest storage reservoir in the Conon scheme. Loch Vaich is just under $3\frac{1}{2}$ miles long and just over $\frac{1}{3}$ of a mile in maximum breadth with a capacity of 2,470,000,000 gallons.

The water from Loch Vaich goes through a small power station at the outlet of the tunnel which carries it to Glascarnoch, the power generated being carried by submarine cable across Glascarnoch to be delivered into the distribution system. Between these high lochs and the tail race of the Torr Achilty power station there is a drop of 830 ft, and all but a few feet is harnessed as the waters pass through three sets of turbines at different levels, Mossford, Luichart and Torr Achilty.

The total scheme is a complicated one harnessing 345 sq. miles of catchment to produce about 290 million units of electricity yearly. There are seven generating stations, seven main dams, 20 miles of tunnels and 15 miles of aqueducts, not to mention 30 miles of public and private roads and a main line railway station.

Loch Glascarnoch is impounded behind 1,670 ft of dam, 92 ft high, and the tunnel which carries its waters to Mossford power station on Loch Luichart is nearly 5 miles in a drop of 530 ft. The site of this power station has grim associations with the force of water, for the original clachan which stood here was obliterated by floods, it is said. The water which falls today produces about 112 million units of electricity.

When Loch Luichart was a natural loch its measurements were 5 miles by 1 mile in maximum breadth, with a maximum depth of 164 ft and a mean of 67 ft. The 45-foot-high dam built at its outlet and stretching 680 ft raised it by 40 ft to 6 miles, though the breadth remains approximately 1 mile. The capacity is estimated at 37,160,000,000 gallons.

The attractive feature of Loch Luichart is its almost Perthshire character, with heather and fine mixed woods to give its low hills colour. Its Highland impact is all the greater because it contrasts so much with the big fields and agricultural lands of the Moray Firth. And as you climb away westward the vegetation changes, brilliantly in autumn when the birches are golden and heather and bracken are rusting.

From the dam the water passes to the Luichart Power Station at the junction of the Meig with the Conon, a fine building in Tarradale stone generating 124 million units of electricity. The big pipelines supplying the station are invisible, buried in the hillside behind the station. Good taste here, like the Meig dam nearby, tunnelling water to top-up Loch Luichart from a narrow reservoir.

The Torr Achilty power house is similar to the one at Pitlochry, in that the dam and power house are in one unit. It not only uses water discharged from all the lochs mentioned, but gets and additional supply from the Orrin power station to the west, to boost the output by 5 million units of electricity.

The Orrin generating station in Strath Conon gets its water supply from a new loch formed behind a dam five miles upstream from the Orrin Falls. This new loch is 5½ miles long by over ½ a mile broad and has a capacity of 13,020,000,000 gallons. The Orrin reservoir is in bare hills, with a spillway level of 840 ft. The dam is 130 ft high on one side of a hill and 50 ft high on the other, the two sections totalling over 2,000 ft. Over 4 miles of

Loch Luichart and pipes to the power station

tunnel takes the water to the power house on Loch Acholockie, the small loch formed by the Torr Achilty dam.

Grasping all this is none too easy, but it is not the whole story. We have still to deal with Loch Fannich remotely situated beneath high mountains and the largest loch within the Cromarty Firth drainage basin. This is in the heart of deer forest country, and has a lodge on its shores which can be reached by private road from Grudie, just west of Loch Luichart. It is a lonely wild track climbing up to over 800 ft with steep rocky peaks rising on the north side.

Good for trout fishing, the old length of the loch was 7 miles by $\frac{3}{4}$ of a mile, with a maximum depth of 282 ft and a mean depth of 109 ft. The rockfill dam built to increase its capacity has increased the length by only half a mile, and the breadth by almost nothing. The surface area today is 2,710 acres compared to the natural 2,300 acres in pre-hydro-electric days. It is a true rock basin of simple form with lots of morainic debris above it on the hills.

The tunnel which leads four miles through the hills to the power station at Grudie Bridge became notable for 'Operation Bathplug'. This was the final blowing out of the 600-ton plug of rock 81 ft below the surface of Loch Fannich through which the water would gush. The underground explosion successfully pulled the plug, and the storage capacity of Loch Fannich today is worth 102 million units of electricity. The neat power station of pink tinged stone is at the west end of Loch Luichart.

Just south of it is the Achanalt Power Station using a barrage with sluice gates across the outlet of Loch a'Chuilinn to regulate the River Bran. The effect has been to combine shallow Loch Achanalt with deeper Loch a'Chuillinn and make one $3\frac{1}{2}$-mile tadpole loch of wriggling shape. The controlled River Bran flowing through the lochs is thus used to drive a 2-megawatt turbine. At the Achanalt Falls there is a fish pass to help the salmon reach their spawning ground.

Loch á Chroisg: you motor along the north shore of this loch if you turn off at Achnasheen for Kinlochewe, and if the surroundings are a bit bleak there are glimpses of nobler things in the rocky peaks of Torridon and Coulin thrusting above the rounder hills. Trending east and west for $3\frac{1}{2}$ miles, the maximum breadth is ½ a mile and the maximum depth of 168 ft occurs near the centre. It is a simple basin containing good trout and char. Loch Maree Hotel has fishing rights.

Loch Gowan: this irregular sheet of water lies between the Kyle of Lochlash road and the railway line a mile south of Achnasheen, and is really two lochs, separated by alluvial material deposited by the Allt Mhartuin stream. Regarded as one loch, the length is 1¾ miles or thereabouts, with the greatest depth in the southern blob at 52 ft, whereas the rather narrower northern basin reaches only 17 ft.

Loch Beannachan: although there is a footpath to this loch from Loch Gowan and the walk is hardly five miles, the only public road is from Strath Conon following up the Meig into the hills nearly as far as you can go. It is a moorland loch, 1¾ miles long by ⅓ of a mile in maximum breadth and the maximum depth near the centre is 176 ft. The feature of the simple basin is the wooded island where the Meig enters and leaves the loch.

Loch Garve: north-east of Loch Luichart and edged by road and railway, Loch Garve occupies a wooded hollow under the hulk of Ben Wyvis, so there is the contrast between an oval of water only 220 ft above sea-level under summits rising to over 3,000 ft. Length 1½ miles, maximum breadth ½ a mile, with a maximum depth of 105 ft near the centre, Loch Garve is a simple basin spilling out eastward by Loch na Croic and the Blackwater. The Rogie Falls should be visited, and are easily reached by footpath from a point near Achilty Inn. It is a colourful place in autumn with the white water pouring over the rocky gorge hung with golden birches.

Once upon a time Loch Garve reached to the site of the present falls, and was lowered naturally by the erosion of the glacial drift deposits and the cutting action of the water draining it back. The present loch is 20 ft above the level of the Falls of Rogie.

Man has had to take a hand in the migration of salmon however, and the runs of 4,000 salmon recorded annually in the Blackwater result from the planting of fry by the North of Scotland Hydro-Electric Board who have a large hatchery at Contin nearby. Fish are caught at the outlet of Loch Garve and other places and stripped of their eggs in autumn, to be hatched indoors during the winter and released as fry in spring, or reared to parr and smolt stages.

Beyond Loch Garve in the River Bran there is a permanent floating trap to catch smolts so that they can be taken downstream to other lochs in the Conon Valley and thus minimise predation. Details of the fishing available in these waters are as follows.

Ross and Cromarty
Water: Loch Achonachie, near Contin, and in specific beats of River Conon between Loch Achonachie and Luichart Power Station.
Tailrace Pool.
Fish: Salmon, trout.
Permits: Loch Achonachie Angling Club.

Loch Garve, edged by road and railway

Water: Loch Meig near Contin.
Fish: Trout.
Permits: Loch Achonachie Angling Club.

Water: Loch Glascarnoch near Garve.
Fish: Trout.
Permits: Altguish Inn, By Garve, Ross-shire.

Water: River Blackwater (Upper Beat) between Loch na Croic outflow and point immediately above Falls of Rogie.
Fish: Salmon.
Permits: Loch Achonachie Angling Club.

Water: River Conon (part).
Fish: Salmon, trout
Permits: Loch Achonachie Angling Club.

Water: River Conon (New Pool, Morrison Pool and Bridge Pool), Conon Bridge.
Fish: Sea trout.
Permits: Dingwall and District Angling Club.

Loch Achilty: situated near Contin this small deep loch is worth a visit, for although it is only 1,500 yds by 700 yds it is 119 ft deep and contains char. The combination of great depth to size and sheltered position allied to small drainage area result in a remarkable range of water temperature, from 63.5°F at the surface to 42.3°F at 70 ft, a range of 21.2° at its most extreme. Delta gravels relating to the 100-ft beach period show that the Conon has filled in the loch to the west and the Blackwater to the east. The hole the loch occupies was probably dug out by glacier ice before the land rose following the period of glaciation.

Loch Glass and Loch Morie do not belong to the Conon Basin drainage, but because they belong to the Cromarty Firth it is expedient to include them lying as they do just north of Ben Wyvis. Both of them are simple rock basins, sinking to a deep point and rising again. In terms of great volume, they are important lochs.

The approach to Loch Glass is from Evanton to the north of

Dingwall, by a narrow track leading in a mile to a strange cleft known as the Black Rock of Novar, a narrow gorge through which the river swirls between twisting puddingstone walls which seem to touch in places. The rock is conglomerate, and adventurous men have forced a way up the river by a combination of rock climbing and inflatable boat. Leave the car and descend to the lip of this impressive ravine if you would see the place. Otherwise follow the track up Glen Glass to the loch in another five miles.

Four miles long and $\frac{2}{3}$ of a mile broad, Loch Glass occupies a sporting hinterland. The road serves shooting lodges sited on its shores. Slightly crescent shaped, and 713 ft above sea-level, the maximum depth is 365 ft with a mean depth of 159 ft. The 300-ft basin runs along the flat bottom for over a mile and the 200-ft basin for 2 miles. A great deal of fluvio-glacial litter bestrews the lower glen, but there is no rock barrier before the Falls of Eillenach.

Loch Morie occupies much lower country than Loch Glass, and has been excavated less deeply, but the character is the same, a narrowish loch among heathery hills. The length here is $2\frac{1}{3}$ miles by just over $\frac{1}{2}$ a mile broad, with a maximum depth of 270 ft and a mean of 125 ft. The outlet stream in this case flows over a barrier of rocks. The best access is from the A836 near Alness.

Loch Damh: if you follow up the river which passes under Bridge of Balgy on the fine road from Loch Torridon to Shieldaig you climb in a short distance to Loch Damh, shaped like a boomerang between impressive hills. Take the track on the east side of the Balgy if you intend to walk the shore for any distance, for the west path peters out at the loch, and the deep burn is quite difficult to ford. In fact you can walk right through the hills south to the public road above Loch Kishorn if you have

Loch Damh above the Bridge of Balgy

a mind. Better still however is just to climb some of the way up Ben Damh for a bird's eye view of the rather secret loch.

The advantage of climbing is that you see the north-south setting in relation to the high peaks of Liathach and Beinn Alligin stretching west to east across Loch Torridon. Four miles long by ¾ of a mile broad, the loch is 206 ft in maximum depth with a mean of 59 ft. The bed is in three basins separated by shallower water. The largest and deepest in the centre of the loch stretches for 2½ miles. The north basin reaches a maximum of only 34 ft, but the southern basin goes down to 135 ft maximum. The fishing for salmon, sea trout, *Salmo ferox* and brown trout is good.

Loch Dhugaill: this little loch lies over the other side of Ben Shieldaig on the public road from Shieldaig to Kishorn and properly belongs to the Applecross peninsula. Situated on the fringes of the most westerly stand of Caledonian pine forest in Scotland, it too contains salmon, sea trout and what I've been told is yellow trout.

Shaped like a narrow triangle pointed north-west the loch is just over ½ a mile long by ¼ of a mile broad at the base, but the maximum depth is 108 ft in the middle with a mean of 38 ft.

Lochs of the Gairloch Basin

Lochs na Houigh, Vallich, á Ghobhainn, Braigh Horrisdale, Badachro, Bad an Sgalaig

North across Upper Loch Torridon behind the peaks of Beinn Alligin and Beinn Dearg lie the strange lochs of the Flowerdale Forest in the roadless country which stretches to the narrow neck of land between Gairloch and Loch Maree.

Loch na h-Oidhche or Loch na Houigh and Loch a Bheallaich or Vallich are the most inaccessible of the lochs, lying on different sides of the 2,869-ft peak of Bus Bheinn. The first named is the higher of the two at 1,250 ft above sea-level and there is a good path to it from a footbridge just east of Loch Bad an Sgalaig on the Gairloch–Loch Maree road. An hour and a half would see you up there in the impressive hollow between steep peaks, Beinn Dearg to the south, and Beinn an Eoin to the east.

The oval loch trending NNW–SSE is 1¾ miles long by ½ a mile in maximum breadth and reaches 121 ft in depth near the centre forming on the whole a simple basin.

Loch Vallich lies only a mile or so westward and can be reached in a rough walk round the end of Bus Bheinn, otherwise you must make the long approach from the north-west at Shieldaig near Badachro. Loch Vallich is narrower and lies at a more westerly angle than the first mentioned. The length is the same, 1¾ miles, but the breadth is less than ½ a mile, the mean being ¼ of a mile. The depth too is less, 92 ft maximum near the middle western portion.

The loch has three basins in its complex formation, each more than 50 ft deep but separated by shallower water coinciding with constrictions in shape. Half a mile from the west end near the southern shore the rocks are covered by only two feet of water.

A short outlet stream no more than 200 yds leads out of Loch Vallich into Loch á Ghobhainn, an elliptical opening only ¾ of a mile long by ⅓ of a mile broad and 28 ft in maximum depth, and the outflow leads to a similar globular water in Loch Gaineamhach. Following down the stream beyond you come to Loch Braigh Horrisdale in four miles. Shallow and roughly triangular in shape the length is ¾ of a mile by ⅓ of a mile in maximum breadth with a greatest depth of 51 ft in the central portion.

Loch Bad a Chroth or Badachro receives the outflow of the above, but the loch is hardly more than an expansion of the river and all of it except 10 per cent is under 10 ft depth, but the maximum is 23 ft. The mean depth of the weedy loch is 6 ft. It is good for salmon and sea trout running up the short distance from the sea.

Loch Bad an Sgalaig: this loch fed from Loch na Houigh, mentioned at the beginning of this section, has been harnessed for electricity with disastrous effects to the Kerrysdale Falls. The impressive cascade is now inside a pipe and the glen is no more than a receptacle for this monstrosity. Such bad taste is not typical of the North of Scotland Hydro-Electric Board whose workings are normally unobtrusive. This is an eyesore running beside the public road replacing a scene of marvellous beauty with ugliness.

The dam at the neck of the glen which contains the water is tiny enough, and its effect has been to join together the Dubh Loch to the south with Loch Bad an Sgalaig in a total length of just over 2 miles by ½ a mile in maximum width. The capacity of the new reservoir is 920,000,000 gallons and the 1,250 kilowatt powerhouse is ½ a mile below the dam.

The Gairloch Angling Club have the fishing rights. There is pike as well as brown trout.

Lochs of the Carron Basin

Lochs Sgamhain and Dhoughaill (Doule)

Leaving Achnasheen and Loch Gowan behind you on the run south-westwards to Kyle of Lochalsh, you pass from the eastward drainage system of the Conon to the western drainage of the Carron, and the first loch of this basin is Loch Sgamhain beneath the 3,000-ft peak of Moruisg. Not a very inspiring country scenically—too much bare foreground and not enough inspiring background, nor is the loch itself of special interest though it is good for salmon, sea trout and char. A mile long by $\frac{1}{3}$ of a mile in maximum width, the maximum depth is 72 ft.

Loch Dhoughaill, or Doule, at Achnashellach is more exciting, set beneath the crags of Fuar Toll where Forestry Commission plantings mingle with Caledonian pines in Coire Lair. Good paths lead into the hills on the north side, with cross-country routes to Torridon, over high or low passes as preferred.

The loch itself is 2 miles long by rather less than $\frac{1}{2}$ a mile in maximum breadth, tapering off until it is merely an expansion of the River Carron. The maximum depth of 179 ft occurs near the top end and like Loch Sgamhain there is salmon, sea trout and char. There are long hard ways east across the hills to Loch Monar.

Salt-water Loch Carron at Plockton, and rising behind it the hills of Applecross

Because the Conon and the Shin drainage basins encroach so far west, the Loch Broom catchment is small leaving only two lochs to be dealt with, Loch a' Bhraoin to the south and Loch Achall to the east of Ullapool. Loch a' Bhraoin, as mentioned in the Gruinard section, lay on the drove road for cattle driving through the hills by the Strath na Sheallag to the Dirrie More. Over 800 ft above sea-level you merely glimpse it from the Braemore–Dundonnell moorland road, but a lover of lochs should leave his car and walk the mile of track leading down to it.

Isle Martin and the Loch Broom basin seen from Ben More Coigach. The distant range centre is the Fannichs

The setting under the steep front of the Fannich peaks is not unrelieved wildness. Scrubby trees grow among the rocks. Shapely peaks rise to the west, the path along the shore steering for them before twisting north for An Teallach and the bothy of Shenavall—a superlative walk. Happy the man who could be dropped here by car and picked up at Gruinard or Dundonnell. Alternatively you could climb the 3,276 ft peak of A' Chailleach as I did and look over the loch into the great Fionn Loch wilderness, or exchange it by a turn of the head for the Beinn Dearg peaks whose eastern glens lead down to the Kyle of Sutherland.

Loch a' Bhraoin is over 2½ miles long by ½ a mile in maximum breadth and its greatest depth of 73 ft is reached half a mile from the outlet. It is a simple basin with a mean depth of roughly half its maximum. The trout are said to be good. The word Broom is from Bhraoin, meaning the place of rain showers.

Loch Achall is a popular trout and salmon fishing loch 2 miles east of Ullapool with Caledonian pines and mixed woodlands. Although you are so close to the Atlantic, the drainage from the next loch only 5 miles further on is to the North Sea. Loch Achall is just over 1¾ miles long by ½ a mile in maximum depth with a greatest depth of 70 ft near the centre. The floor is irregular with shallows among deeper water at the west end.

Lochs of the Garvie Basin

Lochs Lurgain, Bad a' Ghaill and Owskeich

Gavie Bay is an inlet of Enard Bay, the big inlet to the south of Lochinver on the Rhu Coigach and the connected lochs which feed each other are all notable for salmon and trout. To reach them means going north out of Ullapool and west at Drumrunie. This is the road to Achiltibuie and Reiff by Loch Lurgain on the south edge of the Inverpolly Nature Reserve. Go all the way to the sea if you would appreciate the contrasts between the bristling pinnacles of Stac Polly and the rocky grain of the interior, then the transformation of the green coastal fringe with its white crofts and cheerful outlook across the Summer Isles to the big peaks of Ross. The road is narrow and requires careful use of passing places. Beware of caravans.

Loch Lurgain is 4 miles long and just over ½ a mile in maximum breadth with heathery and rocky shores, and is divided into two basins by large islands and shallow water. The maximum depth is 156 ft with a mean of 61 ft. Despite being divided it can be regarded as a true rock basin, even to its outlet.

The east is the deeper basin and is simpler than the western one which in a central constriction has shallows with deeper water on both sides. Loch Lurgain when measured for temperature proved to have a wider range between top and bottom than any other loch in this district, no less than 5.8°, with a fall of 3.4° between 50 and 100 ft.

Loch Bad a' Ghaill: this is another true rock basin and the length is just over 2 miles by ¾ mile in maximum width, with a mean of ½ mile and a maximum depth of 180 ft. It is also in two basins, the south-eastern being deeper and larger.

Loch Owskeich is 1½ miles long by ¾ of a mile in maximum breadth and is a rock basin in low ground. There is deep water under the south-eastern shores which are steep compared to the gentler north-westerly slopes. The maximum depth is 153 ft and occurs 300 yds from the eastern shore.

Visitors who are thinking of climbing Stac Polly should not be put off by its rocky appearance. From the east ridge it is only a walk, all the pinnacles can be by-passed and the return journey can be done easily in two hours. It is worth it for the impression of the watery maze to the north.

Loch Bad a'Ghaill and Loch Owskeich from Ben More Coigach. On right Stac Polly
Lochan Tuath foreground

Lochs of the Polly Basin

Lochan Gainmheich and Loch Sionascaig

These two lochs are almost continuous, and the track in from the cairn and Nature Conservancy notice board on Loch Lurgain near Linneraineach cottage offers one of the finest short walks in the Highlands. Its main charm is the vista which opens before you over the low pass as you see the water maze of the lochs winding over low moor, the feeling of space heightened by monolithic peaks springing up from it, Stac Polly immediately westward, Cul Beag east, and northward Cul Mor and the butt end of Suilven.

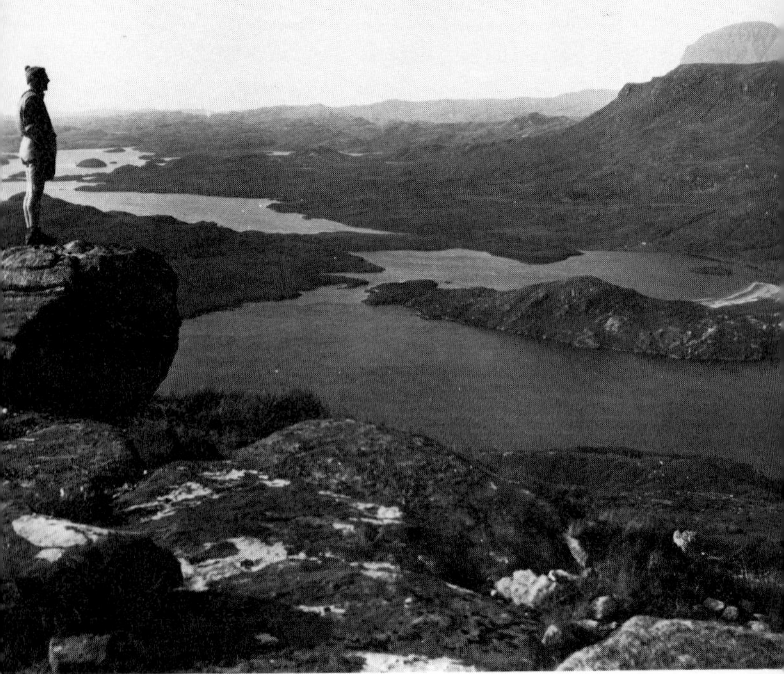

Lochan Gainmheich (foreground) and Loch Sionascaig with Suilven dominating an extraordinary Loch formation

Lochan Gainmheich is a short $1\frac{1}{4}$ miles along the path from Loch Lurgain, but if the day is fine it is better to take the right fork of the path and climb up Cul Mor a little to appreciate the uniqueness of the terrain below, where the squiggly shorelines enclose sandy bays, and densely wooded islands contrast with bare moor and pink Torridonian sandstone.

Lochan Gainmheich is almost divided in two by a headland, so has been measured in two portions, the southerly deeper basin, and the shallower northern one. The details are as follows. Southern portion, length 1 mile from east to west, and nearly $\frac{1}{2}$ a mile in maximum breadth, the centrally placed deepest part being 120 ft. The mean is 42 ft.

The northern part is only $\frac{1}{3}$ of a mile long by $\frac{1}{4}$ of a mile with a maximum depth of 59 ft and a mean of $24\frac{1}{2}$ ft. The bottom is more irregular than the southern portion and the outflow is into Loch Sionascaig. By following the north shore of the loch past the fishing bothy you can cross a plank bridge at the outflow and follow the path back to Loch Lurgain.

You would hardly follow the wriggling shorelines of Loch Sionascaig which are so irregular that they cover 17 miles, though the length measured from the south-east end to the north-west arm is 3 miles, and the mean breadth is $\frac{2}{3}$ of a mile. The *Bathymetric Survey* describes the contour lines of the floor as forming an intricate maze with the maximum depth 216 ft and the mean $60\frac{1}{2}$ ft. There are three main basins:

1 The whole main body of water surrounding the biggest island, Eilean Mor.
2 The north-east arm.
3 The north-west arm.

No. 1 is the largest and the deepest, with two areas exceeding 150 ft, the one to the south of Eilean Mor containing the greatest depth of 216 ft. There are two hills on the bottom to the west of Eilean Mor, the one nearest to the island covered by only 38 ft of water, the other being covered by 41 ft of water. No. 2 has a maximum depth of 137 ft and is much smaller than No. 1. No. 3 has a maximum depth of 66 ft and is cut off from the main basin by very shallow water.

These levels are three feet higher than they would be in nature, due to a sluice built to control the outflow of the loch and stabilise the flow of water for angling. It still operates.

The wooded islands are of outstanding botanical interest, Eilean Mor having large birch trees, and rowan almost pure over several acres, but heavy grazing by deer prevents natural regeneration. The island to the north of it is covered with smaller and more scrubby trees, birch, rowan and willow, with two-foot-high holly bushes in places. Black-throated divers breed and nesting redwings are no longer regarded as uncommon in this part of the world.

The fly fishing for brown trout is good, the average being about ½ lb although weights of 5 lbs and more are not uncommon. There is char in the loch also, but no salmon or sea trout due to an impassable fall. Permits to fish can be obtained from the Estate Manager's Office at Inverpolly, telephone Lochinver 252. There is a charge of £1 per day for each rod, and two boats are available, with or without ghillie.

The grey rocky knolls of Lewisian gneiss entrapping little lochans between them makes this north-westerly point of Ross seem like Sutherland with 8½ per cent of the land surface water. The reason why it was given Nature Reserve status was to conserve its great variety of aquatic, woodland, moorland and mountain habitats and let them evolve naturally with the minimum interference by man, yet exercise scientific control to repair the damage of prolonged misuse by overburning and overgrazing. The surviving trees can be taken as relics of a northern type scrub which once covered the whole region, but now survives only on the islands and in scattered blocks, some wet, and some well drained by their steep slopes.

The outflow of Loch Sionascaig by a miniature box canyon impassable to migratory fish is in contrast to the mile long sluggish flowing section which ends its short course to the sea. The water, running through peat, is deep and a good lie for salmon and sea trout. An electronic counter records that over 1,800 salmon and a few large sea trout go up annually, 70 per cent of them grilse. The tagging of salmon kelts has resulted in 6 previously spawned fish being recovered in other rivers; 1 from the Gruinard, 2 from the Naver, 1 from the Halladale and 2 from coastal nets, which proves that not all fish return to their home rivers.

Pearl fishing is also done in the middle stretches of the Polly where the mussel is abundant, also in the Allt an Strathain a little to the north. Intending pearl fishers should consult Inverpolly Estates. Tinkers or travelling folk are the main pursuers of this ancient craft.

Mention should also be made of the Lower Polly Loch which is only 200 yds away from the parking places on the Lochinver road. This little loch is at the top of the Polly, and July and August are the best months for salmon and sea trout.

Permit holders should consider fishing some of the remoter lochs away from the road, even if it means a walk of a mile or two. These lochs are seldom fished, and for very little trouble the rewards can be high. The Estate Manager at Inverpolly issues a little guide with the permit showing where all the available lochs lie.

There are also hill lochs like Coulin, Adder, Sand, Stack and Loch of the Island which may be fished, so there is no lack of opportunity in this part of the world. Wandering over this big area it soon becomes clear why this rough ground could never support more than just a few crofters growing barley and potatoes and grazing a few black cattle.

Lochs of the Kirkaig Basin

Lochs Borralan, Urigill, Cam Loch, Veyatie, a' Mhiotailt, Fionn Loch

Because Loch Veyatie and the Fionn Loch form the boundary of the Inverpolly National Nature Reserve, Knockan Cliff Visitor Centre at the eastern end is a good place to stop on the run north between Ullapool and Inchnadamph. Here indeed is contrast, where an outcrop of limestone makes an oasis of green in surroundings of bog and rock. The Nature Conservancy have made a big effort to interpret the country for you here, with information, explanation and ideas for walks and motor trails. The jargon name for this is 'Interpretative Conservation'.

Knockan is geologically famous since its exposure of old rocks folded over young played an internationally important role in the understanding of structural geology. The explanation of stresses on the earth's crust forcing old rocks over young was deduced hereabouts and with the aid of the Knockan Cliff Geological Nature Trail pamphlet you can glean something of the nature of these cataclysmic forces.

The name given to it here is the Moine Overthrust and it occurred about 400 million years ago during the Caledonian mountain building movements when a wave of schist a hundred miles long came from the east and over-rode the gneiss in a great crumpling and crushing action, forcing the gneiss onto its crest in places. This petrified sea is all about you here, with quartzite of Cambrian age and infinitely older Torridonian sandstone.

The epitome of all this is expressed in the view from the crofts of Elphin looking over the limestone green to the sandstone Matterhorn of Suilven, rearing up over hummocks of gneiss. Impossible to walk in a straight line to it because of the Kirkaig lochs which form the Assynt frontier. The finest guidebook to it is *The Inverpolly Motor Trail*, written to interpret the wild life and scenery of the 50-mile circuit round Suilven by Skiag Bridge, Lochinver and Drumruinie.

Loch Borralan by Altnacealgach Hotel lies furthest to the east in bare peaty ground and is weedy almost everywhere. Length just over 1 mile by $\frac{1}{4}$ of a mile in maximum breadth, the greatest depth is 21 ft. A good trout loch, its remarkable feature for a shallow loch is its abundance of char. It decants into the Cam

Loch as does Loch Urigill to the south-west.

Loch Urigill like all the other lochs in this basin trends south-east–north–west and it is nearly 2 miles in length with a maximum breadth of $\frac{3}{4}$ of a mile and a maximum depth of 40 ft at the north-west end. Weedy and generally shallow, the mid-loch section is covered by only 3 ft of water. The trout are good.

Cam Loch makes a mirror for the most dramatic view of Suilven, thrusting up in two prongs of sandstone and looking much higher than its 2,399 ft. There is a path along the north side of the loch from Ledbeg, a mile north of the Ledmore junction, but it does not go all the way to the mountain and walking is rough after four miles.

It is a good way to see the Cam Loch which is a shallow rock basin $2\frac{3}{4}$ miles long and $\frac{3}{4}$ of a mile broad, maximum depth 122 ft. Cam, meaning ‘crooked’, is a true description for a

The first plunge of the Eascoul Aulin waterfall which drops 600 ft

miniature Sionascaig even to islands, one of them large, Eilean na Gartaig by name. Another, Eilean na Gaoithe, has a fin of shingly sand projecting 100 yds from its northern point, the islands being situated at the south-eastern end, which is shallow.

The main basin is north-west where two soundings of 122 ft occur separated by a mile. The north-eastern shore with its little cliffs drops steeply, a sounding of 91 ft being taken only 20 ft from the side. The floor of the loch is composed of Archean rocks in the west, with Torridonian and Cambrian strata in the central and east portions. A wild torrent flows out from it into Loch Veyatie.

Loch Veyatie is only half a mile from Elphin and it has good relics of the northern scrub birch along its southerly shore. It is 4 miles long but less than $\frac{1}{2}$ a mile wide and the maximum depth is 126 ft, with a mean of 41 ft. It is a rock basin, and evidence shows it was once connected to the Fionn Loch, when it would be $7\frac{1}{2}$ miles long, with an offshoot arm where Loch a' Mhiotailt is situated.

Uneven on the floor with a few islands dotted along its shores it is dominated by Cul Mor on one side and Suilven on the other, with little Loch a' Mhiotailt lying between it and Loch Sionascaig.

Loch a' Mhiotailt is just over $\frac{1}{2}$ a mile in length, $\frac{1}{4}$ of a mile in maximum breadth and the maximum depth is 69 ft. Lying at right angles to Loch Veyatie the two lochs become one in heavy rainfall when the rock and sand barrier is covered. I have only looked down on it from the top of Cul Mor and Suilven, for the loch is almost imprisoned in steep hillocks of gneiss.

Fionn Loch lies $\frac{3}{4}$ of a mile north-west of Veyatie under Suilven. The easiest walk in is from Inverkirkaig following the river past fine waterfalls to the Fionn Loch in 5 miles of good path. Suilven is hardly more than 2,000 ft above you here, and the scramble up between the two peaks by the gully is easy. No rock climbing is involved and there is no better position for appreciating the watery topography of Inverpolly and Assynt.

Recommended centres for exploration are Ullapool, Inverkirkaig, Achiltibuie and Lochinver. My own choice would be Achiltibuie for the charm of Rhu Coigach and the views west from the crofts over the Summer Isles to the big peaks of Ross.

Lochs of the Inver Basin

Lochs Assynt, Leitir Easaich, Maol a' Choire, Awe, Beannach, Druim Suardalain, na Doire Daraich

Loch Assynt takes its name from the rockiest parish in Britain and is the six-mile remnant of a more horseshoe-shaped loch, before it was silted up by the Loanan at the top and the cutting back of the Inver at the bottom where the alluvial terraces are still traceable. Situated on the Traligill Fault, there are sharp contrasts between the limestone-rich greens of Inchnadamph beneath grey Ben More, highest peak in Sutherland, and the sea of gneiss from which protrudes the eroding tooth of Suilven in an advanced state of decay. When the pink of sunset glows on this strange landscape it responds like snow, paling gradually to bleached bones, leaving only the loch afire. In wind and rain no other part of Scotland is more inhospitable. Yet the magic of Assynt is such that you will want to come back again and again, for it holds so much that is secret.

It has disappearing streams and potholes linked by passageways dangerous because of the speed at which they can flood in an area of 100 in. of rain per annum. It has caves which have been described as '. . . among the most interesting archaeological sites in Scotland'. It has limestone pavements similar to the Burren in Ireland, rich in arctic-alpine flowers, and with a scrub vegetation common in Norway but rare in Scotland. By contrast to this low plateau, the gneiss reaches its highest elevation in Scotland at over 3,000 ft on Ben More.

The caves of the Allt nan Uamh 2 miles south of Loch Assynt have yielded up exciting finds to various excavators, the bones of red deer, reindeer, brown bear, northern lynx, badger, otter, northern vole, arctic lemming and the remains of hundreds of ptarmigan compared to only a few of those of red grouse; evidence that Scotland was a more arctic land when streams began depositing these remains in the caves.

More recent discoveries include the remains of two people belonging to the Mesolithic or even Neolithic period, representing the earliest men in Scotland. Excavations of other caves nearby are yielding similar results but more is likely to come to light as digging goes on. The caves are easily reached by walking for a mile up the south bank of the Allt nan Uamh when you will see them below the north-facing limestone cliff. The connecting channels are dry. The big system of underground passages is higher up with about 1,200 feet of passages.

Behind Inchnadamph Hotel at the top of Loch Assynt the Traligill Burn disappears underground before ending in the loch. Higher up there are more caves and something like 1,500 ft of passages. This is the Cnoc nan Uamh system at 750 ft O.D., and the dry entrance is the 'Cave of the Roaring'—Uamh an Tartair. Going in from here you come to water which plunges down a deep pothole and the 'Cave of the Waterslide'—Uamh an Uisge.

This area is part of the Inchnadamph National Nature Reserve whose boundaries on the north and south are the two streams I have described. Between them lies the undulating limestone plateau with its pavements, sink holes, caves, disappearing streams and willow scrub. Three-quarters of the limestone plateau is composed of an eroding peat cover, where pine trees once grew. The real delight is the flowers. Raven and Walters writing in *Mountain Flowers* (Collins New Naturalist) say,

> There are few botanical centres in Britain more rewarding than Inchnadamph itself, nor any better suited to the indolent. Within a hundred yards of the hotel, on the banks of the Traligill Burn, grow fine clumps of the rare grass *Agropyron donianum*, not to mention an abundance of *Trollius*. Within a quarter of a mile, on the long limestone cliff running southwards, not only purple saxifrage (*S. oppositifolia*) and the *Agropyron* but dark red helleborine (*Epipactis atrorubens*) and the sedge *Carex rupestris* are in unusual plenty. Nearby, in a locality which it is perhaps unwise to define too closely, grows Norwegian sandwort (*Arenaria norvegica*). Barely half a mile to the north of the hotel, on the rabbit-grazed south-facing slopes of a shallow valley, is one of the only two known Scottish stations of *Alchemilla minor*; while on the flat bottom of the valley, which consists of very wet stony patches beside a stream, there grows, amidst a mass of yellow mountain saxifrage (*S. aizoides*), a little of the hair sedge (*Carex capillaris*). Add to this that mountain avens (*Dryas octopetala*) is everywhere abundant, and the attractions of the place should be obvious.

The attractions are plenty, and there is historical interest as well in the skeletal ruins of Ardvreck Castle on a promontory near the head of the loch—the place where the great Montrose was betrayed for £20,000 and 400 bolls of meal, to be led on horseback through the Highlands to Edinburgh and hanged in the Grassmarket on 21 May 1650, a bitter end for one of the least self-seeking men in Scottish history.

You can crawl into the dungeons of Ardvreck Castle and see the cannons beneath the stonework. The osprey used to nest on these ruins. There is another memorial which should be visited, at Inchnadamph on a knoll above the loch where the famous geologists B. N. Peach and J. Horne are commemorated for their outstanding work in this classic area. They also uncovered the earliest human evidence of burnt stones, hearths, split bones and sawn reindeer antlers in the Allt nan Uamh caves, together with remnants of prehistoric fauna described earlier in this section, evidence dating back 8,000 years to the Mesolithic era.

The bareness of Loch Assynt is relaxed as you go west along the 6⅓ miles of its length into lower country with trees and islands to enliven the scene as the shoreline becomes more broken by bays under the fine peaks of Quinag—The Water Stoup. A delightful path crosses low over the west flank to the crofting township of Nedd on the coast road, while a short distance further west is the fault-line of Glen Salach where the narrowing tail end of Loch Assynt makes a sharp dog leg.

Looking at the country it is not surprising to learn that Loch Assynt has an irregular floor of different rock structure, Cambrian and Torridonian at the upper end close to the base of Quinag, while the remainder is Archean gneiss, the whole occupying an ancient consequent valley.

The fishing for trout, sea trout, salmon and *Salmo ferox* is good but the loch has a reputation for being squally. Boats are available at Inchnadamph Hotel, and the fishing to non-residents is 50p per day. Char also occurs in the loch. Nearly a mile broad, with a mean breadth of ½ a mile, Loch Assynt attains a maximum depth of 282 ft with a mean of 101 ft, its area being nearly 2,000 acres. There are four areas exceeding 200 ft, the deepest hole being north of Eilean Assynt. The numerous bays are deep.

Loch leitir Easaich: this small loch at the entrance to Glen Salach and separated from Loch Assynt by only a few yards of streams, was originally a part of the larger loch before its level was lowered by natural means. Now they are separated by a fine waterfall, but the rock basin has only 4 per cent covered by more than 50 ft of water in a maximum length of just over ½ mile by ⅖ mile, with a maximum depth of 70 ft. The fishing is salmon and brown trout and permit arrangements are the same as for Loch Assynt. The local name for the loch is Letteressie and its main feature of interest is its irregularity of outline.

Loch Maol a' Choire is at the Inchnadamph end of the loch and lies inside the Nature Reserve though there is a boat on it and the hotel has the fishing rights. The walk to it by footpath up the Traligill Valley is very fine and fishermen call it the Gillaroo Loch, because, say the Nature Conservancy, '. . . of the alleged resemblance of its trout to the so-called Gillaroo trout of Loughs Neagh and Melcin and the Galway Lakes, in Ireland'. None of these distinctive fishes appears to have been caught for a very long time, possibly because of stocking with trout from other sources. The Gillaroos here had apparently reddish fins but no red spots. Plaster casts of specimens may be seen in the hotel, and the opinion of experts is that the high alkalinity of the water and the abundance of molluscs is reminiscent of the Irish environment.

This hill loch is 600 yds long by 250 yds broad and the maximum depth is 8 ft. South of the loch in the cave pool of the Allt nan Uamh has been found a rare survivor of the Ice Age, the collembolid *Onychiurus schoetti*.

Loch Awe: this small loch, only 7 ft deep and much overgrown, lies just off the road 4 miles south of Inchnadamph, but it is a good salmon loch and fishing arrangements are as for the other lochs. The length is 1,400 yds by 530 yds, and the mean depth is 5 ft.

Loch Beannach: you find this loch north of the stream of the Inver, 2 miles west of Loch Assynt, a fine sinuous loch with wooded islands on a hinterland dotted with lochs stretching all the way to Rhu Stoer and round to Nedd, miles of nothing but watery maze. Beannach is a shallow rock basin in Archean gneiss 1¾ miles long by ⅓ of a mile in maximum breadth with a maximum depth of 38 ft in its south-westerly portion.

Loch Druim Suardalain is another small rock basin, one of a chain in an ancient valley, length $\frac{3}{4}$ of a mile by $\frac{1}{4}$ of a mile with a maximum depth of 31 ft and a mean depth of only 10 ft.

Loch na Doire Daraich: the other name for this is Loch Culag and fishing is available from Culag Hotel for sea trout and brown trout. Lying close to the village of Lochinver, the length is $\frac{1}{2}$ a mile by $\frac{1}{4}$ of a mile, with a mean depth of only $3\frac{1}{2}$ ft and a maximum of 9 ft.

Anglers coming to this district would be well advised to join the Assynt Angling Club for the right to fish over 30 lochs in Assynt. Details can be had from the Commercial Bank, Lochinver, telephone Lochinver 215.

Visitors to the Inchnadamph Nature Reserve should obtain permission from the Assynt Estate Office, Lochinver, telephone Lochinver 203, for any visit between 15 July and 15 October, and for visits by parties of more than six at any time of the year. Research workers from museums and universities are encouraged.

Climbers interested in Suilven will find a good track leading into the hills just north of Loch Culag. The mountain has the hump of a huge haystack from this angle with many verticalities. The easy way is to keep walking until the whole ridge comes into view, then strike up the easy ground between the peaks. It makes a superb and not too strenuous expedition of about 12 miles return journey plus 2,399 ft of ascent.

Walkers should consider making one rather special expedition which has to do with lochs only in passing. It is the Eas Coul Aulin—The Maiden's Tresses—waterfall which drops from a western spur of the Ben More Assynt range into the head of Loch Glencoul. The fall is over 600 ft, and the 'tresses' are where the white column of water splits into two before dividing again into many strands on the dark rocks.

I went to it from Loch Ganvich on the summit of the Inchnadamph–Kylesku road, on a rocky path going eastward to the summit of the Bealach a' Bhurich, high enough to be a fine viewpoint for the wild peaks on both sides. Nor shall I forget the little lochan beneath the pass where sandpipers were flitting and a ring ouzel was sending out its thin cry, mournful as a wader.

The point to remember is not to contour too far to the south-west as you go down. Better to strike off at the first burn by a series of heathery steps on the steepening mountainside. In a short distance you come to a lip of bare rock and the sight of the sparkling water making a rainbow mist against the blue sea-loch far below. On this open hillside the whole atmosphere is of light and brightness, the green glen below adding to that impression.

Go in the sunshine after wind and rain and you won't be disappointed. Lacking big drainage it can drop to a trickle in drought. Nevertheless the walk should not be missed. Allow three hours for the return journey. Reflect too that the Eas Coul Aulin which debouches so close to the sea, is yet within only 3 miles of the easterly drainage by the Gorm Loch Mor and the Cassley, a striking example of the short west coast rivers in relation to those flowing east from the watersheds.

Lochs of the Shin Basin

Lochs Shin, a' Ghriama, Merkland, Fiodhaig, Gorm Loch Mor, Ailsh, Craggie, an Daimh, Migdale, an Lagain, Buidhe

Lairg on the railway is the hub of the mail bus service serving the long straths which lead to the west and north, with connections to such destinations as Bettyhill, Tongue, Durness, Scourie and Lochinver. This is the country where Norse names mix and conjoin with Gaelic. Suilven is an example: Sul is the Norse for Pillar, but Bheinn is the Gaelic for mountain, with 'ben' its shortened form. Sutherland itself comes from the Norse Sudrland, meaning the Southern Land, which it was to the Vikings.

This is the emptiest part of Britain today, as anyone who travels along the long Sutherland straths to the coast will discover. This is the classic ground of the clearances, where crofters were dispossessed from the best land to make way for

Loch Shin since hydro-electrification

sheep and burned out if they resisted. The dates 1814 to 1819 are bitterly remembered in Sutherland as evicted men crossed the Atlantic in overcrowded emigrant ships to try a new life in Canada or tried to eke out a living on the rocky coast. The decline in fertility was rapid due to overgrazing by sheep and overburning to promote grazing growth.

Loch Shin, since hydro-electrification, is the fourth biggest loch in Scotland and has jostled Loch Shiel from that position into fifth place. Narrow and bleak for much of its 17.8 miles it needs the colour of sunset on clouds and hills to be beautiful. Forestry is improving it in places and the views out to Ben More Assynt are fine, but the main attraction of this sheet of water is to anglers. The trout are good, and the Lairg Angling Club supply permits. There is also a Club Hut at the lochside beyond the Lairg Dam where permits and boats can be obtained.

The narrowness of Loch Shin relative to its length makes it akin to Loch Shiel, but the mean breadth is no longer 3 per cent of the length due to the hydro-electric alterations and capture of the headwaters of the rivers Cassley, Brora and other streams. The mean breadth now is 0.7 miles and the maximum 1.3 miles opposite Fiag Bridge. The raise of level was 37 ft, which would make the greatest depth 199 ft, though half the irregular bottom is covered by less than 100 ft.

Hydro-electrification begins at the top western end of the loch where the Cassley, whose natural flow is into Strath Oykell, is diverted by aqueducts to power a small power station before being tunnelled 2½ miles to a main power station on the west shore of Loch Shin. Electricity generated here is carried to the Durness region, the output being 10 megawatts.

Loch Shin itself has a storage capacity of 64.4 million units of electricity contained behind a dam 1,400 ft long and 40 ft high. A mile below the dam there is another dam, and the water contained between them is known as Little Loch Shin, the lower dam being known as the Shin diversion weir. A power station at the outlet of the top dam provides the local electricity supply.

Fish lifts in both dams enable salmon to enter or leave both lochs, or they can be trapped and stripped of their eggs and milt for artificial rearing in the hatchery for subsequent release in tributaries of the Shin. Compensation water to maintain the flow in the river is passed through a small tubular turbine, but the main station is 5 miles down at Iveran.

A 5-mile-long tunnel leads the water down to a concrete-lined shaft 200 ft deep and 45 ft in diameter, feeding into a steel-lined pressure tunnel 1,700 ft long and 13½ ft in diameter ending in twin 9-ft-diameter steel pipes. The Shin station is of Tarradale stone and discharges the water after use through a 1,900-ft open-channel tail race, with an electric screen at its outlet to prevent salmon from entering. The capacity is 12 megawatts.

Group control of all the Shin valley stations is maintained here by power line carrier telephone from Shin to Cassley and Lairg switching stations. A submarine cable crossing Loch Shin for part of the way leads to Cassley. Power from the main station at Shin connects to Beauly in Ross-shire and Mybster in Caithness.

Canoeists can have fun by paddling up Loch Shin and turning north at Loch a' Ghriama and reaching Loch Merkland in about 2 miles of portaging and continuing north-west after crossing the watershed into the Laxford system. A few adventurers do it, and there can be few more worthwhile ways of enjoying a journey of increasing interest as the peaks of Reay draw nearer.

Loch a' Ghriama can be regarded now as the northerly tip of Loch Shin, length in its own right 1½ miles, breadth just over ⅓ of a mile and maximum depth in the centre 64 ft. The brown trout fishing is free to visitors staying in Overscaig Hotel.

Merkland is a narrow ribbon like Shin but has much more character, due to its steeper shores and closing hills, an easy place to watch black-throated divers and listen to their wailing cries. The length is 3 miles but the mean breadth is just ¼ of a mile and the maximum a little over ⅓ of a mile. The maximum depth close to the narrows at the head of the loch is 85 ft and there is an interesting example of the build up of alluvium from burns entering from opposite sides and raising the bottom by their debris. The cone of the Allt nan Albannach on the north-east is smaller than the one laid down by the Garbh Allt to make a shoaling where the depth is only 31 ft, with deep water on both sides of the alluvium. Overscaig Hotel has the brown trout fishing rights.

Loch Fiodhaig, or Fiag, is a hill loch most easily reached from Loch Shin by following up the stream from Fiag Bridge. It is a good moorland trout loch with islands. The length is $1\frac{1}{2}$ miles and the maximum breadth is $\frac{2}{3}$ of a mile. The maximum depth is 71 ft and the mean depth is 26 ft.

Gorm Loch Mor: apart from Loch Shin this mile-long sheet of water on the high plateau east of Ben More Assynt has the distinction of being the deepest in the basin with a maximum sounding of 91 ft. Irregular, and with many islands, the maximum width is just over $\frac{1}{2}$ a mile, though the mean is less than half of that. The streams which feed it are only 3 miles or so from the Atlantic, yet they drain eastward. The loch itself lies relatively close to the big waterfall of the Eas Coul Aulin mentioned in the last section.

The Gorm Loch Mor is a true rock basin in mainly Cambrian quartzite with evidence of glaciation all around it, relics of the times when the ice from Ben More overflowed over this ground into Loch Shin. The islands on the Gorm Loch Mor are themselves moraines—a place to visit for those who are willing to make an effort to get to a wild and remote place.

Loch Ailsh is on the River Oykell whose strath running due west from the Shin Power Station has been described as the most beautiful in the Highlands and was the route followed by the ill-fated Montrose. A track branches north-east to the loch just 2 miles south of Altnacealgach Hotel. This is a trout loch with occasional salmon and it is shallow, being no more than 24 ft in maximum depth in a length of just under 1 mile by $\frac{1}{2}$ a mile in breadth. The Oykell flows through it and it lies wholly within a sporting estate.

Loch Craggie: lies 3 miles south of the above, on the Strath Oykell road and is a true rock basin despite being only $\frac{2}{3}$ of a mile in length, less than $\frac{1}{5}$ of a mile broad and 40 ft in maximum depth.

Loch an Daimh: situated between Ullapool and Oykell Bridge it lies close to the watershed and in the natural course of events will be diverted towards the Atlantic by the cutting action of the Rhidorroch River. Narrow and attractively wooded on the south-east, it makes a fine foreground for the wild peaks of Seana Braigh and the Ben Dearg range which are the highest mountains north of the Grave–Ullapool road.

The loch occupies a fault dislocation and is $1\frac{3}{4}$ miles in length,

$\frac{1}{5}$ of a mile in maximum width and is 52 ft at maximum depth in the centre. The conformation is simple. The trout fishing is good. A cross country walker should be tempted by the overnight accommodation which can be found at either end of this route, at Ullapool and Oykell Bridge with 15 miles of good tracks between.

Loch Migdale is about a mile from Bonar Bridge on the Dornoch Firth and is 2 miles long by $\frac{1}{2}$ a mile broad, the greatest depth being 49 ft and the mean 21 ft. The island at the west end is artificial and there is a passageway to it covered by only shallow water. Burghfield House Hotel, Dornoch, has the brown trout fishing rights.

Loch an Lagain: is a small loch, length 1 mile by $\frac{1}{4}$ of a mile, only 18 ft in maximum depth, lying $3\frac{1}{2}$ miles north-east of Bonar Bridge.

Loch Buidhe lies 5 miles north-east of Bonar Bridge on the Strath Carnoch road to Golspie, and Burghfield House Hotel have the salmon and brown trout fishing rights. The length of the loch is $1\frac{1}{4}$ miles by just under $\frac{1}{4}$ of a mile width, the maximum depth of 36 ft occurring near the centre.

Lochs of the Laxford Basin

Lochs More, nan Ealachan, Stack, na Cla'ise Fearna, nam Bhreac

The Laxford drainage begins just over the watershed from Loch Merkland on the Shin. The distance separating the east and west drainage is only 2 miles, but at Loch More there is an immediate change of scenic contrast, the loch is wider, the shores steeper, natural woodlands cling to the gullies and above everything are the near peaks of pointed Ben Stack and the grey head of Arkle, a great bump of Cambrian quartzite.

Yet Loch More, fine as it is, merely introduces better things to

Loch More and Ben Stack

come. It is too uniform to be really exciting, with straight shores for its 4 miles of length and an unvarying width of ½ a mile. Dropping to 316 ft deep in the centre the conformation could hardly be simpler.

Loch nan Ealachan is the name given to the shallows of the top end, which are separated from the main loch by stepping stones, the maximum depth inside the subcircular basin being no more than 8 ft with a mean of just under 5 ft.

Loch Stack is the gem of the basin and may well be the finest trout, salmon and sea trout loch in Scotland. Add *ferox* and char to that, plus a range of wild life that includes pine marten, otter,

Westminster Estate where deer stalking, salmon fishing, farming and forestry combine at Achfarry

greenshank, black-throated diver, golden eagle, peregrine falcon and some of the finest red deer in Scotland, then look at the rocks and hanging birches hemming you in and you have the epitome of wildest Sutherland—a mixture of savagery and charm.

Sutherland does not give up its secrets lightly. The road goes along the south side of Loch Stack but no road goes round it past the keeper's house at Airdchuilian. Walk from there up the paths which climb the hills east, or go up Ben Stack if you would appreciate the setting. Or you can fish from a boat, at a price, by applying to Cape Wrath Hotel or Scourie or to Westminster Estates. Even without a fish, a day in a boat is worth while here.

The long side of Loch Stack adjoining the public road is 2½ miles and should be regarded as a long stroke of a rough letter H, with a shorter parallel under the grey bulk of Arkle. These two strokes form separate basins joined by no more than a shallow bar of water. Loch Stack is almost two lochs, the greatest depth of 108 ft being in the basin nearest to the road, one mile from the southern end. North-east under Arkle the top basin goes down to 85 ft, but the constriction between the two basins is covered by no more than 16 ft of water.

The big run of salmon occurs in summer, entering from the Laxford River, lax being the Norse word for salmon. The Royal Family sometimes fish here as guests at Loch Stack Lodge, sharing the loch with black-throated divers who are also honoured guests here, and protected against egg thieves.

Loch na Cláise Fearna is on the west road from Laxford Bridge *en route* to Scourie. A wriggly little loch only 38 ft deep with a large central island, the general shape is triangular with a narrow apex pointing north-east.

Loch nam Bhreac. Lies north-west of the last named just off the narrow road that goes to the remote crofting settlement of Foindlemore and not far from Tarbert. A loch which seems to be all arms and promontories with many islands; it is over a mile in maximum length and breadth variable over its 142 acres. The south portion is the widest and it contains the maximum depth of 71 ft, the mean being 28 ft. South-west of the large wooded island the depth is 66 ft, though 54 per cent is covered by less than 25 ft.

Lochs of the Scourie Basin
Loch an Laig Aird and Loch a' Bhaid Daraich

Scourie situated on greensward on hillocks above a sweep of bay is one of the most attractive places in north-west Scotland, its agricultural impact being all the greater for the rocks and bogs which lead to largish walled fields. The hotel has the fishing of some 280 lochs, five of them with salmon and sea trout, free to hotel guests. Fishing in Loch More and Loch Stack can be arranged. In this rocky world of lochs you hardly expect to find palm trees growing in the open, but they are here, proof of the mildness of this coast. They may be the most northerly palms in the world.

I have chosen to describe only two contrasting lochs which are

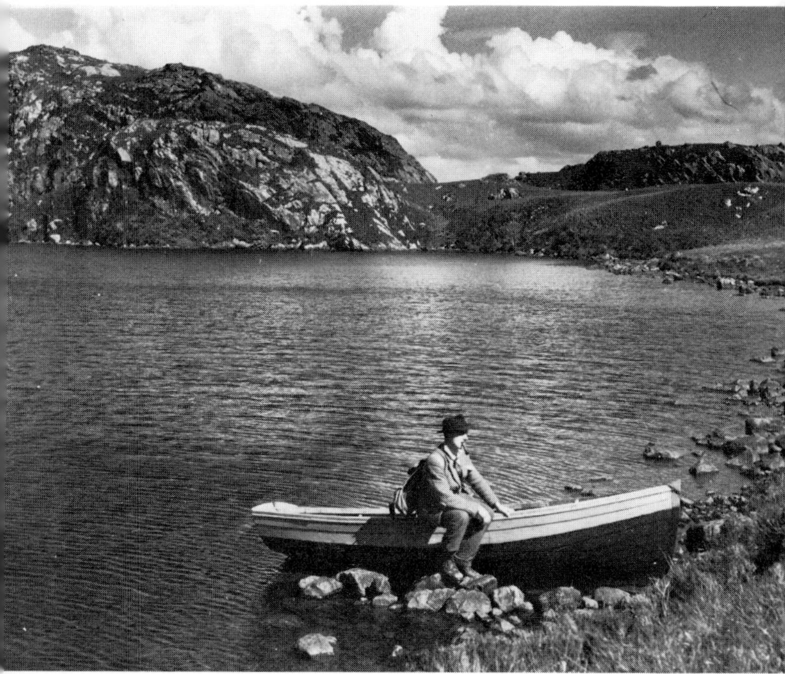

A typical hill loch around Scourie

typical of many. Loch an Laig Aird is a shallow irregular loch covering 67 acres with islands and a projecting promontory. The deepest sounding of 42 ft is south-west of this promontory near the shore. Of the remainder three-quarters of the loch is covered by less than 20 ft.

Loch a' Bhaid Daraich lies almost in the village and has attractive natural birch woods good for birds. A mile long and over one-third of a mile broad it is 121 ft deep in the centre, with a mean depth of $55\frac{1}{2}$ ft. The basin is flat bottomed and simple beneath good rock bluffs north and south.

Walkers who would like more intimate contact with this lochan studded landscape should consider walking the footpath from Duartmore Bridge to Loch Stack Lodge, a distance of seven miles. The daily mail bus would take them back to Scourie, or a return journey could be made by cutting down Strath Stack and hitting off a parallel footpath high above Loch an Leathaid Bhuain.

The tremendous roughness of this hinterland to the south of the Scourie–Laxford Bridge road has to be seen to be appreciated, bosses of gneiss imprisoning lochs each so planed by the passage of ice that the whole landscape has a scalped appearance. And on Eddrachillis Bay there is the same lumpy impression in the black islets where there is said to be one for every day of the year. The probability is that no one has ever visited every loch in this neighbourhood.

Look at the map of the flattish top of Scotland and you will notice three bites out of it towards Cape Wrath. The deepest is Loch Eriboll, with the Kyle of Durness to the west and the Kyle of Tongue to the east. Loch Hope must have been a fourth bite when the sea-level was higher, as raised beaches near its head and foot show. Even today the highest tides reach within a ½ mile of Loch Hope and in distant times must have lapped Ben Hope.

Standing at the outlet you are only 12 feet above sea-level, and the river emerging has only a mile to go to reach the sea; small wonder it is so good for salmon and sea trout. Loch Hope means 'The Loch of the Bay of the Harbour', a perfect description of its connection with Loch Eriboll, where King Haco anchored his fleet in the year 1263 and saw an October eclipse of the sun which

The outlet from Loch Hope

filled him with foreboding. The feeling of ill omen proved true immediately when men he sent ashore were slain by waiting Picts, though it was a trifle in the events which culminated in the Battle of Largs when the elements again played a vital part in the final Viking defeat.

Strange that history should repeat itself 670 years later when other warships assembled at Loch Eriboll, our own this time, to convoy supply ships in the Battle of the Atlantic when Britain was fighting for survival. Unlike the Vikings we did not lose, though the struggle was close at times.

The road that runs south down the east shore of Loch Hope passes the ruins of a drystone tower called Dun Dornadilla. The name Dornadilla is said to be taken from a Princess of the pre-Christian era. It is a good landmark for climbing Ben Hope by the Allt na Caillich Burn, which has considerable geological interest in the folded strata which show the layers of succession unusually clearly.

Look out for the alluvial terraces which are the remains of the 50-ft and 100-ft beach deposits. Just over 6 miles long, the maximum width of Loch Hope is ¾ of a mile with a greatest depth of 187 ft mid-way along its length. The floor is of uneven Lewisian gneiss and deformed schistose rocks with quartzite at the outlet.

Fishing for trout, salmon and sea trout is not absolutely private but can be arranged from Overscaig, Altnaharra, Bettyhill and Durness hotels. Unauthorised fishing is also done by the common seals who take advantage of the short river to hunt in what is almost an extension of the sea. Loch Hope fluctuates to such an extent that between high water in flood and low water in drought there is a difference of as much as 11 ft.

The surveyors who sounded the loch mention seeing the reputed remains of an old castle just above the surface of the water about a mile from the outlet and towards the eastern shore. There is a shallow here, with boulders to the west of it, but nothing seems to be known of the castle or its builders. Despite the uneven floor the mean depth for Loch Hope is high at 61½ ft. Only 45 lochs in Scotland have a higher mean, and in length it is 21st. Loch Assynt and Loch Naver exceed in the latter respect.

Loch Chalum and Loch an Dithreibh (Deerie)

These lochs lie in the remote country between Loch Loyal and Loch Hope. Weedy and with one large island in the middle, Loch Chalum is recognisably a shallow loch, the greater part of it being less than 10 ft deep. Measured from the south-west to the north-east it is $\frac{3}{4}$ of a mile long with a maximum breadth of $\frac{1}{2}$ a mile, with a greatest depth of 30 ft in the western portion. Loch an Deerie into which it drains by a deep burn is a much more exciting proposition, and that evening as I dropped down to it the surface held the yellows and reds of the sunset sky.

No loch I have camped beside has greater character than this one, with golden whins and birches beneath steep bouldery slopes with the drumming of snipe and the wailing of divers adding authentic notes. I climbed Ben Hope and Ben Loyal from here, enjoying warm sun beneath thunder showers, sometimes in a welter of black clouds and stinging hail, other times looking over moorlands glittering with peat hags to the yellow sands of the Kyle of Tongue only 3 miles distant.

The loch is $1\frac{1}{2}$ miles long and has a uniform width of $\frac{2}{3}$ of a mile with a narrower arm crooking to the north-east. It is deep, with a mean of 66 ft and a maximum in the centre of 157 ft. It is a true rock basin in gneiss, which is exposed on the great crag on its east side. Between the crook of the north-eastern arm and the main basin there is a rise in bottom which gives a sounding of 49 ft, deepening again to give a maximum of 59 ft to the smaller basin. Under the east face of Ben Hope lie many attractive lochans.

Loch Coulside drains into Loch Loyal by a mile of river. A mile long by only 250 yds broad, the maximum depth is only 14 ft with a mean of $7\frac{1}{2}$ ft.

Loch Loyal with the road running along its west shore under a striking peak has been perfectly described as being like a Wellington boot with the toe pointing west and the leg north. The length is $4\frac{1}{2}$ miles, with a maximum breadth of nearly a mile and a maximum depth of 217 ft. There are two deep basins separated by shallows about $2\frac{1}{2}$ miles from the foot of the loch.

Loch Loyal, looking north-east

The northern one contains the maximum depth, while the top basin reaches 137 ft. Altnaharra Hotel has salmon and trout fishing rights.

Loch Creagach (Craggie): only a short stream separates this loch from Loch Loyal and they must have been joined at one time; the barrier between is a mixture of morainic material and alluvium deposited by the stream. A terrace above the lochs points to their one-time continuity. The rock formation is mainly granite.

Length $1\frac{1}{2}$ miles by $\frac{1}{2}$ a mile, it resembles Loch Loyal in that there are two basins separated by shallow water, the deeper being the southern portion which has a maximum depth of 84 ft. The top end where the Borgie emerges is known as Loch Slain. The pleasant village of Tongue is only a short distance away, and near it is a small loch where a cow once picked up a French gold piece, a relic of the time when a French ship bringing money to assist the Jacobites foundered. The men escaped and were rounded up but the gold was never found. The cow seems to prove the story that it was thrown into the loch and later recovered by somebody local—all but an odd gold piece or two perhaps.

Lochs Naver, na Meide, a' Bhealaich, Choire, Syre

Loch Naver is 6 miles long by $\frac{2}{3}$ of a mile broad with a maximum depth of 108 ft in the widest part a mile from the western end. The mean is 39 ft on an irregular floor. Fishing for salmon, trout and sea trout can be arranged at Altnaharra, Bettyhill and Garvault Hotel, Kinbrace.

Loch na Meide is on the Loch Hope–Altnaharra road about 10 miles south of Tongue and its $3\frac{1}{3}$ miles is almost halved by a constriction in the middle. Over a mile wide at the southern end where it is deepest, maximum 63 ft, it is a true rock basin in Moine schists scooped out by ice radiating from the Ben Loyal and Ben Hope ice cauldron. Irregular in outline with little islands in the southern part the constriction which divides it is covered by only 2 ft of water.

Loch a' Bhealaich and Loch Choire: these two interesting lochs lie parallel to Loch Naver on the other side of Ben Klibreck and, separated by only 200 yds of stream, can be regarded as remnants of one continuous loch. The height difference between them is only 2 ft, and the deepest water of both lochs is nearest to their point of separation. The total length of the two is $4\frac{3}{4}$ miles of which Loch a' Bhealaich forms over $1\frac{1}{2}$ miles with a maximum depth of 80 ft. The maximum breadth is only $\frac{1}{4}$ of a mile, and the enclosed effect of the steep ground hemming it in is of a corrie loch.

Loch Choire is twice the length and breadth and nearly twice as deep at 151 ft. Tracks lead in from the west near Crask Inn, but from the east there is a road leading off the B871 to the shooting lodge at the wooded north-eastern end of Loch Choire.

Loch Syre: this small loch lies to the north of Loch Naver and has some little islands on its shallow water. The length is $\frac{3}{4}$ of a mile with a maximum breadth of just over $\frac{1}{2}$ a mile. The maximum depth is 12 ft and the mean $5\frac{1}{2}$ ft. The Naver should be followed down to the sea from this point for some exploration of the coast west of Bettyhill where at the end of minor branch roads are some of the remotest crofting communities in Scotland.

Altnaharra at the west end of Loch Naver

Lochs of the Brora Basin

Loch Brora

Loch Brora seen from the top of the bold Carrol Rock is constricted into three nearly separate blobs, the biggest to the north. These narrows are caused by the build-up of alluvium from the entering streams, the total length being 3½ miles, with a maximum breadth of nearly ½ a mile near the head, though the mean is only ¼ of a mile. The maximum depth of 66 ft is in the middle; the mean is 22½ ft.

The *Bathymetric Survey* records four basins in order from the outlet as follows:

1 A shallow basin with a maximum depth of 31 ft shallowing to 7 ft.
2 The basin which contains Eilean nam Faoileag, an island once fortified, and used in a later period by the Earl of Sutherland as a hunting lodge. The maximum depth is 43 ft shallowing to 9 ft.
3 The third and deepest basin containing the maximum depth of 66 ft shallowing to 4 and 7 ft.
4 In the fourth the depth is 59 ft to the south-east and 64 ft to the north-east.

The fishing for salmon, sea trout and brown trout is good, May and June being the best months. Burghfield House Hotel and the Sutherland Arms Hotel have fishing rights.

From the wooded loch a little excursion can be made by a path up the Blackwater to a Pictish broch known as Castle Cole on a narrow neck above the river in a fine defence situation of crag and defile. There are remains of fortifications also on Craig Bar on the south side of Loch Brora and numerous tumuli in the neighbourhood, green hummocks without history.

Lochs of the Helmsdale Basin

Lochs an Ruathair, Coire nan Meann, Leum a' Chlamhain, Araich-Lin, Truid air Sgithiche, nan Cuinne, a' Chlair, Baddanloch, Allt an Fheàrna, na Moine

These moorland sheets of water lie in the rather featureless country between Strath Ullie, noted for its gold, and Strath Halladale which drops enchantingly to Melvich Bay on the north coast; and in springtime if you motor this single-track road you have to watch out for lambs for the place is jumping with them. Rail and road run together to Forsinard, where the line swings away east to Caithness over roadless peat-hags. Immediately south of Forsinard and half way to Kinbrace lies Loch an Ruathair.

This is the loch nearest to the source of the Helmsdale and it contains trout and char in its rather shallow oval of water. Length 1½ miles, breadth ¾ of a mile and maximum depth 26 ft with a mean of half that amount, the bottom is flattish, its overspill joining the Helmsdale below Kinbrace.

Loch Coire nan Meann: famed for its good trout, this shallow loch which also contains char, is most easily reached from the branch road which goes west into Strathnaver. Roughly circular in shape with a diameter of ½ a mile it drains by a short stream into the next loch to be mentioned. It is a simple basin with a maximum depth of 33 ft and a mean of 11½ ft.

Loch Leum a' Chlamhain: only ¼ of a mile separates this loch from the above, and it too is good for large trout. The length is 1⅔ miles with a maximum breadth of just over ½ a mile, and the bottom is in two basins covered by shallower water between. The maximum depth of south and north basins is nearly the same, 51 ft and 50 ft respectively, the mean for the whole loch being 19½ ft.

Loch Araich-Lin or Arichlinie is a tiny loch immediately north-west of Kinbrace and contains trout and char in its shallow waters whose maximum depth is only 7 ft with a mean of 4½ ft. The length is ¾ of a mile and the breadth ⅓ of a mile. Inflowing streams are gradually silting the loch with alluvium.

Truid air Sgithiche, or Truderscaig, is another fine trout loch, and presumably private like all the rest. Lying due east of Ben Kliberick, the outline is triangular with the apex pointing north-east out of which the burn flows to Loch nan Cuinne. The length is just under a mile with a maximum width of $\frac{2}{3}$ of a mile and a maximum depth of 12 ft. Shallow and flat-bottomed, the mean depth is 6 ft.

Loch nan Cuinne: known locally as Rimsdale Loch. Garvault Hotel, Kinbrace have brown trout fishing rights, and must include Lochs a' Chlair and Baddanloch for these waters are virtually continuous, though 100 yards of stream separates the first from the other two.

Loch nan Cuinne is 3 miles long and of variable width, the mean being just over $\frac{2}{3}$ of a mile, though the central portion is $\frac{3}{4}$ of a mile broad. The maximum depth is 28 ft in the widest part, with an overall mean of $12\frac{1}{2}$ ft.

Loch a' Chlair: the passage between the first loch and this one is 5 ft deep and there is a great feeling of space, given presence by the distant peaks of Hope, Loyal, Morven and nearby Kliberick and Armine. This irregular water which is continuous with the next is measured separately. The length east to west is just over $1\frac{1}{2}$ miles with a north to south width of $1\frac{1}{3}$ miles, the mean being $\frac{3}{4}$ of a mile. The maximum depth is 32 ft with a mean of $13\frac{1}{2}$ ft.

Loch Baddanloch: this appendage is $1\frac{3}{4}$ miles long and 1 mile in maximum width, with a maximum depth of 42 ft and a mean of 17 ft. The level of these lochs can rise fairly quickly.

Loch Allt an Fheàrna: this mile-long loch of pear shape is $\frac{1}{2}$ a mile in maximum width and is 36 ft at deepest with a mean of 14 ft. It lies close to the above named into which it flows by a short stream.

Loch na Moine: the Helmsdale River emerges from this loch which is only $2\frac{1}{2}$ miles from Kinbrace. Only 8 ft in maximum depth, with a mean of $4\frac{1}{2}$ ft, it contains salmon and trout in its 1 mile long by $\frac{3}{4}$ of a mile wide waters. Its smallness is remarkable considering that it received drainage from an area 400 times greater than its size. One of the delights of this neighbourhood is the preponderance of greenshank in the wild floes, their sharp echoing cries a perfect complement to the wailing pipes of golden plover. On smaller lochs which must go unmentioned I have found the common scoter breeding, and there may be the odd wood sandpiper nesting if you know where to look.

The scene of the first goldrush was the Kildonan Burn after a round piece of gold weighing over half an ounce was found in the gravelly bed. The Duke of Sutherland had a ring made from it, but although a great deal of searching was done, nothing more was found for half a century until a native prospector Robert Gilchrist returned from Australia. He found gold near Kildonan Farm, alerted other prospectors who soon made a strike in the Suisgill Burn just to the north. Strikes were soon being made in other burns at Kinbrace and Berridale.

The goldrush settlements of tents was called Baile-an-Oir, 'City of Gold', and a signpost marks the spot today. The cost of staking a 40-square-foot claim in 1869 was £1 sterling per month. Regulations stipulated that one tenth of any gold found had to go to the Crown, and excisemen were on hand to extract their due.

The Bank of England analysed a sample and valued it at 759.9 gold, 22.7 silver, with alloy present at 17.4, including copper. Well-equipped miners were getting enough to give them 50p a day, though casual 'panners' were not so successful. But the 500 miners produced a local trade boom in Helmsdale and even the great Duke was pleased enough to send an ox and a cask of beer from Dunrobin Castle. He even organised a dinner for 300 miners at which the man who had sparked off the strike carved the joint.

The big goldrush did not survive the winter. It might have done if the miners had been permitted to explore towards the loch systems described in this chapter, but the sheep farmers and the sportsmen and gamekeepers wanted rid of the miners and were glad to see them go down the valley. The Excise figure of the gold taken was put around £11,000, but it would be a poor Highlander who would declare everything to the Crown. No doubt a few fortunes were made, and they may be made again by modern exploration companies who are showing renewed interest.

Caithness—Lochs of the Wick Basin

Lochs Scarmclate, Watten and Hempriggs

Ask nine out of ten people where the most northerly point of the British mainland lies and they will tell you John o'Groats. They would be wrong, for the true north point is Dunnet Head. South and west of it lie the low level lochs of the county which the Norsemen named Caithness when they colonised it about AD 880. The local tribes displaced fought like wildcats, and are remembered by the word Caithness which is derived from Catti. The boundary between Sutherland and Caithness follows closely the geological division of the old red stone where the peaks come to an end in Morvern and moorlands.

But it is by no means as dreary as Volume XV of the new *Statistical Account of Scotland* makes out, which reads:

> The general appearance of the county is flat and uninteresting; the only hills of any eminence forming the boundary with Sutherland. A great proportion of the ground consists of flat moor and heath, and there being no extent of trees, the interior has a dreary appearance. Along the sea coast, which is generally bold and rocky, the appearance improves; and, from the improvements now going on in various quarters, a more cheerful and pleasant aspect is given to it, especially along the high road from the south towards Thurso. There are a few sheets of water, but none of any extent or peculiar beauty of appearance, and there are no navigable rivers.

Travel there and you come across Norse names like Tister, Stemster, Wester and Hoy. There is even a 'Greenland', and no false description either to mislead any innocent to become a colonist, for it is a truly fertile place of swaying grasses loud with the trilling of skylarks, a farming rather than a crofting country, with broad fields full of sheep and cattle until you come to Brough, where the feeling is of being suddenly transported to the Hebrides, with dozens of white houses dotting the green strips and large peat stacks by every door. The blue sea and the rocky headland beyond the sweep of Dunnet Bay add to the feeling.

And like the Outer Hebrides, there is sharp contrast when suddenly the crofting land peters out and you are in a world of peaty hills and bog cotton lochs—except that this little world ends in a plunge of over 340 feet of cliff, and perched on the very brink is the dazzling pencil-stalk of Dunnet Head lighthouse.

What of the lochs? Loch Scarmclate is a typical shallow Caithness loch in boulder clay whose maximum depth is only 5 ft. Triangular in shape with a maximum length of nearly a mile, the maximum breadth is just over $\frac{1}{2}$ a mile. Situated in farming land, its floor used to be dredged for a white and calcareous mud found to the south of the island. Spread on the fields it marled the land.

Loch Watten: this 3-mile-long loch as a larger superficial area than any other Caithness loch. Situated mid-way between Wick and Thurso the maximum breadth is $\frac{3}{4}$ of a mile and the

Caithness—a country of moors and shallow lochs

maximum depth is 12 ft, though half of it is less than 6 ft deep. Salmon, sea trout and brown trout fishing are available.

Loch Hempriggs: situated 2 miles south-west of Wick, this sub-circular loch has a maximum depth of 8 ft and a diameter of ¾ of a mile.

For fishing Loch Watten apply:
Lochview Farmhouse, Watten. Telephone Watten 663
Portland Arms Hotel, Lybster. Telephone Lybster 208.

Loch of Wester, Heilen and St. John's

Loch of Wester is a mile long and is so close to sea-level at Sinclair's Bay that high tides find their way into the freshwater and make it salt for a time. Only 3 ft deep and shallower than the short river connecting it to the sea, it contains salmon, brown trout and sea trout. Permits are available from Lochview Farmhouse, Watten and Mr. Charles Dunnet, Aukhorn, Lyth.

Loch Heilen: two miles east of Dunnet Bay, this 1½-mile-long by ½-mile broad loch has a maximum depth of 5 ft and contains brown trout. Permits from Mr. Pottinger, Loch End Farm, Barrock, also Loch Watten Farmhouse.

St. John's Loch: this small sub-circular loch has a mean depth of only 4½ ft and a maximum of 7 ft in its less than ½ a mile diameter. Fishing permit from Northern Sands Hotel, Dunnet. Castle Mey, residence of the Queen Mother, lies east along the coast.

Lochs of the Thurso Basin

Loch More is another sub-circular loch less than ½ a mile in diameter with a maximum depth of 7 ft, half of the flat bottom being covered by less than 5 ft of water. Thirteen miles south of Thurso, it has a big reputation for salmon and trout fishing which is private.

Lochs of the Forss Basin

Loch Shurrey: this 1¼-mile-long loch lies 7 miles south of Reay in moorland country. Width less than ½ a mile, the maximum depth is 7 ft with a mean of 4 ft.

Loch Calder is the deepest loch in Caithness, and it was on its shore that Earl Rognvald Kali, founder of St. Magnus Cathedral and ruler of Orkney and Shetland, was struck on the face and killed. That incident occurred on 20 August 1158 at a place called Forsie, but his relics and the mutilated skull were not found until the last century in a cavity high in the north pillar of the Cathedral choir. This great find in the cathedral was to be rivalled in 1919 during restoration work when it was noticed that some stones high in the south pillar of the choir needed attention. They revealed a cavity containing bones and the battered skull of Earl Magnus who 804 years before, almost to the day, had been executed in a manner of his choice, by being struck on the middle of the head. The skull in the box showed the axe wound to be as described in the Orkneyinga Saga thus confirming the account of the execution which took place on Egilsay in 1115.

Think of the good Earls then, when you go to this loch which is a true rock basin in Caithness flagstones with a bottom of 85 ft. The length is $2\frac{1}{3}$ miles with a breadth of nearly 1 mile. The fishing is for brown trout, and permits are available from Lochview Farmhouse, Watten, or from 'The Tackle Shop', 23 Sinclair Street, Thurso.

There are plenty of other good fishing lochs in Caithness, mostly small and all of them shallow in a variety of settings where the main feature is the vast horizon and open skies. Water permits and further information can be obtained by writing to the County Development Officer, Wick, or to Thurso Fisheries Ltd, Thurso East, Thurso.

Account too should be taken of the numerous brochs of Caithness, sited near some of the lochs and at places where landings could be made from the sea as at Dounreay, Lybster, Scrabster, Castletown, Ham, Kirk o'Tongue, Borrogie, Skirsa Head, Freswickn Nybster, Tong Head, Keiss, Ackergill, Staxigoe, Papigoe, Hempriggs, Ulbster, Bruan, Occumster, Latheron, etc.

The brochs are one of the mysteries of Scotland, for they occur nowhere else in the world and a great weight of literature has grown up round them. Whoever built them in Caithness took full advantage of the Caithness flagstones which are so easily worked here that they do service as fences in some fields. The Old Red Sandstone of which the flags are composed is rich in fossil fish forms, and the thickness of the series is estimated at 14,500 feet.

The numerous chambered cairns in Caithness are of two types, long horned cairns and round cairns with the same features of those in Argyll. It is thought that the builders of these ancient burial cairns came from the south-west. Norse burial finds in the cairns reveal connections with the regions of Møre, Rogaland and Trondelag in West Norway, dating from the ninth century.

Mull, like Skye, is much indented by the sea and rich in variety but has only two notable fresh-water lochs, both of them fairly close to Salen, north and south of the short neck which separates Loch na Keal and the Sound of Mull; Loch Frisa in an open valley, Loch Ba pushing into a ring of fine peaks which close its head.

Loch Frisa was the scene of some of the first measuring work tried by the Bathymetric Survey of Sir John Murray and Fred Pullar but the results were never published because the plumbing instrument proved untrustworthy, so they designed a new machine called the Pullar Sounding Machine which is still in use

Terraces of volcanic rock at Balmeanach, Mull

at the Loch Lomond Field Station after 70 years of splendid work.

The new machine showed Loch Frisa to be in 3 separate 150-ft basins separated from each other by shallower water, the deepest where the loch is widest in the middle of the loch, being 205 ft deep. Fast moving ice dug these basins in the tertiary volcanic rock, the openness of the valley assisting the process. Length 4½ miles by just over ½ a mile, its north-west–south-east orientation is exactly the same as Loch Ba, though the outlets are at opposite ends. Large scale forestry has been changing the upper shores of Loch Frisa since 1925.

Loch Frisa and Loch Ba, including their rivers, are covered by the same fishing permits for trout, sea trout and salmon. The Manager, Killiechronan Office, Aros; telephone Aros 54, deals with applications. Loch Ba is 3 miles long and ¾ of a mile broad with a maximum depth of 144 ft in its widest portion to the north. It is a rock basin in granophyre whose water level has been heightened by a dam of raised beach material at the outlet. There are fine natural oakwoods on the south shore and a good track for walking, with shapely peaks rising in a horseshoe round the head. Two good hill paths cross the range from Loch Ba, one by Glen Clachaig over the shoulder of Ben More—a notable view point. The one from the head of the loch joins with Glen More further east.

Mull is made up of great terraces of volcanic rock which break down to good soil, their greensward in places like Balmeanach smooth as carpets under dark headlands, a landscape spattered with cattle and fronted by islands, Ulva, Staffa and the Treshnish. The good car ferry service from Oban is opening up its charms. Second of the Inner Hebrides after Skye, it is a place to explore.

It is paradoxical that it is tourism which keeps the crofting system alive in Skye, since it is the tiny fields and the linear pattern of the whitewashed houses which give such an alpine feel to the sea-level communities dominated by the most abrupt peaks in Britain—the Cuillin. Look from the crofts of Elgol across the water to that eye-catching crest of 20 rock peaks. See how they are linked one to another in a continuous spine impossible to traverse except by rock climbing. Over there 3,000 feet below the highest serrations lies the 'Corrie of the Waters'—Coruisk—

Skye, crofting beneath Blaven

carved from the naked gabbro in a rock basin without parallel in Scotland.

You can sail to it from Elgol in summer; there are daily fishing boat trips to the landing at Loch Scavaig. A short walk up the outlet stream and you are there. Far better, however, to walk the shore path by the 'Bad Step'. The track, easy to find, begins in the township, half way up the hill, a grassy path running along the side of Ben Cleat and gradually dropping to thread the sea-cliffs. Keep your mind on your feet and stop if you want to look at arctic terns flickering on sea-swallow wings or watch eiders or red-breasted mergansers in the little bays below.

The crofters graze their cattle here. Look out for the bull loaned by the Department of Agriculture for the summer. A favourite grazing place is the big sandy bay just before Camusunary. Over the greensward rise the exciting contrasts between the Red Cuillin in pink granite and the Black Cuillin in grey gabbro. There is a shooting lodge here, and an easier but not so interesting way to reach this point is by motor track from Strathaird on Loch Slapin.

Round the bay and over the river by suspension bridge the true wilderness begins as Sgurr na Stri rises ever more steeply and the path rises to a rocky notch, beyond which are bare gabbro slabs dotted with erratic blocks like curling stones where the melting glaciers stranded them. The 'Bad Step' lies just ahead where a curving rock slab goes straight into the sea. A little islet is a useful landmark for the place.

It is no more than an easy scramble, and a way of avoiding it has been marked with white paint on the rocks. The alternative route was marked because so many people get into trouble here. In fact the 'Bad Step' by any approach is no harder than the alternative. To cross the 'Bad Step' from the south, the important thing is not to keep too high. The beginning is obvious for the rock makes a pavement, from which you step on to an inclined slab split by a convenient crack in the form of a natural gangway. This crack gradually ascends to holdless rock but you have to break off leftward about half way along. In other words keep your traverse low, and don't be misled by the right forking crack. Go left easily and you strike a comfortable shelf leading to heather. The route is much easier to find coming from the opposite direction (north).

To avoid the 'Bad Step' you follow the 'Diversion' arrows by striking straight uphill for a couple of hundred feet, traverse a heathery ledge, then strike down again. A short distance on through more rocks and you are at Coruisk, whose only urbanisation is a mountain hut and a collapsed footbridge. If possible you should take yourself right round the head of the loch to savour its savagery of bog and rock. The circuit will occupy up to two hours.

That pioneer physicist J. D. Forbes of Pitsligo did some useful thinking when he walked here, pondering on how ice masses moved in this rock basin. He it was who discovered that the

Approaching the Bad Step on the Loch Coruisk path

middle of a glacier moves faster than its sides, and that the upper portions move faster than the lower. An alpinist, he applied what he saw in Norway and Switzerland to formulate theories and stimulate research in Scotland. At Coruisk he saw how the abrasion and plucking effect of the moving ice had given a smooth effect to the rocks when you looked downhill, reversed when you looked up-valley to their plucked ragged edges. Forbes, who died in 1868, had foresight years ahead of his time.

Loch Coruisk is 1¾ miles long with a maximum breadth of just over ¾ of a mile and a maximum depth of 125 ft, and there is no doubt that it provides excellent sea-trout fishing, with a few salmon. Once upon a time netting used to be done at the outflow into Loch Scavaig. Its most notable feature however is the ferocity of its midges, and there is a fine echo to prolong the screams of the afflicted.

The tertiary basalt country of the Storr is quite the opposite of sterile Loch Coruisk. Here in Trotternish in the north of Skye the weird pinnacles of rotten rock rise from garden-like turf cropped by sheep and rabbits. The basalt is friable but base-rich in minerals on which alpine plants thrive—roseroot, globe flowers, saxifrages of several kinds, alpine ladies' mantle, holly fern, white rock cress and one special to this place found nowhere else in Britain, *Koenigia islandica*, the Iceland purslane.

The Storr is a collapsed mass of basalt worn into a confusion of volcanic pinnacles, the 'Old Man' tilted as if about to fall, while others are worn so thin that holes of daylight gape through them. The 'Old Man' is 160 ft high and has been climbed by two improbable routes, the first in 1955, the second in 1969. The pioneer ascent was by Don Whillans, later to distinguish himself on Annapurna by the south-west face.

A 600-ft cliff lies above these pinnacles giving out on a plateau which can be reached easily by traversing northward to avoid the rocks. From the top you can look north-west on the coast at Uig Bay where Flora Macdonald landed with the Prince in his disguise as her maid Betty Burke.

On the east side of the Storr beneath the high road lie the Storr Lochs, now forming one reservoir behind 170 ft of gravity dam 36 ft high, the water being led through 2,800 ft of tunnel to a power station on the sea-edge below. Producing 7,000,000 units a year, the spillway level is 456 ft, the combined length of the lochs being just over $2\frac{1}{2}$ miles by $\frac{1}{2}$ a mile broad.

Five boats are available for brown trout fishing on the Storr Lochs, permits from Macdonald & Fraser, Solicitors, National Bank Buildings, Portree, telephone Portree 39. The best catch of recent years however was a fossil lizard of seventy million years ago, 10 feet of vertebrae proving it to be Ichthyosaurus. You can see the rock impression of it in the Royal Scottish Museum, Edinburgh. Another interesting find near here was some tenth-century silver and some Samarkand coins, the loot of a far travelled Norseman who finished up here no doubt when this was Viking land. The Norse place names remain.

The 'Old Man of Storr' above the Storr lochs

Before leaving this part of the world a visit should be made to the Quirang above the crofts of Staffin, another weird place of slipped basalt worn into fantastic shapes and rich with wild flowers. A track leads in from Loch Langaig, a neat gem like so many lochans in Skye.

Lochs of interest to fishermen by permit are as follows:

Loch	*Trout*	*Hotel*
Bernisdale	Brown	Skeabost
Claigan	Brown and sea	Dunvegan
Connan	Brown	Ullinish Lodge
Duagrich	Brown	Ullinish Lodge
Ravag	Brown	Ullinish Lodge

Lochs of the Outer Hebrides

Lewis, Harris, North Uist, Benbecula, South Uist, Eriskay and Barra

In the Highland Development Board booklet *Game Fishing in the Outer Hebrides*, author James Coutts prefaces his chosen lochs with the words that '. . . to list all the lochs in these islands would require a book of telephone directory dimensions'. A look at a large scale map is enough to show why even the energetic men of the *Bathymetrical Survey of the Scottish Fresh-water Lochs* baulked the task by picking only a representative sample from Lewis, Benbecula and North Uist, pointing out that of many hundreds of lochs of all shapes and sizes, few are straight valley lochs and that a great many of them are brackish.

The fertile Orkneys and the rugged and indented Shetlands are simple compared to the contrasts of the Western Isles, with their mountains of gneiss and machairs of shell sand, the east side offering anchorages and harbours, the west side open to the Atlantic and rich in pasture. Between these different worlds lie mazes of lochs, many named, but many more unnamed. What the Orkneys, the Shetlands and the Outer Hebrides have in common is inexpensive and excellent fishing easily accessible by air or sea.

You can be in Benbecula in one hour from Glasgow, or you can take you car on the ferry from Uig in Skye to Lochmaddy in North Uist, or go on across the Sound of Harris to Tarbert to explore the biggest island in Britain even if the names Lewis and Harris makes it sound like two islands.

The Outer Islands, from Barra Head to the Butt of Lewis is the Gaelic-speaking stronghold of Scotland where the crofting tradition is very much alive and much combined with weaving tweed and fishing. Stornoway is the only town, centre of the Harris tweed industry, with a population of 2,000 in the Burgh and 5,000 in the town. A full third of all the people in Lewis live here, yet this is what Martin Martin wrote in 1703: 'There is a village called Stornoway, at the head of the bay of that name; it consists of about sixty families; there are some houses of entertainment in it, as also a church and school in which Latin and English are taught.'

Lewis is not so much a peat blanket, as a wrinkled cap enclosing water in its numerous folds. Loch Suainaval is the deepest loch, a Lewisian gneiss rock basin dropping to 219 ft. Breadth $\frac{1}{2}$ a mile maximum, there are two deep basins, one of 212 ft in this broadest part, and another containing the maximum depth just south of the centre of the loch, the overall mean depth being $108\frac{1}{2}$ ft which is three times more than that of any other loch in Lewis. Length $2\frac{2}{3}$ miles it is one of the longest lochs, with fine mountains to the west, and to the east over a ridge, Loch Grunavat—now a reservoir of the North of Scotland Hydro-Electric Board.

Loch Stacsavat: this loch intervenes between Loch Suainaval and the sea, and is roughly triangular, length $\frac{3}{4}$ of a mile by $\frac{1}{3}$ of a mile with a maximum depth of 40 ft and a mean of $17\frac{1}{2}$ ft. A rock basin like its large neighbour, it discharges into one of the loveliest bays in the Hebrides at Uig Sands, a place hallowed by the find of 1831 of a set of superbly carved chessmen of walrus

Stornoway harbour, with Lewis Castle, looking towards Broad Bay

ivory, almost certainly Norse. They may be seen in the Scottish National Museum, Edinburgh. The finest rock climbing in Lewis can be found in the hills rising immediately south. To the east through rocky Glen Valtos lies Valtos and its magnificent bays which should not be missed. See the situation of these clustering crofts and you know why people want to live in the Hebrides. Alas, there is little in the way of accommodation here but there is no restriction on camping or caravanning.

Not very far away, at the foot of East Loch Roag are the Standing Stones of Callanish described by the unemotional Department of the Environment as 'A cruciform setting of megaliths unique in Scotland and outstanding in Great Britain'. In fact its only rival is the celebrated Stonehenge on Salisbury Plain, as was discovered in the middle of the last century when 5½ ft of peat was dug out to reveal the true height and

Lewis. A typical croft at Loch Erisort

proportions of not just a normal circle but a cross of stones. The depth of peat had accumulated since it was built around 1500 BC when the pattern of settlement on the isles was vastly different from what it is today if we are to judge from another seven stone circles within a short radius of Callanish.

This stone temple must have been one of great importance, the tallest megalith being 15 ft 6 in. high by a cairn in the centre of a circle of 13 large stones approached by an avenue of 19 stones, with projections east and west of the circle to form a cross. The climate was better and no doubt the land was more fertile when prehistoric people built these monuments. Today in Lewis, apart from the settlement of Achmore, everybody lives away from the peat blanket of the interior by the sea where the land can be

Dun Carloway, the best preserved broch in the Western Isles

worked, though a treatment of surface seeding is winning land from the peat.

Just to the north of Callanish above Loch an Duin is the best preserved broch in the Western Isles, Dun Carloway, now shaped rather like a pinnacle, its highest point 30 ft above the base with galleries within the thick walls. This broch could be called the culmination of dry-stone building in the Western Isles, no doubt evolving from the simpler duns which are so common on lochs on islands in these parts, pre-dating the brochs. Similarly the Standing Stones of Callanish are thought to have evolved from a simple cairn to a stone circle and then a cross.

The Neolithic and the Iron Age people left their memorials in stone, the Norsemen in the place names of hills and lochs such as *Langavat*, meaning 'long water', well named from the way it wriggles from the Harris border into the Lochs district of Lewis, that peat and water maze which extends from Loch Seaforth to Stornoway. Loch Langavat by its shortest measurement is 7¼ miles of zig-zagging rock basins excavated by the glaciers which scooped them out from weaker rocks. Maximum breadth ¾ of a mile, the maximum depth is 98 ft in the southern basin nearest the big hills where the loch is straight for almost 3 miles. Then it shallows to 9 ft beyond which is the mid-basin.

There is a constriction here where the loch forks north-east, soon attaining a depth of 90 ft and shallowing before another change of direction east to the third basin which is over 3 miles long, much islanded and irregular of shoreline, with a maximum depth of 65 ft. Situated remotely and difficult to comprehend from its winding shores, the best way of viewing the loch is to take the path from Vigadale Bay on Loch Seaforth and walk west for a couple of miles to a pass commanding a fine view of the head of the wild loch, whose foot is another maze of lochs stretching almost to Callanish.

Loch Benisval to the west of Langavat is another remotely situated loch and at 95 ft maximum depth is the third deepest in Lewis, with a mean of 35 ft which is higher than Langavat, though the length is only ¾ of a mile by ½ a mile, the form being a rough oblong with a little protruding tail end. It takes its name from the peak Benisval rising 350 ft above it and shelving steeply into it.

Loch More Barvas is an example of a very different kind of Hebridean loch, a shallow sheet of water ponded by shell sand on grassy machair with crofting fields sloping down to its shores, with a short salmon river running from it into the sea. A mile long from east to west and ½ a mile broad, the mean depth is only 4½ ft with a maximum of 8 ft, nothing more than a sandbar separating it from the sea where seals lurk to poach salmon, and are shot at by the jealous onlookers waiting to net the running fish. Like many of the best lochs in Lewis, waters are preserved, but there is plenty of good free and inexpensive fishing round Stornoway.

Among some lochs which may be fished free of charge near Stornoway are the following:

Loch Airigh nan Gleann 3½ miles south of the town and good for trout.
Loch Beag a' Ghrianain lies adjacent to above named and is recommended.
Mar a' Ghrianain in the same neighbourhood, smallish trout.
Loch Breugach 5 miles from Stornoway, boats available, enquire at Ship Chandler R. Morrison, 5 Bank St., Stornoway. Trout are said to be big.
Loch Beag na Craoibhe, adjacent to above named, small trout but plenty of them.
Loch Leiniscall (Ghost Loch), near the above named, slightly larger fish than na Craoibhe.
Loch a' Bhuna and Loch an Eilein on the Stornoway–Uig road 6 miles from the town.
Loch Mar a' Chocair and Loch Vatandip on the Stornoway–Pentland Road are also recommended.

Harris is less Norse in place names, no doubt because the high hills left less scope for settlement. The population today is around 3,000, and the old truism that the finest scenery makes the poorest agriculture is very much in evidence, especially around the Clisham and the weird peaks of Strone Ulladale in the forest of Harris—meaning deer forest, for this is very much sporting territory.

A walk *par excellence* I would recommend is from

Amhuinnsuidhe on the Husinish road north by Loch Chliostair following on past Loch Ashavat to look at the overhanging snout of Strone Ulladale, a great crag that looks as if it was in the act of falling, but the rock is gneiss, polished and hard, and under the threatening beak lies Glen Ulladale broken by a loch of the same name. By cutting east a keen walker can return by adjacent Glen Meavaig in a longish but not too strenuous expedition. Loch Chliostair is a reservoir now with a spillway level at 542 ft for hydro-electricity, length nearly 1 mile by $\frac{1}{5}$ of a mile broad.

Tarbert is the car ferry terminal for Harris, the route being via North Uist or Uigin Skye. Tarbert means a narrow neck of land dividing water, and the narrowness of the constriction here almost makes two islands of North and South Harris. The hotel

Salmon netting on the short river between Loch More Barvas and the sea

has the fishing rights in Laxdale lochs just 2 miles east, with boats and ghillie available.

Magnificent fishing can also be had from Borve Estate who control a large area of excellent lochs holding salmon, sea trout and brown trout. Unfortunately, they are often let for the whole season, but an inquiry to the Factor, Borve Lodge Cottage, Scarista, Harris will obtain the necessary information.

South Harris is two different worlds, curving with sands and grasslands to the west, and carved out of rocks on the east where the soil has to be scraped together and built up into lazybeds to grow tiny patches of oats and potatoes. But the little bays make good anchorages for lobster boats, and descendants of people dispossessed from better land continue to live the old way. In the small rectangle of South Harris there is every kind of Hebridean landscape, ending at the southern tip with the early sixteenth-century church of St. Clement, described by the Department of the Environment as being '. . . the only church of a monumental character in the outer isles'. Ornate in architectural detail, it is an appropriate masterpiece with which to leave, and cross the Sound of Harris to North Uist out of whose 12 by 16 miles, 8,000 acres is fresh-water, and 20,000 acres foreshore and tidal waters.

To capture the flavour of North Uist it is only necessary to take a sip, not drink the whole bottle, for no more bewildering region of lochs exists in Britain. Take Loch Scadavay, so labyrinthine in its maze that although the length is only 4¼ miles by 2 miles broad, the shoreline is 50 miles—a ratio of circumference to length unequalled by any other loch. Yet it is so beset with islands that there is no extent of open water visible, and while the maximum depth is 50 ft, the mean is a mere 9 ft. Containing one island nearly a mile long, while others have ancient dun fortifications reached by submerged causeways, it is not unrepresentative of the lochs straggling in such confusion down the east side of North Uist and nearly encircling Eaval—Ey Fjall to give it its Norse name, which means Island Hill because it is so nearly cut off. So to climb the highest hill you almost need a boat to reach its base.

An easier sip however, if you would have a golden eagle's view of North Uist, is to go north out of Lochmaddy by car or bicycle and climb the 625 ft of Ben Mhor opposite Harris. Only by getting up can you appreciate the hidden contrasts of this flat land, not only the dramatic differences between east and west, but realise the magnitude of desert sands and watery topography spread out before you in an extraordinary map drawn in relief and coloured by sky and sea.

Westward stretch the great sands, mile upon curving mile, ridged inland by dunes and becoming floral pastures, the machair lands where the township cattle graze in large herds, joyous with birds and flowers in summer, in winter provided with great tangles of weed, blown in on Atlantic gales for fertilising the fields. Lochmaddy is on the east side because of the harbour and shelter opposite Skye where the car ferry operates. But the life of North Uist is the machair lands where townships like Tighgarry, Houghgarry and Paible send up their peat reek. Other townships

Outer island lochscape, North Uist. The view from Ben Mhor looking southwards to Lochmaddy

are on tidal islands or out on Bernera. The population has dropped from 5,000 in 1821 to the more reasonable figure of 1,800 now, though the impression you may get if you keep to the main road is of an almost deserted island, for the crofts and most delightful bays lie off it.

The Tourist Office in Lochmaddy will give you some addresses if you are looking for accommodation, and if you are an angler temporarily resident on the island join the North Uist Angling Club and get the right to fish by fly in a big variety of waters from the bank. Permits for those North Uist Estate fishings outwith Club waters are obtainable from the Manager, Loch Maddy Hotel, Isle of North Uist, telephone Lochmaddy 331.

Salmon waters with boats include Lochs nan Geireann, Skealtar and Ciste. Sea trout, Lochs Oban na Fiadh, Dusary, Horisary, Grogarry, na Clachan and Geireann Mill. Brown trout lochs with boats, Lochs Strumore, Scadavay, a' Bharpa, Tormasad, Eaval, Hosta and Obisary.

Loch Obisary which half encircles the highest peak, Eaval, is the largest loch by volume in North Uist and at 151 ft is twice as deep as Loch a' Glinne-Dorcha, the second deepest, though the mean depth of the latter is higher. Loch Obisary is so complex that it has fifteen rock basins. One of its islands even has a small lochan. Crescent shaped with a length of 3 miles along its axis, the greatest breadth is 1 mile, though the presence of islands reduces the extent of open water to half that amount. The deepest basin is between Eilean Mor and the burn running north into Loch Eport. Some of the other basins are 51, 57, 50, 65 and 58 ft deep. Like many another loch in North Uist it is affected by tides, rendering the deeper water salty and enabling marine and fresh-water organisms to overlap. When it was tested for temperature by the Bathymetric surveyors the temperature was found to be one degree lower at 50 ft than at the bottom, an interesting example of a temperature inversion.

Loch an Duin is an example of a different kind of brackish loch, fresh at one end and salt at the other, mostly shallow in its squiggling expansions, but reaching 35 ft deep in the north though the mean is 6 ft. Nearly 1 mile long and $\frac{2}{3}$ of a mile broad, the name comes from 3 duns—stone fortifications—and the broch of Dun Torcuill whose walls are 10 ft high and the best-preserved on the island. A very little rise in sea-level would reduce the brackish and fresh-water lochs of North Uist drastically. It has happened before, for undoubtedly the great east coast inlets of Loch Eport and Loch Maddy were once fresh-water lochs, and in those times North Uist must have been a much more extensive island without peat.

Loch an Duin is on the Newton Estate which controls the other half of the angling on North Uist and their territory is in the wilder country north of the A865. The Department of Agriculture and Fisheries for Scotland deal with enquiries from their office at Balivanich, telephone Benbecula 346. There is a wide range of fishing at modest cost, and some of the lochs quoted are as follows:

Loch an Duin, brown trout.
Loch na Ceardaich and Dead Man's Loch.
Loch Fada, one boat available.
Loch nan Geadh and Loch Tergavat, as above but bank fishing only, brown trout.
Loch Vergavat, brown trout as above.
Loch Traigh Ear.

Wildlife and the Uists are synonymous, and these islands may seem strange places to find bird sanctuaries, but the building of connecting roads and car ferries meant a steep rise in tourist traffic, so the Royal Society for the Protection of Birds with the co-operation of landowners and crofters established 1,500 acres of reserve at Balranald on the north-west tip of North Uist to safeguard marsh birds like the red-necked phalarope which needs shallow water and marshes for feeding and breeding.

Balranald is just this kind of nutrient-rich marsh with plenty of wildfowl food plants, as well as having an Atlantic beach, sand dunes, floral machair and Loch nam Feithean for waterfowl. Here is a list of some of the birds which breed, or have bred here: little grebe, mallard, teal, gadwall (probably), wigeon, shoveller, tufted duck, pochard, eider, red-breasted merganser, shelduck, mute swan, water rail, corncrake, moorhen, coot, oystercatcher, lapwing, ringed plover, red-necked phalarope, snipe, common sandpiper, redshank, dunlin, common gull, black-headed gull, common tern, arctic tern, little tern, cuckoo, skylark, hooded crow, wren, wheatear, sedge warbler, meadow pipit, rock pipit, starling, twite, corn bunting, reed bunting, house sparrow and tree sparrow—a total of 43 species—not to mention wintering species such as geese and whooper swans.

There are also Atlantic seals breeding on the little island of Causamul which is inside the reserve. The reserve is wardened and visitors wanting to learn about the birds should contact the RSPB representative at nearby Houghgarry crofting township.

From North Uist you drive across a strand to Benbecula on a good road, or you can fly direct there from Glasgow or Stornoway. Balivanich is the airport and, despite the general flatness the division between machair on the west and moorland to the east is very much the same as on North Uist, nor are the lochs any easier to grasp. They are just as irregular and bouldery, the longest being Langavat, just over 2 miles long but a mere tenth of a mile in mean breadth, maximum depth 34 ft and mean 8 ft. It is a rock basin almost cut in half by a canal 5 ft deep, and its islands are elongated along the strike of the Lewisian gneiss.

On this abnormally windy island live men of the South Uist rocket range who, if they were here long enough, would no doubt stoop like the islanders from the effects of the unrelenting blast. Shelter there is none, except perhaps on the steep curve of Culla Bay on the west coast where the Highland chief Clanranald wisely built his house though he threw caution aside in joining Bonny Prince Charlie to find himself alone, unsupported by other island chiefs. The grey stones at Nunton still defy the winds of the pancake isle whose highest hill is Rueval projecting like a pyramid in the middle of nothing.

I liked W. H. Murray's description of the view from the summit, with Benbecula looking 'like a well-fired crumpet pitted with holes by the hundred'. The holes of course are lochs, and beneath the top there is a famous cave where the Prince hid, waiting for Flora MacDonald to come back from Clanranald's house with the fancy dress which would enable him to escape dressed as Betty Burke. The whole world knows the story of the escape to Skye, but few people know the cave on the 'Mountain of the Fords'—the literal description of the name Benbecula.

The 'North Ford' leading to North Uist, and the 'South Ford' leading to South Uist are tamed by bridge and causeway now, making it all too easy to clear out of Benbecula whereas, not so long ago, crossing the dangerous strands called for skill and cunning, knowledge of the tides and weather. Ironically it was the easier crossing of the South Ford which cost the most lives, because people took it more casually, whereas the longer difficulties of the North Ford and its quicksands commanded more respect and care.

Creagorry Hotel is the recommended centre of fishing on Benbecula, controlling a number of lochs and able to arrange private fishing. There are so many lochs to choose from that it is not worth mentioning specific names, though West Loch Olavat is highly spoken of, not to mention sea trout fishing in the sea pools.

In South Uist the strings of lochs which make this the anglers' paradise of the Western Isles are on the rich sandy soil of the machairs, stretching 20 miles as a broad Atlantic fringe against the inhospitable peat hills rising east and devoid of population. Fishermen become poetic when they talk about South Uist. Trout fishing is free to guests staying at Lochboisdale Hotel and is described by Mr. James Coutts in *Game Fishing in the Outer Hebrides* as '. . . the best value available anywhere'. Day tickets, when available, can be had from the Factor, Benbecula, and South Uist Estate Office, Askernish. Fishing on the salmon and trout lochs of Fada, Roag, Schoolhouse and Castle is of the best, available from Lochboisdale Hotel.

The Howmore river is the most famous stream in the Outer Hebrides for monster sea trout, but owing to drought when I was there the keeper was spending his time carrying up baths of salmon and sea trout stranded in the lower pools, some of the trout weighing up to 14 lbs. He reckoned the fish were in such poor condition that they had nothing like their usual fight left in them. 'You can pull them in like cod,' he said. However the rain came that night, and round Loch a' Machair at dusk fishermen stood glorying in it, listening to the crying of whimbrel and golden plover wheeling with a vast flock of lapwings.

Loch Druidibeg has the status of a National Nature Reserve, thanks to the co-operation of crofters and the South Uist Estates. The total area is 4,145 acres, about half of which is owned by the Nature Conservancy. The reserve, comprising grass and heather moor, lochs with islands and sand dunes, shore and machair lies within the crofting townships of Dremisdale and Stilligarry. It is a perfect example of an unspoiled Hebridean system, of fertile and infertile land and water. It is the main nesting ground of Grey Lag geese in Britain.

In describing the Loch Druidibeg Nature Reserve you have a fragment that will do for a general description of the topography of South Uist west side, with the highest point on the ground a mere 100 ft above sea-level and the deeply indented Loch Druidibeg with its many islets and peninsulas a mere 15 ft above high water. Man-made channels connect it through other lochs to the Howmore River, making Castle Loch, Loch Rigarry, Loch Stilligarry and Loch a' Machair a continuous network.

These sluggish outlet streams of Druidibeg giving out on the grassy machair, and lochs with interconnecting streams beloved of birds, are separated from the pebble and sand beach by dunes, the whole on a bed rock of Lewisian gneiss much grooved by the scraping of the glaciers which over-rode them. May is the sunniest month, June the driest, but the wind can blow all the time, making the temperature feel lower and the rain wetter, though in fact neither is extreme. Rainfall is a mere 50 in., and records show that the difference in mean temperature between summer and winter is around 9°F which is small compared to most places. The wind of course is a great aid to agriculture by raising the evaporation rate which means good drying at harvest time. The prone and distorted trees of the small plantation on the reserve show the debit side of the wind factor.

Only the islands on the loch carry natural scrub, birch, rowan, willow, juniper, bramble and wild rose with a fine mixture of herbs and ferns and lots of moss. The water itself is not rich in mineral content, but the islands give security to the adult pairs of geese, while the fertile machair lochs provide the goslings with food once they hatch and are taken down there by the parent birds. Conservation would be impossible without the nurseries as well as the breeding loch, hence the nature reserve agreement with the crofters who love the birds. Herons also breed on an island here, while on the machair there are good tern colonies. Brown trout and sea trout enter the loch from the Howmore River to spawn at the eastern end where the fast flowing streams from the hills enter.

It is worth following the maze of Druidibeg's channels east and continuing on to Loch Skiport to where half a dozen families live by lobstering and seaweed gathering, with a pier and a good harbour facing out to Skye. It was from here in cattle droving days that the beasts were loaded on to schooner-rigged vessels holding perhaps fifty, to be landed at Loch Dunvegan in Skye. From there they were walked to the Crieff market after swimming the narrows at Kyle Rhea to gain the Scottish mainland.

Orkney and its Lochs

Lochs Stenness, Harray, Bosquoy, Sabiston, Isbister, Kirkbister, Tankerness, Swannay, Boardhouse, Hundland, Skaill, Muckle Water, Peerie and Hoglins

A sail of only 28 miles from Scrabster in Caithness takes you to Stromness in Orkney passing the Old Man of Hoy on the way. Step along the flagstoned street where the gable-ends point to the sea and narrow lanes lead steeply down to little harbours and you have the feeling of being abroad, a feeling emphasised if someone asks you if you come from Scotland. Orkney, which was Scandinavian until the fifteenth century, still regards itself as being different. And so it is.

Man exploring from the Mediterranean was quick to discover the advantages of the Orkneys, as the Stone Age village of Skara Brae on the Bay of Skail testifies. Within a very short distance of Stromness the various stages of man's culture can be traced for 4,000 years through megalithic tombs and stone circles to the chapels of early Christians. The Norsemen left us a wonderful literature in the Orkneyinga Saga. They built St. Magnus Cathedral in Kirkwall, in sound of whose bells live one fifth of the 19,000 or so people who inhabit the islands today.

The small population relative to the amount of good land explains some of the prosperity of modern Orkney, which is a countryside of small farms, not crofts. Sixty years ago when the population was 30,000 the average land holding was 16½ acres. Today it is 35 acres, which in Orkney means good soil made of red sandstone, which is porous and retains heat. This is no peaty acid soil as in the Outer Hebrides, where the hard gneiss allows no proper drainage. Also the rainfall in Orkney is only 35 in. a year compared to 60 in. in Lewis. In Orkney 35 acres can support 35 or more Jersey or Ayrshire cows without being overstocked.

The milk goes to Kirkwall Creamery, a favourite retreat of holiday visitors on wet days. This is where the Claymore butter and Orkney cheese are made, and skim milk is converted into powder by modern machinery. The local distillery has the biggest pot-still in Scotland. Straw-backed Orkney chairs are still being hand-made.

Hoy today is the saddest island, almost empty now that Lyness is no longer a naval base. The social and operational centre of

20,000 servicemen is now a ghost town littered with concrete debris and other sad remains. The health of the various communities scattered between the North Isles and the South Isles of Orkney is better, centring on the land and sea, not on the whims of the navy or industry. On these green islands there are 3,000 good farms owning between them the biggest number of tractors and motor cars to be found anywhere in Europe—

Stone Age dwelling at Skarabrae

proportionate to population. Their people are workers, so energetic that they find time to gather seaweed and export it to South Uist in spare hours of their days. From these islands sailed the home fleet in war. Stromness was once the northern port of call for rice ships, and here the Hudson Bay whaling fleet used to take on water and men. Nowadays planes from the Continent call to buy Orkney lobsters. There is always a stir in Stromness or Kirkwall because they exist to serve the islands, shuttling forth the imports and exports which keep Orkney alive. The pace of life is fast on Mainland where the creamery is a factory clock gearing everyone to its time for collecting the milk and handling it. On the smaller islands such as Westray there is no clock, the emphasis is

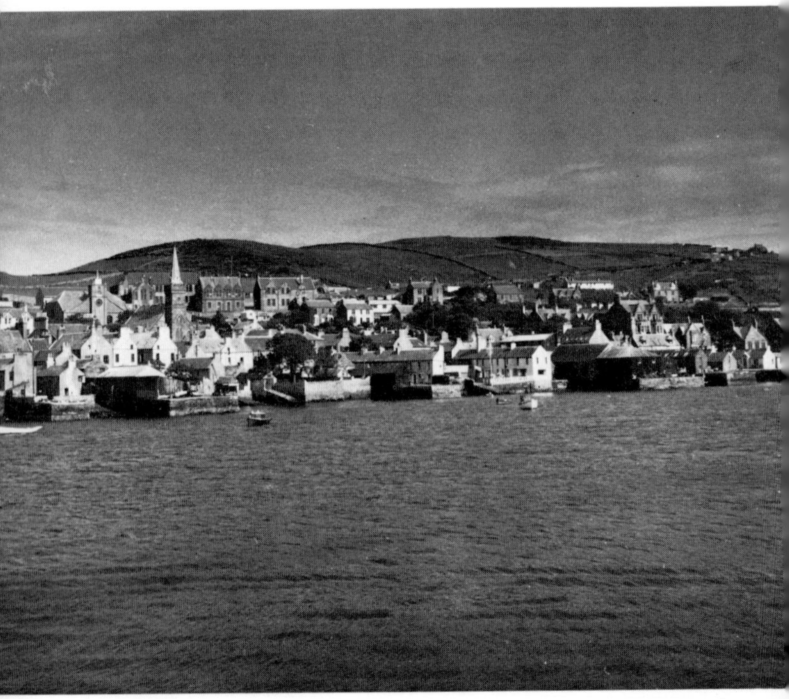

Stromness, Orkney

on beef cattle, so nobody appears to be in a hurry, but they have an inter-island plane service which is a great asset.

When an Orkney man talks about Mainland he does not mean the country across the Pentland Firth but the biggest of the seventy islands which scatter over a large area of sea. Only Mainland in the group has changed its shape of recent times by acquiring a tail in the shape of Burray and South Ronaldshay which are linked by causeways known as the Churchill Barriers. A road runs over the top, and as you drive along the top reflect that this was where the Royal Oak was sunk by a U-boat with a loss of 800 lives early in the war, while on land the first British civilian was killed by air attack.

It is on Mainland which comprises about 200 sq. miles and has over 200 miles of good motoring roads that we find the important lochs, all of them good for fishing and all of them free, hence the description of Orkney as 'This Angling Paradise'. Even the salmon here are free, for they are mostly taken in salt water or at burn-mouths by rod and line using lob worms. The locals go for them in September and do well, even if the fish are advanced in spawn.

Where the burns enter the sea is also good for sea trout on their way to spawn. The worm is the favourite local bait and average fish are from 1½ to 2 lbs though fish three times that size are frequently taken. Now for the lochs, which are so good for sea trout and brown trout and of such high general interest.

Loch of Stenness and Loch of Harray are separated from each other only by a narrow neck of land on which, with a fine sense of the dramatic, early man built one of the most exciting monuments in Britain, the Ring of Brogar, a gaunt Stonehenge giving brooding character to the great expanse of water and low land under the great changing skies, Harray to the east and Stenness to the west with a sea passage only a short distance southward.

Loch of Stenness is in fact salt, and its salinity affects Loch Harray, though this has been controlled to a great extent by the Orkney Angling Association fitting flaps at the Bridge of Brogar outflow to reduce the sea water entering. The tide which does the damage enters from the Bay of Ireland under Bridge of Waith, and it seems to suit the brown trout for the largest on record from Orkney was taken from the Loch of Stenness, weight

Fishing the Loch of Stenness

29½ lbs, and its cast is in Stromness Museum.

Length 4 miles and breadth 1½ miles in the bulging centre, the water is fresh only at the surface, the maximum depth of 17 ft occurring at the south-eastern extremity, while the mean is 10½ ft. On the shore just north of where the sea plunges in at Bridge of Waith is Unston Cairn, one of the most famous of the Orkney burial cairns because of the pottery found here, unburnt and burnt, with human and animal bones.

The pottery, found in 1884, has been estimated to date from at least 1500 BC and is akin to that discovered in the lowest stratum of Windmill Hill in Wiltshire. This largest collection of Neolithic pottery ever found at one site in Scotland is enshrined in the term 'Unston Ware' to indicate this special type of ornate vase. Barley marks on the shards show that grain must have been cultivated in the Stone Age. No doubt the vases originally contained food to see the dead on their last journey.

Loch of Harray: this wide water, 4⅔ miles by 1¾ miles, is the

The ring of Brognar between Lochs Harray and Stenness

largest and most renowned of the Orkney fishing lochs. Situated in a lowland mixture of moorland, wet meadows and farmland, it is a shallow rock basin in Middle Old Red Flagstones, maximum depth 14 ft and mean 9 ft. The feeding must be good, for the growth rate of fish is said to be ahead of all the other lochs. May and June are the best months for brown trout, the average weighing around 1 lb. Wading in the rocky islets of the west shore is not difficult, but a ghillie is recommended for boating because of the rocky shore. Apart from Merkister Hotel, the local farmers have boats for hire.

Just a step from the southern tip of Loch Harray lies the sun-hat shape of the grassy knoll known as Maes Howe, 24 ft high and 115 ft in diameter with a tunnel leading into the heart of the finest Megalithic burial cairn in the British Isles. A stone tomb of superb construction, with cells opening off the main chamber, its interest is heightened by the fact that it contains the runic scribblings of the Norsemen who raided it, the greatest number of these scrawls to be found anywhere in the world.

One of them reads: 'These runes were incised by the best runester in the west, using the axe that Gauk Trandilsson once owned in the south of Iceland.'

Another reads: 'The Jerusalem pilgrims broke in here.'

Still another: 'Ingigerd is the sweetest woman there is.'

As well as the branch-like strokes of the runic writing there are drawings of a lion, a walrus, and a serpent-knot, a unique historical record which makes mention of treasures removed from the tomb and gives bits of information which tie up with the Sagas. The craftsmanship of the building is said to be unsurpassed in Western Europe.

Loch of Bosquoy: situated near the north-east tip of Loch Harray in boggy meadow this small shallow loch is fishable when the weather is too stormy for the bigger waters. Length $\frac{2}{3}$ of a mile by $\frac{1}{3}$ of a mile, the depth is 5 ft maximum with a mean of $2\frac{1}{2}$ ft. Weeds in mid-summer make fishing difficult. The fish average half a pound or less.

Loch of Sabiston: lies $1\frac{1}{2}$ miles north of Loch Harray on a boggy flat under the Hill of Greenay, length $\frac{1}{2}$ a mile, breadth $\frac{1}{4}$ of a mile, maximum depth 3 ft. Keep an eye open for hen harriers and short-eared owls wavering over the moor. Their main prey is the Orkney vole and both are ground nesters. The elegant hen harrier, flickering on long wings, may take a vicious swipe at you if you get too close to its young and may strike and draw blood, the right kind of action to deter the trespasser, I would say.

Loch of Isbister: situated near the village of Twatt in boggy ground this small loch is $\frac{2}{3}$ of a mile long by nearly $\frac{2}{3}$ of a mile broad, the maximum depth being 3 ft and the mean $1\frac{1}{2}$ ft. Trout of 1 lb and over are taken here in May and June.

Loch of Kirkbister: this loch, 5 miles south-west of Kirkwall, is in the Parish of Orphir and is recommended for beginners in fishing, for the stock of small trout is so great that failure to bring home something is almost impossible. Length $1\frac{3}{4}$ miles by $\frac{1}{2}$ a mile broad, the maximum depth is 6 ft and the mean 4 ft. Any visit there should take account of the round church of Orphir, a remaining fragment of a twelfth-century church built to the model of the Church of the Holy Sepulchre in Jerusalem. It is attributed to Earl Hakon who put to death Earl Magnus.

Here is a passage from the Orkneyinga Saga, amply supported by evidence on the ground:

> At Orphir there was a large drinking-hall, with a door in the south side-wall right at the eastern gable; facing this door was a magnificent church, and some steps led down from the hall to the church.

Look beyond the semi-circular apse of the sanctuary and you can trace the stone foundations of that hall, together with an opening at the eastern end where steps led down to the church, the place where that 'Ultimate Viking' Svein Asleifsson committed murder after rowing across the Pentland Firth in his galley on Christmas Eve. The ruins and the runes as at Maes Howe, here and elsewhere, square with the Sagas whose authenticity is beyond doubt. No ancient history in stone has been invested with so much life, thanks to the Icelandic storytellers.

Loch of Tankerness lies east of Kirkwall across Inganess Bay on a peninsula. Roughly triangular in shape this mile-long loch by $\frac{1}{2}$ a mile has a maximum depth of 7 ft and a mean of $4\frac{1}{2}$ ft.

Loch of Swannay: this large elliptical loch is the most northerly on Mainland and is popular for fishing competitions.

One angler has taken out 42 brown trout in a day weighing 69 lb 10 oz. Boats are readily available and the west shore is recommended as safest for wading. The length is 2 miles with maximum breadth of $\frac{2}{3}$ of a mile and the maximum depth is 16 ft with a mean of 9 ft. Shallows and rocks occur at various points, so fishermen using outboard motors on their boats have to be careful. The main road round the island skirts the top of the loch so access is easy.

Loch of Boardhouse is at the north-west tip of Mainland half a mile east of Birsay. The Orkney Angling Association have a boat house here on the west shore and an evening competition is held on this good fishing loch every May. The length is 2 miles, the maximum breadth is $\frac{2}{3}$ of a mile, the maximum depth is 9 ft and the mean 6 ft. Boats are available from the Barony Hotel and from various local people in Birsay.

Loch of Hundland: this triangular loch lies between the last two described and like the other two tends to be weedy after June. The length is $1\frac{1}{3}$ miles and the breadth just over $\frac{1}{2}$ a mile, with a maximum depth of 7 ft and a mean of 4 ft.

Loch of Skaill: a small loch due north of Stromness near the Bay of Skaill, one of the most interesting places in Orkney. Triangular-shaped and containing an artificial island of flat stones, the length of the loch is nearly 1 mile by $\frac{1}{2}$ a mile broad, the maximum depth being 4 ft and the mean 2 ft. Muddy bottomed and reedy, the outflow used to power a corn mill. The real interest about here is Skara Brae on the Bay of Skaill beyond the boggy flats.

This Stone Age village is the finest example of its kind and shows us the kind of furniture our forbears used, and the way they built their huts, linking them by passages. The settlement is in a remarkable state of preservation, thanks to the sand that buried the ruins until they were revealed after a great storm last century.

Dated by fragments of pottery found, these huts must go back to 1500 BC at least, yet only the roofs have caved in, the rectangular rooms with the rounded corners, the hearths and the drains remain to indicate to us how a people who tended cows and sheep lived.

Muckle Water, Rousay: just north-east of Mainland lies

Rousay, another island rich in archaeological monuments. This narrow loch, 1 mile long by $\frac{3}{4}$ of a mile broad has a maximum depth of 20 ft and a mean of 11 ft and lies 322 ft above sea level just north of the Peerie Water.

Peerie Water: Muckle means large, and Peerie means small, the loch in question being no more than $\frac{1}{2}$ a mile long by $\frac{1}{6}$ of a mile broad. The maximum depth is 10 ft and the mean 6 ft.

Hoglins Water, Isle of Hoy: this tiny rock basin has the distinction of being the deepest loch in the Orkneys at 57 ft maximum, with a mean of 26 ft. The length is only $\frac{1}{3}$ of a mile and the breadth $\frac{1}{5}$ of a mile. The greater height of the hills of Hoy and the resultant down-cutting of ice in glacial times no doubt account for the great depth of the Hoglins basin in the Upper Old Red Sandstone, excavated when the Scottish ice flowing north-westwards over-rode the Orkneys from Caithness.

Facing out to the Pentland Firth, the great crags of Hoy are now attracting the finest rock climbers in the country. The Old Man of Hoy, that finger of rock rising 400 ft from the sea, was climbed in the sixties as a television spectacular and now it is a popular route. Then the 1,200-ft challenge of St. John's Head North Wall was accepted, giving two crack climbers, Edwin Drummond and Oliver Hill 'the most difficult climb ever attempted in Britain'. They succeeded after nearly a week hanging on the face, and they called their climb 'The Longhope Route', after the men of that village in Hoy who went out on a lifeboat mission and who never came back.

Today there is a new lifeboat in Hoy and another crew ready to take to the sea when called upon.

Lochs of Shetland

Lochs Cliff, Snarravoe, Stourhoull, Watlee, Spiggie, Clickhimin, Girlsta, Tingwall, Asta, Strom, Roer Water, Papil Water, Winyadepla, Funzie

If you want to fish or bird-watch around the most northerly loch in Britain then you must go to Loch Cliff of Unst in Shetland which is considerably nearer to Bergen in Norway than to Aberdeen in Scotland. Ponded by gravel where the Burra Firth indents the last land in Scotland, there is little more beyond this loch except Hermaness and the stacks of Muckle Flugga where the Atlantic and the North Sea fight it out round the great gannet cliffs. Of the hundred Shetland islands extending seventy miles, none produces such an overwhelming feeling of timeless austerity as Unst which in some mysterious way reminded a friend of mine of East Africa—nor was he thinking of darkness, rather of the vastness.

The land and seascapes of Shetland are less friendly than the green fertility of the Orkneys, with ruggedness everywhere more pronounced, in cliffs and heather, the whole cut up by innumerable fjords called voes. Here in summer the sun is below the horizon for only five hours in mid-June, and above it for only five hours in mid-December. More fertile than the Faroes, they have a similar predominance of gales and fogs, and like them it is fishing rather than agriculture which holds the population.

The Norse accent is unmistakable. When the Shetlander greets you with 'Due is wylkomm', it is almost the Norwegian 'De er velkommen'. Shetland tongue is a mixture of the old Norn language plus Scots, English, German and Dutch. The Faroese people have no difficulty in understanding it since they share the common inheritance.

There was a little corner of Shetland which was still Norwegian in 1940 when the National Flag flew from the mast of Lerwick Tower to show that one Norse garrison was still out of enemy hands. It was from these islands that the Viking invasion went into reverse when 'The Shetland Bus' began shuttling between Scalloway and the Norwegian coast, to take men out and bring men in under the noses of the enemy, just part of the war of nerves which pinned down the occupying army and destroyed its morale. The story has been well told by David Howarth in *The Shetland Bus*.

The story of the Scandinavian invasion of Shetland begins in the Ice Age when the islands were over-ridden by glaciers radiating from Norway. Subsequent local glaciations deepened the valleys; the longest loch in Shetland, Loch Cliff of Unst, occupies such a trough, length 3 miles from north to south, with a long weedy leg thrusting south-east for $\frac{3}{4}$ of a mile.

The whole loch is shallow, the maximum depth being only 21 ft at the widest part, which is just over $\frac{1}{4}$ of a mile, the narrow off-shoot being less than 10 ft deep. The north end is good for sea trout, while the biggest brown trout are found in the south end, though these are unlikely to be more than 8 oz, and double that

Lerwick, capital of Shetland

size is considered very good. Boats are available from the Springfield Hotel.

There is evidence in the blanket bog around Loch Cliff that trees grew here around 500 BC before the climate became wetter and peat began to form. Today the rainfall averages out at 45 in. which is half that of Loch Maree in Western Ross, and the peat is eroding. Despite being nearly 61° north, in the same latitude as South Greenland, snow lies on only 12 to 15 days a year and frost is an infrequent occurrence, owing to the benign influence of the Gulf Stream.

No one who goes to Unst should miss the chance of exploring Hermaness, the 3-mile peninsula projecting north of Loch Cliff where you run the gauntlet of aggressive Great and Arctic skuas

Scalloway, the former capital of the Shetlands

in the rough ground which they defend in the breeding season, the 'Bonxies' big as buzzards giving vicious 'coughs' as they drive in for a low flying attack. More vicious are the smaller swallow-tailed Arctic skuas, dive-bombing from above, and much more liable to strike hard. The population could be 1,600 Bonxies and 150 or so Arctics—which is a big success story in protection since numbers were down to only 7 pairs of Bonxies in 1895. The RSPB maintain a watcher and Hermaness itself is a National Nature Reserve.

The cliffs, which drop to the sea west of the Warden's Hut on Hermaness Hill and continue in chaotic tenements of birds to Muckle Flugga, have been well documented since 1917 when a few pairs of gannets bred for the first time, rising to 1,000 pairs by 1937, increasing to 3,000 in 1949 and to over 5,000 pairs in the next 20 years. Beginning on Vesta Skerry they gradually spread to Muckle Flugga and Hermaness pushing out guillemots and kittiwakes, as they did on Noss near Lerwick.

They repeated the success story of the fulmar which nested here in 1897 for the first time and is now abundant, together with tens of thousands of snub-nosed puffins and large guillemot colonies. Razorbills are scarcer. There is also a local race of moths, darker than those on the Scottish mainland, having evolved that way as a result of isolation. Amongst these Caradrinidae are the following: 'True Lovers' Knot, Northern Rustic, Autumnal Rustic, Square-spot Rustic; while the dark characteristics can also be seen in the Hydriomenidae and the Hepialidae.

The Management Plan of the Nature Conservancy on Hermaness is to perpetuate the undisturbed conditions of this fascinating place and study the bird populations and inter-relationships—important in these days when sea birds all over the world are being badly affected by pollution.

Loch of Snarravoe at the opposite end of Unst, in the south-west, is in peat-free ground and is noted for its golden trout weighing about $\frac{3}{4}$ lb. Triangular in shape and $\frac{1}{2}$ a mile at its broadest, the maximum depth is 29 ft. Loch of Stourhoull just north of the above mentioned has a reputation for large fighting fish. Loch of Watlee close to the A968 is a safe wading loch with good fishing and is the second biggest water in Unst.

Since it is impossible within the scope of one chapter to deal with all the lochs of Shetland, I am going to jump for contrast from the extreme north to Loch of Spiggie in south Mainland, in the friendly parish of Dunrossness only a few miles north of the airport of Sumburgh. Plenty of variety here, with farms, croftlands, the big cliffs of Fitful Head, the excavated wonders of the Jarlshof, and St. Ninian's Isle with its evidence that the Shetland Picts were converted to Christianity long before St. Columba landed on Iona.

Loch of Spiggie is notable in its own right, not only for being the only large loch in south Mainland but for being the fourth largest in the Shetlands at 1⅓ miles long by ½ a mile broad, with a maximum depth of 41 ft. And it has a big reputation among fishermen, early in the season for brown trout and from late August onwards for sea trout. It contains arctic char and is so shallow in the north end that it can be waded from shore to shore, but boats are available from the hotel.

Loch of Spiggie and its surroundings of croft houses, bays, cliffs and islands is one of the best ornithological centres in Shetland with variety in plenty, from water birds including the red-necked phalarope to skuas on the moor, arctic terns on the sands to stormy petrels on the near island of Colsay. And the boat for Fair Isle leaves from Grutness Pier just south of Sumburgh Airport less than five miles distant, close to Jarlshof, which the Department of the Environment describes as one of the most remarkable archaeological sites in Britain.

What makes Jarlshof, on a green headland above a sandy beach, unique is that within 3 acres is a chronology in stone of the people who occupied this place from Bronze and Iron Age times to the Viking period, including a broch and courtyard protecting partly roofed wheelhouses, the best examples of their kind dating from the first centuries AD.

Much in the period puzzle has still to be elucidated, between the first ovals of the stone huts, preserved in sand as at Skara Brae in Orkney, through the different structures modified by successive waves of people who re-used the stones for their own constructions. But plenty of pottery with Neolithic affinities was found. Then from the period of stone and bone implements to that of bronze swords, axes and knives, even to the smithy where they were made, with stocks of clay and the quern for preparing it.

The broch came later, to be abandoned and its stones used for other structures, one of them a large round house, which in turn became wheelhouses. Following that came the Viking foundations of the most complete settlement yet found in Britain, its growth over 2 acres revealing its evolution from the ninth to the thirteenth century, the original settlers hailing from the More-Trondelag regions of Norway, most probably. In the wheelhouse phase preceding the Vikings it would appear that Shetland was occupied by the northern Picts.

St. Ninian's Isle 2 miles north of Loch of Spiggie was the scene

Jarlshof near Sumburgh

of exciting excavations from 1955–9 when beneath a mediaeval church was found the ruins of a pre-Norse church and a wooden box turned upside down. It hid a silver treasure of 12 brooches, 8 bowls and 9 other objects, one inscribed in Latin and Pictish, valuables of the church hidden in haste, possibly around AD 800. The green island is accessible by a strand from Bigton and St. Ninian's Well is still a clear stream.

Of the total population of Shetland numbering around 21,000, about one third lives in Lerwick, a town on a hill, of sharp angles where the gable ends of houses tower one above the other and canyons lead between narrow walls. The flagstones paving the main street and the constant stir of boats in Bressay Sound give it a delightfully foreign atmosphere.

You could describe Loch of Clickhimin as being in the suburbs, only ten minutes from Commercial Street with a broch on a bouldery promontory to give it character.

The broch at Clickhimin was found in 1953 to be built beside the internal structures of an earlier stone fort, of a type from which the brochs evolved, dating back to the fourth and second century BC. The excavations revealed for the first time the domestic arrangements of an early Celtic fortress by people with the same culture as the Bronze Age and Iron Age people of Jarlshof. A change of loch level, causing flooding, enforced changes in fort construction.

What seems to be accepted about the brochs from the most recent excavations is that they were the strongholds of an agricultural population of 2,000 years ago and were part of a village complex for refuge. Also, that when their use passed, they were pulled down or converted into other uses. Mousa standing 40 ft high and unbroken is the best example in existence, and can be reached by boat from Sandwick, 14 miles south of Lerwick.

Loch of Clickhimin is ½ a mile long by ¼ of a mile broad, with a maximum depth of 10 ft and a mean of 5–6 ft, and although tidal, the south shore is rich in fresh-water shrimps and good brown trout are caught without wading.

Loch of Girlsta: six miles north of Lerwick, this loch contains three times as much water as any other loch in Shetland with a maximum depth of 74 ft and a mean of 31 ft in 1½ miles of length and ⅓ of a mile in bredth. Situated among heathery hills, it is a true rock basin, contains char and has a reputation for big brown trout. Spinning for them is allowable here, but not elsewhere on any Association Water. Two boats are available to permit holders at the south end.

Loch of Tingwall: this fertile spot was an important place in Norse times, for it was in this attractive valley 4 miles from Lerwick that justice was meted out at a special Lawting presided over by the Lord of Shetland or the King of Norway. Tingvallur in Iceland is held to be the place where the first 'Parliament' in the world met to govern in democratic fashion. The same principles held in Shetland. At Tingwall trial of criminals was by

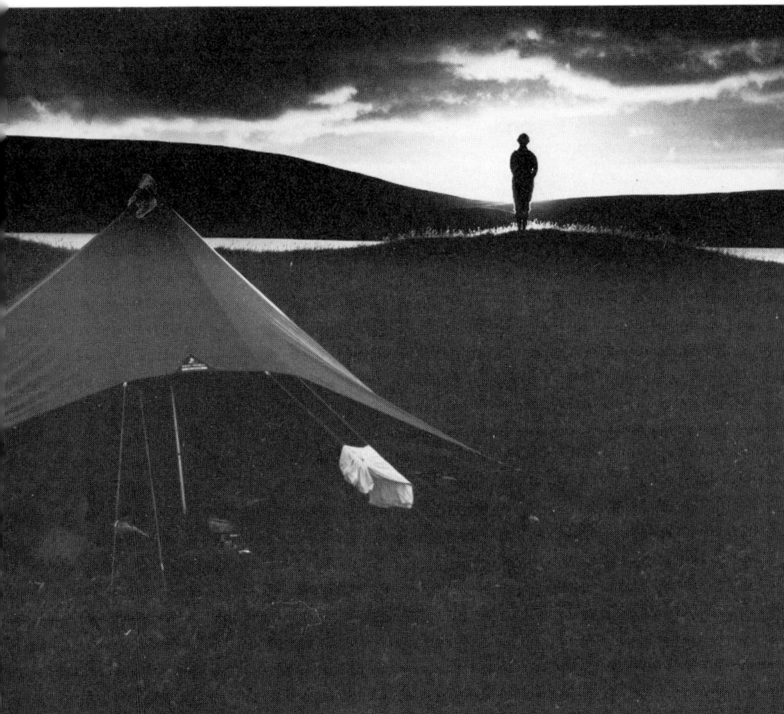

Midsummer midnight on Shetland

jury, and the guilty had their backs broken on a stone. Quarrels were sometimes solved by fighting it out in a boxing ring on a little peninsula of Tingwall Loch when the first man to shed blood on the ground lost.

The valley preserves its air of civilization and the long loch gives excellent fishing in a charming location of green fields and rolling croftlands. The loch has six boats on it, and lots of 1-lb fish and twice that weight are taken, though the average is 11 oz or so. The length is over 1 mile, the breadth $\frac{1}{4}$ of a mile, with shallows at mid-length where the depth is only 9 ft, while around the island the depth goes down to 2–3 ft.

The loch then is in two basins, the north being shallower, with a maximum depth of 40 ft though it is mostly flat bottomed and 7–9 ft deep. The southern basin is quite different, with a maximum of 60 ft in a simple rock basin whose mean is 19 ft.

Loch of Asta is almost linked to Tingwall Loch on the south and is $\frac{1}{2}$ a mile long by $\frac{1}{8}$ of a mile broad, with a mean depth of only 5 ft and a maximum of 13 ft near the north end. As well as brown trout there is a run of sea trout from East Voe.

Loch of Strom at $2\frac{1}{2}$ miles in length is one of the longest lochs in Shetland with a breadth of only $\frac{1}{3}$ of a mile and it is a rock basin into which the tide enters, but with little effect on its level. Studded with little islands, it is in two basins, whose maximum depth is 12 ft in the north and 13 ft in the south. It has a good reputation for sea trout and grilse, especially at the head of the loch.

Roer Water: this loch lies beneath Ronas Hill, the highest in the Shetlands at 1,476 ft, and a view from that top will show the impossibility of dealing with more than just a few lochs where there are so many. But as this is the largest loch in North Roe it must be mentioned.

Length $\frac{2}{3}$ of a mile by $\frac{1}{3}$ of a mile, the maximum depth is 32 ft with a mean of 10 ft and it is a rock basin, easily fished from the shore, but there is a boat obtainable from Mr. W. Moat, Burra Voe.

Fetlar is perhaps the most fertile island of the Shetlands, and is said to have been the first to be colonised by the Norse. There are three good fishing lochs, Papil Water, Loch of Winyadepla and Loch of Funzie, the first and last named containing sea trout as well as brown trout. Permission can be obtained locally.

There is no space left to deal with the excellent fishing lochs of Yell, peatiest and least beautiful of the Shetlands, but with some of the most charming people you are likely to meet in these enchanted islands of the far north, whose treasure now is the black, black oil. Sullom Voe, the largest oil-terminal in Europe, is just across Yell Sound.

Game Fishing in Mainland Ross & Cromarty W. Brown, Highland Development Board booklets.

The Shetland Isles A. T. Clunes, Robert Hale 1956

The Highlands and Islands Fraser F. Darling and J. Morton Boyd, Collins 1964

West Highland survey Fraser F. Darling, Oxford University Press 1955

Highways and Byways in West Highlands Seton Gordon, Macmillan 1935

Highways and Byways in the Central Highlands Seton Gordon, Macmillan 1949

The drove roads of Scotland A. R. B. Haldane, Edinburgh University Press 1968

The Picts Isabel Henderson, Thames & Hudson 1967

The Great Orme of Loch Ness F. M. Holiday, Faber and Faber 1968

The Canals of Scotland Jean Lindsay, David & Charles 1968

A hundred years in the Highlands O. Mackenzie, Bles 1965

A description of the Western Isles of Scotland Martin Martin (1703) reprint James Thin (1970)

The Merrick and neighbouring hills J. M. McBain, Stephen and Pollock

Galloway: the spell of its hills and glens Andrew McCormick, John Smith 1947

Bathymetrical Survey of the Scottish Fresh-water Lochs J. Murray and L. Pullar, vols 1–2 1910

The companion guide to the West Highlands of Scotland W. H. Murray, Collins 1968

The Hebrides W. H. Murray, Heinemann 1966

The Evolution of Scotland's Scenery J. B. Sissons, Oliver & Boyd 1967

Studies on Loch Lomond Harry D. Slack and Peter Maitland, vols 1–2, University of Glasgow, 1957 vol 1 1966 vol 2 Blackie & Sons Ltd

Power from the Glens North of Scotland Hydro-Electric Board, Edinburgh

Index